GHANA

ENERGY POLICY, LAWS AND REGULATIONS HANDBOOK

VOLUME 1

STRATEGIC POLICIES AND REGULATIONS

International Business Publications, USA
Washington DC, USA - Ghana

GHANA

ENERGY POLICY, LAWS AND REGULATIONS HANDBOOK

VOLUME 1 STRATEGIC POLICIES AND REGULATIONS

UPDATED ANNUALLY

We express our sincere appreciation to all government agencies and international organizations which provided information and other materials for this handbook

Cover Design: **International Business Publications, USA**

2018 Updated Reprint International Business Publications, USA
ISBN 1-4330-7160-6

For additional analytical, business and investment opportunities information, please contact Global Investment & Business Center, USA at (703) 370-8082. Fax: (703) 370-8083. E-mail: ibpusa3@gmail.com Global Business and Investment Info Databank - www.ibpus.com

Printed in the USA

For additional analytical, business and investment opportunities information, please contact Global Investment & Business Center, USA at (703) 370-8082. Fax: (703) 370-8083. E-mail: ibpusa3@gmail.com Global Business and Investment Info Databank - www.ibpus.com

GHANA

ENERGY POLICY, LAWS AND REGULATIONS HANDBOOK

VOLUME 1

STRATEGIC POLICIES AND REGULATIONS

TABLE OF CONTENTS

STRATEGIC AND DEVELOPMENT PROFILES

BASIC INFORMATION

Capital and largest city	Accra 5°33′N 0°12′W
Official languages	English[2][3]
National languages	• Asante Twi, Akuapem Twi, Bono, Dagaare, Dagbani, Dangme, Ewe, Ga, Gonja, Kasem, Fante, Nzema, Wasa, Talensi, Frafra, Hausa, Ghanaian Sign Language
Ethnic groups	• 47.5% Akans (11.5 mln) • 16.6% Dagbani / Mole (4 mln) • 13.9% Ewe (2.9 mln) • 7.4% Ga-Adangbe (1.8 mln) • 5.7% Gurma (0.7 mln) • 5.0% Fulani (0.5 mln) • 3.7% Guan / Gonja (0.3 mln) • 2.5% Gurunsi (0.1 mln) • 1.1% Bissa / Mande (0.1 mln) • 1.6% Other (0.1 mln)
Demonym	Ghanaian
Government	Unitary presidential constitutional republic
• President	Nana Akufo-Addo
• Vice-President	Mahamudu Bawumia
Legislature	Parliament
Independence from the United Kingdom	
• Declared	6 March 1957
• Republic	1 July 1960
• Current constitution	28 April 1992
Area	
• Total	239,567 km^2 (92,497 sq mi) (80th)
• Water (%)	4.61 (11,000 km^2 / 4,247 mi^2)
Population	
• 2014 estimate	27,043,093[5] (45th)
• 2010 census	24,200,000
• Density	101.5/km^2 (262.9/sq mi) (103rd)
GDP (PPP)	2017 estimate
• Total	$130.208 billion (70th)
• Per capita	$4,604[7] (126th)
GDP (nominal)	2017 estimate
• Total	$45.464 billion (69th)
• Per capita	$1,607 (126th)
Gini	42.8 medium
HDI	▲ 0.579[9] medium · 139th
Currency	Ghana cedi (GH₵) (GHS)

Time zone	GMT (UTC+0)
Drives on the	right
Calling code	+233
ISO 3166 code	GH
Internet TLD	.gh

Ghana officially called the **Republic of Ghana**, is a sovereign multinational state and unitary presidential constitutional democracy, located along the Gulf of Guinea and Atlantic Ocean, in the subregion of West Africa. Ghana is the 82nd largest country in the world and 33rd largest country on continental Africa by land mass, and Ghana has a land mass of 238,535 km^2, with 2,093 kilometres of international land borders. The country is bordered by the Ivory Coast in the west, Burkina Faso in the north, Togo in the east and the Gulf of Guinea and Atlantic Ocean in the south. The word *Ghana* means "Warrior King".

Ghana is a constitutional democracy divided into ten administrative regions, and the world's 45th−most inhabited nation and Africa's 11th−most inhabited nation with a population of approximately 27 million as of 2014. Ghana's varied geography includes savannas, woodlands, forests, a coastal line, springs, cave systems, mountains, estuaries, wildlife parks, and nature reserves. The coast of Ghana stretches 560 kilometres (350 miles) and includes a rich assortment of culturally significant castles, forts, ports and harbours. Prior to colonisation by the British empire in the early-20th century, Ghana was the site of numerous kingdoms and empires; the most powerful being the Akan Kingdom of Ashanti. In 1957, it became the first African nation to declare independence from European colonisation. This made Ghana a symbol of black achievement and helped to inspire other African nations to seek independence. It also had a major influence on Pan-Africanism and the Black Pride movements in the United States of America.

Ghana is the 7th-best governed country, 5th-most stable country and rated thirteenth-highest HDI on continental Africa. Ghana's economy is the 6th-largest on the Africa continent by purchasing power parity and Nominal GDP and is one of the fastest growing in the world. In terms of purchasing power parity per capita income, Ghana has the highest per capita income in the subregion of western Africa and Ghana has the tenth−highest per capita income on continental Africa. Ghana is one of only five countries in Africa with a free press.

Ghana has been a significant petroleum and natural gas producer since December 2010, and one of the world's largest gold and diamond producers, and is projected to be the largest producer of cocoa in the world as of 2015. Ghana is home to Lake Volta, the largest artificial lake in the world by surface area. Ghana's sweet crude oil reserves, ranks at 5th on continental Africa and 21st–25th globally and Ghana's natural gas reserves, ranks at 6th on continental Africa and 49th globally. Ghana ranks as the 61st most peaceful country in the world. Ghana is a regional power in West Africa and on continental Africa, a founding member of the Non-Aligned Movement, and a member of both the Economic Community of West African States (ECOWAS) and the Group of 24 (G24).

Background: Formed from the merger of the British colony of the Gold Coast and the Togoland trust territory, Ghana in 1957 became the first country in colonial Africa to gain its independence. A long series of coups resulted in the suspension of the constitution in 1981 and the banning of political parties. A new constitution, restoring multiparty politics, was approved in 1992.

GEOGRAPHY

Location: Western Africa, bordering the Gulf of Guinea, between Cote d'Ivoire and Togo
Geographic coordinates: 8 00 N, 2 00 W
Map references: Africa
Area:
total: 238,540 sq km
land: 230,020 sq km *water:* 8,520 sq km
Area - comparative: slightly smaller than Oregon

Land boundaries: *total:* 2,093 km
border countries: Burkina Faso 548 km, Cote d'Ivoire 668 km, Togo 877 km

Coastline: 539 km

Maritime claims:
contiguous zone: 24 nm *continental shelf:* 200 nm
exclusive economic zone: 200 nm
territorial sea: 12 nm

Climate: tropical; warm and comparatively dry along southeast coast; hot and humid in southwest; hot and dry in north

Terrain: mostly low plains with dissected plateau in south-central area

Elevation extremes:
lowest point: Atlantic Ocean 0 m
highest point: Mount Afadjato 880 m

Natural resources: gold, timber, industrial diamonds, bauxite, manganese, fish, rubber, hydropower

Land use:
arable land: 12%
permanent crops: 7%
permanent pastures: 22%
forests and woodland: 35%
other: 24%

Irrigated land: 60 sq km
Natural hazards: dry, dusty, harmattan winds occur from January to March; droughts

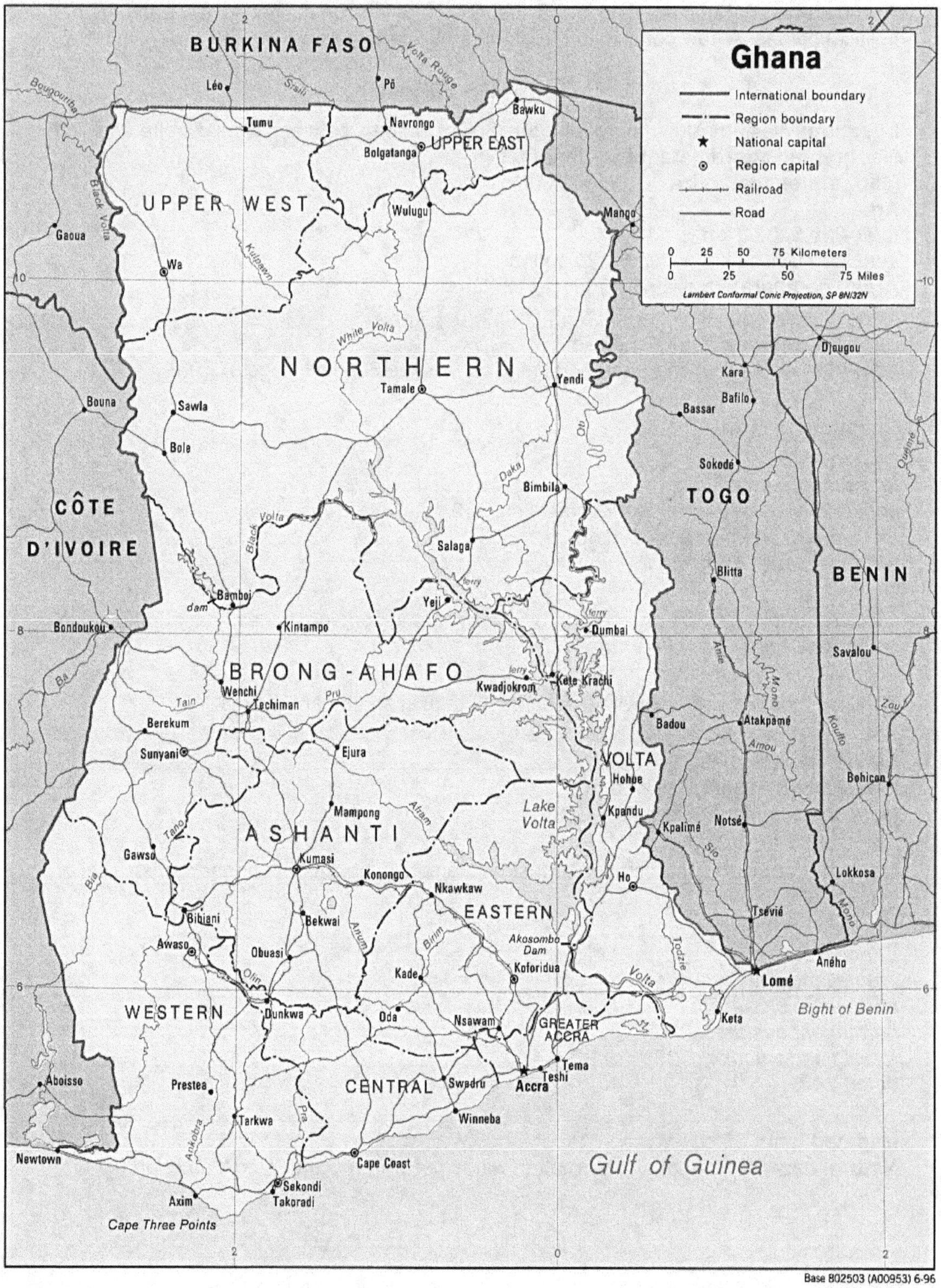

Base 802503 (A00953) 6-96

Environment - current issues: recent drought in north severely affecting agricultural activities; deforestation; overgrazing; soil erosion; poaching and habitat destruction threatens wildlife populations; water pollution; inadequate supplies of potable water

Environment - international agreements:
party to: Biodiversity, Climate Change, Desertification, Endangered Species, Environmental Modification, Law of the Sea, Nuclear Test Ban, Ozone Layer Protection, Ship Pollution, Tropical Timber 83, Tropical Timber 94, Wetlands
signed, but not ratified: Marine Life Conservation

Geography - note: Lake Volta is the world's largest artificial lake; northeasterly harmattan wind (January to March)

PEOPLE

Population: 19,533,560
note: estimates for this country explicitly take into account the effects of excess mortality due to AIDS; this can result in lower life expectancy, higher infant mortality and death rates, lower population and growth rates, and changes in the distribution of population by age and sex than would otherwise be expected (July 2000 est.)

Age structure:
0-14 years: 42% (male 4,120,240; female 4,063,960)
15-64 years: 55% (male 5,290,675; female 5,391,175)
65 years and over: 3% (male 318,890; female 348,620)

Population growth rate: 1.87%
Birth rate: 29.81 births/1,000 population
Death rate: 10.22 deaths/1,000 population
Net migration rate: -0.89 migrant(s)/1,000 population

Sex ratio:
at birth: 1.03 male(s)/female
under 15 years: 1.01 male(s)/female
15-64 years: 0.98 male(s)/female
65 years and over: 0.91 male(s)/female
total population: 0.99 male(s)/female

Infant mortality rate: 57.43 deaths/1,000 live births

Life expectancy at birth:
total population: 57.42 years
male: 56.07 years
female: 58.82 years

Total fertility rate: 3.95 children born/woman

Nationality:
noun: Ghanaian(s)
adjective: Ghanaian

Ethnic groups: black African 99.8% (major tribes - Akan 44%, Moshi-Dagomba 16%, Ewe 13%, Ga 8%), European and other 0.2%
Religions: indigenous beliefs 38%, Muslim 30%, Christian 24%, other 8%
Languages: English (official), African languages (including Akan, Moshi-Dagomba, Ewe, and Ga)

Literacy:
definition: age 15 and over can read and write
total population: 64.5%
male: 75.9%
female: 53.5%

GOVERNMENT

Country name:
conventional long form: Republic of Ghana
conventional short form: Ghana
former: Gold Coast

Data code: GH
Government type: constitutional democracy
Capital: Accra
Administrative divisions: 10 regions; Ashanti, Brong-Ahafo, Central, Eastern, Greater Accra, Northern, Upper East, Upper West, Volta, Western
Independence: 6 March 1957 (from UK)
National holiday: Independence Day, 6 March (1957)
Constitution: new constitution approved 28 April 1992
Legal system: based on English common law and customary law; has not accepted compulsory ICJ jurisdiction
Suffrage: 18 years of age; universal

Executive branch:

chief of state: President Nana Addo Dankwa AKUFO-ADDO (since 7 January 2017); Vice President Mahamudu BAWUMIA (since 7 January 2017); the president is both chief of state and head of government

head of government: President Nana Addo Dankwa AKUFO-ADDO (since 7 January 2017); Vice President Mahamudu BAWUMIA (since 7 January 2017)
cabinet: Council of Ministers; nominated by the president, approved by Parliament
elections/appointments: president and vice president directly elected on the same ballot by absolute majority popular vote in 2 rounds if needed for a 4-year term (eligible for a second term); election last held on 7 December 2016 (next to be held in December 2020)
election results: Nana Addo Dankwa AKUFO-ADDO elected president; percent of vote - Nana Addo Dankwa AKUFO-ADDO (NPP) 53.8%, John Dramani MAHAMA (NDC) 44.4%, other 1.8%

Legislative branch:
description: unicameral Parliament (275 seats; members directly elected in single-seat constituencies by simple majority vote to serve 4-year terms)
elections: last held on 7 December 2016 (next to be held in December 2020)
election results: percent of vote by party - NA; seats by party - NPP 171, NDC 104

Judicial branch:

highest court(s): Supreme Court (consists of a chief justice and 12 justices)
judge selection and term of office: chief justice appointed by the president in consultation with the Council of State (a small advisory body of prominent citizens) and with the approval of Parliament; other justices appointed by the president upon the advice of the Judicial Council (an 18-member independent body of judicial, military and police officials, and presidential nominees) and on the advice of the Council of State; justices can retire at age 60, with compulsory retirement at age 70
subordinate courts: Court of Appeal; High Court; Circuit Court; District Court; regional tribunals

Political parties and leaders:
note: Ghana has more than 20 registered parties; included are 5 of the more popular parties as of May 2017
Convention People's Party or CPPm [Edmund DELLE]
National Democratic Congress or NDC [Kofi PORTUPHY]
New Patriotic Party or NPP Nana AKUFO-ADDO]
People's National Convention or PNC Edward MAHAMA]
Peoples Progressive Party or PPP [Dr. Papa Kwesi NDOUM]

Political pressure groups and leaders:
public policy think tanks: Institute for Democratic Governance (IDEG); IMANI Center for Policy and Education; Ghana Center for Democratic Development; Institute for Economic Affairs
professional and trade groups: Ghana Bar Association; Ghana Trades Union Congress; American Chamber of Commerce; British Chamber of Commerce; and a host of religious organizations
other: wide range of international and domestic human rights and policy advocacy groups, environmental groups, business organizations, traditional leaders and youth groups

International organization participation:
ACP, AfDB, AU, C, ECOWAS, EITI (compliant country), FAO, G-24, G-77, IAEA, IBRD, ICAO, ICC (national committees), ICCt, ICRM, IDA, IFAD, IFC, IFRCS, ILO, IMF, IMO, IMSO, Interpol, IOC, IOM, IPU, ISO, ITSO, ITU, ITUC (NGOs), MIGA, MINURSO, MINUSMA, MONUSCO, NAM, OAS (observer), OIF, OPCW, UN, UNAMID, UNCTAD, UNESCO, UNHCR, UNIDO, UNIFIL, UNISFA, UNMIL, UNMISS, UNOCI, UNWTO, UPU, WCO, WFTU (NGOs), WHO, WIPO, WMO, WTO

Diplomatic representation in the US:
chief of mission: Ambassador Barfour ADJEI-BARWUAH (since 21 July 2017)
chancery: 3512 International Drive NW, Washington, DC 20008
telephone: [1] (202) 686-4520
FAX: [1] (202) 686-4527
consulate(s) general: New York

Diplomatic representation from the US:
chief of mission: Ambassador Robert P. JACKSON (since 4 February 2016)
embassy: 24 Fourth Circular Rd., Cantonments, Accra
mailing address: P.O. Box 194, Accra
telephone: [233] 030-274-1000
FAX: [233] 030-274-1389

Flag description: three equal horizontal bands of red (top), yellow, and green with a large black five-pointed star centered in the yellow band; uses the popular pan-African colors of Ethiopia; similar to the flag of Bolivia, which has a coat of arms centered in the yellow band

ECONOMY

Ghana has a market-based economy with relatively few policy barriers to trade and investment in comparison with other countries in the region, and Ghana is well-endowed with natural resources. Ghana's economy was strengthened by a quarter century of relatively sound management, a competitive business environment, and sustained reductions in poverty levels, but in recent years has suffered the consequences of loose fiscal policy, high budget and current account deficits, and a depreciating currency.

Agriculture accounts for about 20% of GDP and employs more than half of the workforce, mainly small landholders. Gold and cocoa exports, and individual remittances, are major sources of foreign exchange. Expansion of Ghana's nascent oil industry has boosted economic growth, but the fall in oil prices since 2015 reduced by half Ghana's oil revenue. Production at Jubilee, Ghana's offshore oilfield, began in mid-December 2010. The country's first gas processing plant at Atubao is also producing natural gas from the Jubilee field, providing power to several of Ghana's thermal power plants.

As of 2017, key economic concerns facing the government include the lack of reliable electricity and the high debt burden. The AKUFO-ADDO administration has made some progress by committing to fiscal consolidation, but much work is still to be done in 2018. Ghana signed a $920 million extended credit facility with the IMF in April 2015 to help it address its growing economic crisis. The IMF fiscal targets require Ghana to reduce the deficit by cutting subsidies, decreasing the bloated public sector wage bill, strengthening revenue administration, and boosting tax revenues. Priorities for the new administration include rescheduling some of Ghana's $31 billion debt, stimulating economic growth, reducing inflation, and stabilizing the currency. Prospects for new oil and gas production and follow through on tighter fiscal management are likely to help Ghana's economy in 2018.

GDP (purchasing power parity):

$130.2 billion (2017 est.)
$123 billion (2016 est.)
$118.8 billion (2015 est.)
note: data are in 2017 dollars
country comparison to the world: 81

GDP (official exchange rate):
$45.46 billion (2017 est.)

GDP - real growth rate:
5.9% (2017 est.)
3.5% (2016 est.)
3.8% (2015 est.)
country comparison to the world: 27

GDP - per capita (PPP):
$4,600 (2017 est.)
$4,500 (2016 est.)

$4,400 (2015 est.)
note: data are in 2017 dollars
country comparison to the world: 172

Gross national saving:
7.9% of GDP (2017 est.)
7.8% of GDP (2016 est.)
9% of GDP (2015 est.)
country comparison to the world: 166

GDP - composition, by end use:
household consumption: 82.1%
government consumption: 8.7%
investment in fixed capital: 13.9%
investment in inventories: 0.7%
exports of goods and services: 40.3%
imports of goods and services: -45.7% (2017 est.)

GDP - composition, by sector of origin:
agriculture: 18.3%
industry: 24.5%
services: 57.2% (2017 est.)

Agriculture - products:
cocoa, rice, cassava (manioc, tapioca), peanuts, corn, shea nuts, bananas; timber

Industries:
mining, lumbering, light manufacturing, aluminum smelting, food processing, cement, small commercial ship building, petroleum

Industrial production growth rate:
7.4% (2017 est.)
country comparison to the world: 23

Labor force:
12.49 million (2017 est.)
country comparison to the world: 47

Labor force - by occupation:
agriculture: 44.7%
industry: 14.4%
services: 40.9% (2013 est.)

Unemployment rate:
11.9% (2015 est.)
5.2% (2013 est.)
country comparison to the world: 155

Population below poverty line:
24.2% (2013 est.)
Household income or consumption by percentage share:
lowest 10%: 2%
highest 10%: 32.8% (2006 est.)

Distribution of family income - Gini index:
42.3 (2012-13 est.)
41.9 (2005-06 est.)
country comparison to the world: 54

Budget:
revenues: $9.236 billion
expenditures: $12.38 billion (2017 est.)
Taxes and other revenues:
20.3% of GDP (2017 est.)
country comparison to the world: 151

Budget surplus (+) or deficit (-):
-6.9% of GDP (2017 est.)
country comparison to the world: 184

Public debt:
76.8% of GDP (2017 est.)
78.1% of GDP (2016 est.)
country comparison to the world: 45

Fiscal year:
calendar year

Inflation rate (consumer prices):
11.8% (2017 est.)
17.5% (2016 est.)
country comparison to the world: 206

Central bank discount rate:
25.5% (31 December 2016 est.)
26% (31 December 2015 est.)
country comparison to the world: 2

Commercial bank prime lending rate:
30% (31 December 2017 est.)
31.3% (31 December 2016 est.)
country comparison to the world: 8

Stock of narrow money:
$6.909 billion (31 December 2017 est.)
$6.472 billion (31 December 2016 est.)
country comparison to the world: 92

Stock of broad money:
$14.93 billion (31 December 2017 est.)
$13.75 billion (31 December 2016 est.)
country comparison to the world: 99

Stock of domestic credit:
$14.23 billion (31 December 2017 est.)
$13.67 billion (31 December 2016 est.)
country comparison to the world: 99

Market value of publicly traded shares:
$12.55 billion (31 December 2016 est.)
$15.05 billion (31 December 2015 est.)
$3.465 billion (31 December 2012 est.)
country comparison to the world: 69

Current account balance:
-$2.643 billion (2017 est.)
-$2.866 billion (2016 est.)
country comparison to the world: 163

Exports:
$12.16 billion (2017 est.)
$11.06 billion (2016 est.)
country comparison to the world: 82

Exports - commodities:
oil, gold, cocoa, timber, tuna, bauxite, aluminum, manganese ore, diamonds, horticultural products

Exports - partners:
Switzerland 17.6%, India 14.7%, UAE 13.4%, China 8.9%, Vietnam 5.2%, Netherlands 4.2%, Burkina Faso 4% (2016)
Imports:
$12.73 billion (2017 est.)
$12.75 billion (2016 est.)
country comparison to the world: 90

Imports - commodities:
capital equipment, refined petroleum, foodstuffs
Imports - partners:
China 17.3%, UK 9.7%, US 7.7%, Belgium 5.1%, India 4.6% (2016)
Reserves of foreign exchange and gold:
$7.345 billion (31 December 2017 est.)
$6.162 billion (31 December 2016 est.)
country comparison to the world: 83

Debt - external:
$23.1 billion (31 December 2017 est.)
$21.95 billion (31 December 2016 est.)
country comparison to the world: 90

Stock of direct foreign investment - at home:
$19.85 billion (31 December 2013 est.)
$118 million (31 December 2012 est.)
country comparison to the world: 78

Stock of direct foreign investment - abroad:
$16.62 billion (31 December 2013 est.)
$109 million (31 December 2012 est.)
country comparison to the world: 56

Exchange rates:
cedis (GHC) per US dollar -

4.385 (2017 est.)
3.909 (2016 est.)
3.909 (2015 est.)
3.712 (2014 est.)
2.895 (2013 est.)

ENERGY

Electricity - production:
8.764 billion kWh (est.)
country comparison to the world: 97

Electricity - consumption:
6.122 billion kWh (est.)
country comparison to the world: 105

Electricity - exports:
752 million kWh (est.)
country comparison to the world: 60

Electricity - imports:
198 million kWh (est.)
country comparison to the world: 86

Electricity - installed generating capacity:
1.985 million kW (est.)
country comparison to the world: 102

Electricity - from fossil fuels:
40.6% of total installed capacity (est.)
country comparison to the world: 169

Electricity - from nuclear fuels:
0% of total installed capacity (est.)
country comparison to the world: 95

Electricity - from hydroelectric plants:
59.4% of total installed capacity (est.)
country comparison to the world: 33

Electricity - from other renewable sources:
0% of total installed capacity (est.)
country comparison to the world: 131

Crude oil - production:
72,580 bbl/day (2011 est.)
country comparison to the world: 53

Crude oil - exports:
14,000 bbl/day (est.)
country comparison to the world: 53

Crude oil - imports:
43,000 bbl/day (est.)
country comparison to the world: 59

Crude oil - proved reserves:
660 million bbl (1 January est.)
country comparison to the world: 45

Refined petroleum products - production:
27,260 bbl/day (est.)
country comparison to the world: 92

Refined petroleum products - consumption:
61,590 bbl/day (est.)
country comparison to the world: 94

Refined petroleum products - exports:
7,275 bbl/day (est.)
country comparison to the world: 92

Refined petroleum products - imports:
24,390 bbl/day (est.)
country comparison to the world: 95

Natural gas - production:
0 cu m (est.)
country comparison to the world: 134

Natural gas - consumption:
120 million cu m (est.)
country comparison to the world: 105

Natural gas - exports:
0 cu m (est.)
country comparison to the world: 203

Natural gas - imports:
120 million cu m (est.)
country comparison to the world: 74

Natural gas - proved reserves:
22.65 billion cu m (1 January 2012 est.)
country comparison to the world: 75

Carbon dioxide emissions from consumption of energy:
10.58 million Mt (est.)
country comparison to the world: 100

COMMUNICATIONS

Telephones - fixed lines:
total subscriptions: 251,490
subscriptions per 100 inhabitants: 1 (July 2016 est.)
country comparison to the world: 121

Telephones - mobile cellular:
total: 38,305,078
subscriptions per 100 inhabitants: 142 (July 2016 est.)

country comparison to the world: 38

Telephone system:
general assessment: primarily microwave radio relay; wireless local loop has been installed; outdated and unreliable fixed-line infrastructure heavily concentrated in Accra
domestic: competition among multiple mobile-cellular providers has spurred growth with a subscribership of more than 140 per 100 persons and rising

international: country code - 233; landing point for the SAT-3/WASC, Main One, and GLO-1 fiber-optic submarine cables that provide connectivity to South Africa, Europe, and Asia; satellite earth stations - 4 Intelsat (Atlantic Ocean); microwave radio relay link to Panaftel system connects Ghana to its neighbors

Broadcast media:
state-owned TV station, 2 state-owned radio networks; several privately owned TV stations and a large number of privately owned radio stations; transmissions of multiple international broadcasters are accessible; several cable and satellite TV subscription services are obtainable

Internet country code:
.gh

Internet users:
total: 9,328,018
percent of population: 34.7% (July 2016 est.)
country comparison to the world: 49

TRANSPORTATION

Railways:
total: 953 km (undergoing major rehabilitation)
narrow gauge: 953 km 1.067-m gauge (32 km double track)

Highways:
total: 39,409 km
paved: 11,653 km (including 30 km of expressways)
unpaved: 27,756 km

Waterways: Volta, Ankobra, and Tano Rivers provide 168 km of perennial navigation for launches and lighters; Lake Volta provides 1,125 km of arterial and feeder waterways
Pipelines: 0 km
Ports and harbors: Takoradi, Tema
Merchant marine:
total: 6 ships (1,000 GRT or over) totaling 13,484 GRT/18,583 DWT
ships by type: petroleum tanker 2, refrigerated cargo 4
Airports: 12
Airports - with paved runways:
total: 6
2,438 to 3,047 m: 1
1,524 to 2,437 m: 3
914 to 1,523 m: 2
Airports - with unpaved runways:
total: 6
1,524 to 2,437 m: 1

914 to 1,523 m: 3
under 914 m: 2

MILITARY

Military branches:
Ghanaian Army, Ghanaian Navy, Ghanaian Air Force (2010)

Military service age and obligation:
18 years of age for voluntary military service; no conscription (2008)

Manpower available for military service:
males age 16-49: 5,802,096
females age 16-49: 5,729,939 (est.)

Manpower fit for military service:
males age 16-49: 3,849,113
females age 16-49: 3,840,083 (est.)

Manpower reaching militarily significant age annually:
male: 272,954
female: 266,186 (est.)

Military expenditures:
0.8% of GDP (2006 est.)
country comparison to the world: 151

TRANSNATIONAL ISSUES

Disputes - international:
Ghana struggles to accommodate returning nationals who worked in the cocoa plantations and escaped fighting in Cote d'Ivoire

Refugees and internally displaced persons:
refugees (country of origin): 35,653 (Liberia); 8,517 (Togo)

Illicit drugs:
illicit producer of cannabis for the international drug trade; major transit hub for Southwest and Southeast Asian heroin and, to a lesser extent, South American cocaine destined for Europe and the US; widespread crime and money laundering problem, but the lack of a well developed financial infrastructure limits the country's utility as a money laundering center; significant domestic cocaine and cannabis use

IMPORTANT INFORMATION FOR UNDERSTANDING GHANA

Official Name: Republic of Ghana

PROFILE

Geography

Area: 238,538 sq. km. (92,100 sq. mi.); about the size of Illinois and Indiana combined.
Cities: *Capital*--Accra (metropolitan area pop. 3 million est.). *Other cities*--Kumasi (1 million est.), Tema (250,000 est.), Sekondi-Takoradi (200,000 est.).
Terrain: Plains and scrubland, rain forest, savanna.
Climate: Tropical.

People

Nationality: *Noun and adjective*--Ghanaian(s).
Population : 17.7 million.
Density: 74/sq. km. (192/sq. mi.).
Annual growth rate : 2.3%.
Ethnic groups: Akan, Ewe, Ga.
Religions: Christian 35%, indigenous beliefs 31%, Muslim 27%, other 7%.
Languages: English (official), Akan 44%, Mole-Dagbani 16%, Ewe 13%, Ga-Adangbe 8%.
Education: *Years compulsory*--9. *Literacy*--64.5%.
Health: *Infant mortality rate* -- 80/1,000. *Life expectancy*--56 yrs.
Work force: 4 million: *Agriculture and fishing*--54.7%. *Industry*--18.7%. *Sales and clerical*--15.2%. *Services, transportation, and communications*--7.7%. *Professional*--3.7%.

Government

Type: Democracy.
Independence: March 6, 1957.
Constitution: Entered into force January 7, 1993.
Branches: *Executive*--President popularly elected for a maximum of two four-year terms. *Legislative*--unicameral Parliament popularly elected for four-year terms. *Judicial*--Independent, Supreme Court Justices nominated by President with approval of Parliament. Subdivisions: 10 regions.
Political parties: National Democratic Congress, New Patriotic Party, People's Convention Party, National Convention Party, People's National Convention, et alia. Names, slogans, and symbols of parties existing prior to 1992 are banned by law.
Suffrage: Universal at 18.
Flag: Three horizontal stripes of red, gold, and green, with a black star in the center of the gold stripe.

Economy

GDP : $6.01 billion.
Real GDP growth rate : 5.5%.
Per capita GDP : $340.
Inflation rate : 27%.
Natural resources: Gold, timber, diamonds, bauxite, manganese, fish.
Agriculture: *Products*--cocoa, coconuts, coffee, pineapples, cashews, pepper, other food crops, rubber. *Land*--70% arable and forested.
Business and industry: *Types*--mining, lumber, light manufacturing, fishing, aluminum, tourism.
Trade : *Exports*--$1.6 billion: cocoa ($600 million), aluminum, gold, timber, diamonds, manganese. *Imports*--$1.9 billion: petroleum ($272 million), food, industrial raw materials, machinery, equipment. *Major trade partners*--U.K., Germany, U.S., Nigeria.
Fiscal year: Calendar year.

GEOGRAPHY

Ghana is located on West Africa's Gulf of Guinea only a few degrees north of the Equator. Half of the country lies less than 152 meters (500 ft.) above sea level, and the highest point is 883 meters (2,900 ft.). The 537-kilometer (334-mi.) coastline is mostly a low, sandy shore backed by plains and scrub and intersected by several rivers and streams, most of which are navigable only by canoe. A tropical rain forest belt, broken by heavily forested hills and many streams and rivers, extends northward from the shore, near the Cote d'Ivoire frontier. This area, known as the "Ashanti," produces most of the country's cocoa, minerals, and timber. North of this belt, the country varies from 91 to 396 meters (300-1,300 ft.) above sea level and is covered by low bush, park-like savanna, and grassy plains.

The climate is tropical. The eastern coastal belt is warm and comparatively dry; the southwest corner, hot and humid; and the north, hot and dry. There are two distinct rainy seasons in the south--May-June and August-September; in the north, the rainy seasons tend to merge. A dry, northeasterly wind, the Harmattan, blows in January and February. Annual rainfall in the coastal zone averages 83 centimeters (33 in.).

Volta Lake, the largest man-made lake in the world, extends from the Akosombo Dam in southeastern Ghana to the town of Yapei, 520 kilometers (325 mi.) to the north. The lake generates electricity, provides inland transportation, and is a potentially valuable resource for irrigation and fish farming.

PEOPLE

Ghana's population is concentrated along the coast and in the principal cities of Accra and Kumasi. Most Ghanaians descended from migrating tribes that probably came down the Volta River valley at the beginning of the 13th century. Ethnically, Ghana is divided into small groups speaking more than 50 languages and dialects. Among the more important linguistic groups are the Akans, which include the Fantis along the coast and the Ashantis in the forest region north of the coast; the Guans, on the plains of the Volta River; the Ga- and Ewe-speaking peoples of the south and southeast; and the Moshi-Dagomba-speaking tribes of the northern and upper regions. English, the official and commercial language, is taught in all the schools.

Primary and junior secondary school education is tuition-free and mandatory. The Government of Ghana support for basic education is unequivocal. Article 39 of the Constitution mandates the major tenets of the free, compulsory, universal basic education (FCUBE) initiative. Launched in 1996, it is one of the most ambitious pre-tertiary education programs in West Africa. Since 1987, the Government of Ghana has increased its education budget by 700%. Basic education's share has grown from 45% to 60% of that total.

Students begin their 6-year primary education at age six. Under educational reforms implemented in 1987, they pass into a junior secondary school system for 3 years of academic training combined with technical and vocational training. Those continuing move into the 3-year senior secondary school program. Entrance to one of the five Ghanaian universities is by examination following completion of senior secondary school. School enrollment totals almost 3 million.

HISTORY

The history of the Gold Coast before the last quarter of the 15th century is derived primarily from oral tradition that refers to migrations from the ancient kingdoms of the western Soudan (the area of Mauritania and Mali). The Gold Coast was renamed Ghana upon independence in 1957 because of indications that present-day inhabitants descended from migrants who moved south from the ancient kingdom of Ghana.

The first contact between Europe and the Gold Coast dates from 1470, when a party of Portuguese landed. In 1482, the Portuguese built Elmina Castle as a permanent trading base. The first recorded English trading voyage to the coast was made by Thomas Windham in 1553. During the next three centuries, the English, Danes, Dutch, Germans, and Portuguese controlled various parts of the coastal areas.

In 1821, the British Government took control of the British trading forts on the Gold Coast. In 1844, Fanti chiefs in the area signed an agreement with the British that became the legal steppingstone to colonial status for the coastal area.

From 1826 to 1900, the British fought a series of campaigns against the Ashantis, whose kingdom was located inland. In 1902, they succeeded in establishing firm control over the Ashanti region and making the northern territories a protectorate. British Togoland, the fourth territorial element eventually to form the nation, was part of a former German colony administered by the United Kingdom from Accra as a League of Nations mandate after 1922. In December 1946, British Togoland became a UN Trust Territory, and in 1957, following a 1956 plebiscite, the United Nations agreed that the territory would become part of Ghana when the Gold Coast achieved independence.

The four territorial divisions were administered separately until 1946, when the British Government ruled them as a single unit. In 1951, a constitution was promulgated that called for a greatly enlarged legislature composed principally of members elected by popular vote directly or indirectly. An executive council was responsible for formulating policy, with most African members drawn from the legislature and including three ex officio members appointed by the governor. A new constitution, approved on April 29, 1954, established a cabinet comprising African ministers drawn from an all-African legislature chosen by direct election. In the elections that followed, the Convention People's Party (CPP), led by Kwame Nkrumah, won the majority of seats in the new Legislative Assembly.

In May 1956, Prime Minister Nkrumah's Gold Coast government issued a white paper containing proposals for Gold Coast independence. The British Government stated it would agree to a firm date for independence if a reasonable majority for such a step were obtained in the Gold Coast Legislative Assembly after a general election. This election, held in 1956, returned the CPP to power with 71 of the 104 seats in the Legislative Assembly. Ghana became an independent state on March 6, 1957, when the United Kingdom relinquished its control over the Colony of the Gold Coast and Ashanti, the Northern Territories Protectorate, and British Togoland.

In subsequent reorganizations, the country was divided into 10 regions, which currently are subdivided into 110 districts. The original Gold Coast Colony now comprises the Western, Central, Eastern, and Greater Accra Regions, with a small portion at the mouth of the Volta River assigned to the Volta Region; the Ashanti area was divided into the Ashanti and Brong-Ahafo Regions; the Northern Territories into the Northern, Upper East, and Upper West Regions; and British Togoland essentially is the same area as the Volta Region.

Post-Independence Politics

After independence, the CPP government under Nkrumah sought to develop Ghana as a modern, semi-industrialized, unitary socialist state. The government emphasized political and economic organization, endeavoring to increase stability and productivity through labor, youth, farmers, cooperatives, and other organizations integrated with the CPP. The government, according to Nkrumah, acted only as "the agent of the CPP" in seeking to accomplish these goals.

The CPP's control was challenged and criticized, and Prime Minister Nkrumah used the Preventive Detention Act (1958), which provided for detention without trial for up to 5 years (later extended to 10 years). On July 1, 1960, a new constitution was adopted, changing Ghana from a parliamentary system with a prime minister to a republican form of government headed by a powerful president. In August 1960, Nkrumah was given authority to scrutinize newspapers and other publications before publication. This political evolution continued into early 1964, when a constitutional referendum changed the country to a one-party state.

On February 24, 1966, the Ghanaian Army and police overthrew Nkrumah's regime. Nkrumah and all his ministers were dismissed, the CPP and National Assembly were dissolved, and the constitution was suspended. The new regime cited Nkrumah's flagrant abuse of individual rights and liberties, his regime's corrupt, oppressive, and dictatorial practices, and the rapidly deteriorating economy as the principal reasons for its action.

POST-NKRUMAH POLITICS

The leaders of the February 24 coup established the new government around the National Liberation Council (NLC) and pledged an early return to a duly constituted civilian government. Members of the judiciary and civil service remained at their posts and committees of civil servants were established to handle the administration of the country.

Ghana's government returned to civilian authority under the Second Republic in October 1969 after a parliamentary election in which the Progress Party, led by Kofi A. Busia, won 105 of the 140 seats. Until mid-1970, the powers of the chief of state were held by a presidential commission led by Brigadier A.A. Afrifa. In a special election on August 31, 1970, former Chief Justice Edward Akufo-Addo was chosen president, and Dr. Busia became prime minister.

Faced with mounting economic problems, Prime Minister Busia's government undertook a drastic devaluation of the currency in December 1971. The government's inability to control the subsequent inflationary pressures stimulated further discontent, and military officers seized power in a bloodless coup on January 13, 1972.

The coup leaders, led by Col. I.K. Acheampong, formed the National Redemption Council (NRC) to which they admitted other officers, the head of the police, and one civilian. The NRC promised improvements in the quality of life for all Ghanaians and based its programs on nationalism, economic development, and self-reliance. In 1975, a government reorganization resulted in the NRC's replacement by the Supreme Military Council (SMC), also headed by now-General Acheampong.

Unable to deliver on its promises, the NRC/SMC became increasingly marked by mismanagement and rampant corruption. In 1977, General Acheampong brought forward the concept of union government (UNIGOV), which would make Ghana a non-party state. Perceiving this as a ploy by Acheampong to retain power, professional groups and students launched strikes and demonstrations against the government in 1977 and 1978. The steady erosion in Acheampong's power led to his arrest in July 1978 by his chief of staff, Lt. Gen. Frederick Akuffo, who replaced him as head of state and leader of what became known as the SMC-2.

Akuffo abandoned UNIGOV and established a plan to return to constitutional and democratic government. A Constitutional Assembly was established, and political party activity was revived. Akuffo was unable to solve Ghana's economic problems, however, or to reduce the rampant corruption in which senior military officers played a major role. On June 4, 1979, his government was deposed in a violent coup by a group of junior and non-commissioned officers--Armed Forces Revolutionary Council (AFRC)--with Flt. Lt. Jerry John Rawlings as its chairman.

The AFRC executed eight senior military officers, including former chiefs of state Acheampong and Akuffo; established Special Tribunals that, secretly and without due process, tried dozens of military officers, other government officials, and private individuals for corruption, sentencing them to long prison terms and confiscating their property; and, through a combination of force and exhortation, attempted to rid Ghanaian society of corruption and profiteering. At the same time, the AFRC accepted, with a few amendments, the draft constitution that had been submitted, permitted the scheduled presidential and parliamentary elections to take place in June and July, promulgated the constitution, and handed over power to the newly elected president and parliament of the Third Republic on September 24, 1979.

The 1979 constitution was modeled on those of Western democracies. It provided for the separation of powers among an elected president and a unicameral parliament, an independent judiciary headed by a Supreme Court, which protected individual rights, and other autonomous institutions, such as the Electoral Commissioner and the Ombudsman. The new president, Dr. Hilla Limann, was a career diplomat from the north and the candidate of the People's National Party (PNP), the political heir of Nkrumah's CPP. Of the 140 members of parliament, 71 were PNP.

The PNP government established the constitutional institutions and generally respected democracy and individual human rights. It failed, however, to halt the continuing decline in the economy; corruption flourished, and the gap between rich and poor widened. On December 31, 1981, Flight Lt. Rawlings and a small group of enlisted and former soldiers launched a coup that succeeded against little opposition in toppling President Limann.

THE PNDC ERA

Rawlings and his colleagues suspended the 1979 constitution, dismissed the president and his cabinet, dissolved the parliament, and proscribed existing political parties. They established the Provisional National Defense Council (PNDC), initially composed of seven members with Rawlings as chairman, to exercise executive and legislative powers. The existing judicial system was preserved, but alongside it the PNDC created the National Investigation Committee to root out corruption and other economic offenses, the anonymous Citizens' Vetting Committee to punish tax evasion, and the Public Tribunals to try various crimes. The PNDC proclaimed its intent to allow the people to exercise political power through defense committees to be established in communities, workplaces, and in units of the armed forces and police. Under the PNDC, Ghana remained a unitary government.

In December 1982, the PNDC announced a plan to decentralize government from Accra to the regions, the districts, and local communities, but it maintained overall control by appointing regional and district secretaries who exercised executive powers and also chaired regional and district councils. Local councils, however, were expected progressively to take over the payment of salaries, with regions and districts assuming more powers from the national government. In 1984, the PNDC created a National Appeals Tribunal to hear appeals from the public tribunals, changed the Citizens' Vetting Committee into the Office of Revenue Collection and replaced the system of defense committees with Committees for the Defense of the Revolution.

In 1984, the PNDC also created a National Commission on Democracy to study ways to establish participatory democracy in Ghana. The commission issued a "Blue Book" in July 1987 outlining modalities for district-level elections, which were held in late 1988 and early 1989, for newly created district assemblies. One-third of the assembly members are appointed by the government.

Under international and domestic pressure for a return to democracy, the PNDC allowed the establishment of a 258-member Consultative Assembly made up of members representing geographic districts as well as established civic or business organizations. The assembly was charged to draw up a draft constitution to establish a fourth republic, using PNDC proposals. The PNDC accepted the final product without revision, and it was put to a national referendum on April 28, 1992, in which it received 92% approval. On May 18, 1992, the ban on party politics was lifted in preparation for multi-party elections. The PNDC and its supporters formed a new party, the National Democratic Congress (NDC), to contest the elections. Presidential elections were held on November 3 and parliamentary elections on December 29 of that year. Members of the opposition boycotted the parliamentary elections, however, which resulted in a 200 seat Parliament with only 17 opposition party members and two independents.

The Constitution entered into force on January 7, 1993, to found the Fourth Republic. On that day, Flt. Lt. Jerry John Rawlings was inaugurated as President and members of Parliament swore their oaths of office. In 1996, the opposition fully contested the presidential and parliamentary elections, which were described as peaceful, free, and transparent by domestic and international observers. In that election, President Rawlings was re-elected with 57% of the popular vote. In addition, Rawlings' NDC party won 133 of the Parliament's 200 seats, just one seat short of the two-thirds majority needed to amend the Constitution, although the election returns of two parliamentary seats face legal challenges.

GOVERNMENT

The Constitution that established the Fourth Republic provided a basic charter for republican democratic government. It declares Ghana to be a unitary republic with sovereignty residing in the Ghanaian people. Intended to prevent future coups, dictatorial government, and one-party states, it is designed to establish the concept of powersharing. The document reflects lessons learned from the abrogated constitutions of the 1957, 1960, 1969, and 1979, and incorporates provisions and institutions drawn from British and American constitutional models. One controversial provision of the Constitution indemnifies members and appointees of the PNDC from liability for any official act or omission during the years of PNDC rule. The Constitution calls for a system of checks and balances, with power shared between a president, a unicameral parliament, a council of state, and an independent judiciary.

Executive authority is established in the Office of the Presidency, together with his Council of State. The president is head of state, head of government, and commander in chief of the armed forces. He also appoints the vice president. According to the Constitution, more than half of the presidentially appointed ministers of state must be appointed from among members of Parliament.

Legislative functions are vested in Parliament, which consists of a unicameral 200-member body plus the Speaker. To become law, legislation must have the assent of the president, who has a qualified veto over all bills except those to which a vote of urgency is attached. Members of Parliament are popularly elected by universal adult suffrage for terms of four years, except in war time, when terms may be extended for not more than 12 months at a time beyond the four years.

The structure and the power of the judiciary are independent of the two other branches of government. The Supreme Court has broad powers of judicial review. It is authorized by the Constitution to rule on the constitutionality of any legislation or executive action at the request of any aggrieved citizen. The hierarchy of courts derives largely from British juridical forms. The hierarchy, called the Superior Court of Judicature, is composed of the Supreme Court of Ghana, the Court of Appeal, the High Court of Justice, regional tribunals, and such lower courts or tribunals as Parliament may establish. The courts have jurisdiction over all civil and criminal matters.

PRINCIPAL GOVERNMENT OFFICIALS

Principal Government Officials

Pres., **John Dramani MAHAMA**
Vice Pres., **Kwesi AMISSAH-ARTHUR**
Min. of Agriculture, **Clement Kofi HUMADO**
Min. of Chieftancy & Traditional Affairs,
Min. of Communications, **Edward Omane BOAMAH**
Min. of Defense,
Min. of Education, **Naana Jane OPOKU-AGYEMAN**
Min. of Employment & Labor Relations, **Nii Armah ASHIETEY**
Min. of Energy & Petroleum, **Emmanuel Armarh Kofi BUAH**
Min. of Environment, Science, Technology, & Innovation, **Oteng ADJEI**
Min. of Finance, **Seth TERPKER**
Min. of Fisheries & Aquaculture Development,
Min. of Foreign Affairs & Regional Integration, **Hanna TETTEH**
Min. of Gender, Children, & Social Protection, **Nana Oye LITHUR**
Min. of Health, **Hanny Sherry AYITTEY**
Min. of Information, **Mahama AYARIGA**
Min. of Interior,
Min. of Justice & Attorney Gen., **Marietta BREW-APPIAH-OPPONG**
Min. of Lands & Natural Resources, **Inusah FUSEINI**
Min. of Local Govt. & Rural Development, **Akwasi Oppong FOSU**
Min. of Roads & Highways, **Amin Amidu SULEMANI**
Min. of Tourism, Culture, & Creative Arts,
Min. of Trade, Industry, & Private-Sector Development,
Min. of Transportation, **Dzifa ATTIVOR**
Min. of Water & Natural Resources, **Collins DAUDA**
Min. of Youth & Sports, **Elvis AFRIYIE-ANKRAH**
Min. of State, Office of the Pres.,
Min. of State, Office of the Pres.,
Governor, Bank of Ghana,
Ambassador to the US, **Daniel Ohene AGYEKUM**
Permanent Representative to the UN, New York, **Kenneth Kweku KANDA**

Ambassador to the United States--Daniel Ohene Agyekum
Permanent Representative to the United Nations--Nana Effah-Apenteng

Ghana maintains an embassy in the United States at 3512 International Drive, NW., Washington, D.C. 20008 (tel. 202-686-4500). Its permanent mission to the United Nations is located at 19 E. 47th Street., New York, N.Y. 10017 (tel. 212-832-1300).

ECONOMY

Currency	Cedi (GHS)
Fiscal year	Calendar year 1 January to 31 December

Statistics

GDP	▲$103 billion (estimate, PPP) ▲$50 billion (estimate, nominal)
GDP growth	8.5% 8.2%
GDP per capita	▲$5,150 (2013 estimate, PPP) ▲$2,500 (2013 estimate, nominal)
GDP by sector	▲Services: 50.6% ▲Industry: 28.1% ▼Agriculture: 21.3%
Inflation (CPI)	▲14.5% (2014 March)
Population below poverty line	▼3%
Gini coefficient	19.2 (2009)
Labor force	▲12.83 million
Labor force by occupation	▲Services: 28% ▲Industry: 20% ▼Agriculture: 52%
Unemployment	▼1.9%
Average gross salary	▲¢29,669.16 / $10,483.8 (per year)
Average net salary	▲¢2,472.43 / $873.65 (per month)
Main industries	List
Ease-of-doing-business rank	▼67th
External	
Exports	▬$13.73 billion
Export goods	Gold Bullion 44% List
Main export partners	List
Imports	▲$17.56 billion (
Import goods	Military technology Industrialization equipment
Main import partners	List
FDI stock	▼$4.9 billion
Gross external debt	▲$46.4 billion (1 July 2014 est.)
Public finances	
Public debt	▲61% of GDP (2014 est.)
Revenues	▲9.282 billion
Expenses	▲14.13 billion

The **economy of Ghana**, has a diverse and rich resource base with a primary manufacturing and exportation of digital technology goods combined with automotive and ship construction and exportation, as well as exportation of diverse and rich resource hydrocarbons, industrial minerals among many others makes Ghana attain one of the highest GDP per capita in Africa. Ghana is one of the top-ten fastest growing economies in the world, and the fastest growing economy in Africa.

The Ghanaian domestic economy in 2012 revolved around services, which accounts for 50% of GDP and employs 28% of the work force. Growing output towards economic industrialization has made Ghana remain one of the more economically sound countries in all of Africa.

Ghana embarked on a currency re-denomination exercise, from Cedi (¢) to the new currency, the Ghana Cedi (GH¢) in July 2007. The transfer rate is 1 Ghana Cedi for every 10,000 Cedis. Ghana embarked upon an aggressive media campaign to educate the public about what re-denomination entails. Value added tax is a consumption tax administered in Ghana. The tax regime which started in 1998 had a single rate but since September 2007 entered into a multiple rate regime. In 1998, the rate of tax was 10% and amended in 2000 to 12.5%. The top income tax and corporate tax rates are 25%. Other taxes included with value-added tax (VAT), are national health insurance levy, and a capital gains tax. The overall tax burden amounts to 12.1% of Ghana's total domestic income, and the budget of Ghana has fallen to the equivalent of 39.8% of GDP

By West African standards, Ghana has a diverse and rich resource base. The country is mainly agricultural, however, with a majority of its workers engaged in farming. Cash crops consist primarily of cocoa and cocoa products,which typically provide about two-thirds of export revenues, timber products, coconuts and other palm products, shea nuts, which produce an edible fat, and coffee. Ghana also has established a successful program of nontraditional agricultural products for export, including pineapples, cashews, and pepper. Cassava, yams, plantains, corn, rice, peanuts, millet, and sorghum are the basic foodstuffs. Fish, poultry, and meat also are important dietary staples.

Minerals--principally gold, diamonds, manganese ore, and bauxite--are produced and exported. The only commercial oil well has been closed after producing 3.5 million barrels over its seven-year life, but signs of natural gas are being studied for power generation, while exploration continues for other oil and gas resources.

Ghana's industrial base is relatively advanced compared to many other African countries. Import-substitution industries include textiles; steel (using scrap); tires; oil refining; flour milling; beverages; tobacco; simple consumer goods; and car, truck, and bus assembly.

Tourism has become one of Ghana's largest foreign income earners (ranking third in 1997), and the Ghanaian Government has placed great emphasis upon further tourism support and development.

ECONOMIC DEVELOPMENT

At independence, Ghana had a substantial physical and social infrastructure and $481 million in foreign reserves. The Nkrumah government further developed the infrastructure and made important public investments in the industrial sector. With assistance from the United States, the World Bank, and the United Kingdom, construction of the Akosombo Dam was completed on the Volta River in 1966. Two U.S. companies built Valco, Africa's largest aluminum smelter, to use power generated at the dam. Aluminum exports from Valco are a major source of foreign exchange for Ghana.

Many Nkrumah-era investments were monumental public works projects and poorly conceived, badly managed agricultural and industrial schemes. With cocoa prices falling and the country's foreign exchange reserves fast disappearing, the government resorted to supplier credits to finance many projects. By the mid-1960s, Ghana's reserves were gone, and the country could not meet repayment schedules. To rationalize, the National Liberation Council abandoned unprofitable projects, and some inefficient state-owned enterprises were sold to private investors. On three occasions, Ghana's creditors agreed to reschedule repayments due on Nkrumah-era supplier credits. Led by the United States, foreign donors provided import loans to enable the foreign exchange-strapped government to import essential commodities.

Prime Minister Busia's government (1969-72) liberalized controls to attract foreign investment and to encourage domestic entrepreneurship. Investors were cautious, however, and cocoa prices began declining again while imports surged, precipitating a serious trade deficit. Despite considerable foreign assistance and some debt relief, the Busia regime also was unable to overcome the inherited restraints on growth posed by the debt burden, balance-of-payments imbalances, foreign exchange shortages, and mismanagement.

Although foreign aid helped prevent economic collapse and was responsible for subsequent improvements in many sectors, the economy stagnated in the 10-year period preceding the NRC takeover in 1972. Population growth offset the modest increase in gross domestic product, and real earnings declined for many Ghanaians.

To restructure the economy, the NRC, under General Acheampong (1972-78), undertook an austerity program that emphasized self-reliance, particularly in food production. These plans were not realized, however, primarily because of post-1973 oil price increases and a drought in 1975-77 that particularly affected northern Ghana. The NRC, which had inherited foreign debts of almost $1 billion, abrogated existing rescheduling arrangements for some debts and rejected other repayments. After creditors objected to this unilateral action, a 1974 agreement rescheduled the medium-term debt on liberal terms. The NRC also imposed the Investment Policy Decree of 1975--effective on January 1977--that required 51 % Ghanaian equity participation in most foreign firms, but the government took 40% in specified industries. Many shares were sold directly to the public.

Continued mismanagement of the economy, record inflation (more than 100% in 1977), and increasing corruption, notably at the highest political levels, led to growing dissatisfaction. The post-July 1978 military regime led by General Akuffo attempted to deal with Ghana's economic problems by making small changes in the overvalued cedi and by restraining government spending and monetary growth. Under a one-year standby agreement with the International Monetary Fund (IMF) in January 1979, the government promised to undertake economic reforms, including a reduction of the budget deficit, in return for a $68 million IMF support program and $27 million in IMF Trust Fund loans. The agreement became inoperative, however, after the June 4 coup that brought Flight Lieutenant Rawlings and the AFRC to power for 4 months.

In September 1979, the civilian government of Hilla Limann inherited declining per capita income; stagnant industrial and agricultural production due to inadequate imported supplies; shortages of imported and locally produced goods; a sizable budget deficit (almost 40% of expenditures in 1979); high inflation, "moderating" to 54% in 1979; an increasingly overvalued cedi; flourishing smuggling and other black-market activities; unemployment and underemployment, particularly among urban youth; deterioration in the transport network; and continued foreign exchange constraints.

Limann's PNP government announced yet another (2-year) reconstruction program, emphasizing increased food production and productivity, exports, and transport improvements. Import austerity was imposed and external payments arrears cut. However, declining cocoa production combined with falling cocoa prices, while oil prices soared. No effective measures were taken to reduce rampant corruption and black marketing.

When Rawlings again seized power at the end of 1981, cocoa output had fallen to half the 1970-71 level and its world price to one-third the 1975 level. By 1982, oil would constitute half of Ghana's imports, while overall trade contracted greatly. Internal transport had slowed to a crawl, and inflation remained high. During Rawlings' first year, the economy was stagnant. Industry ran at about 10% of capacity due to the chronic shortage of foreign exchange to cover the importation of required raw materials and replacement parts. Economic conditions deteriorated further in early 1983 when Nigeria expelled an estimated 1 million Ghanaians who had to be absorbed by Ghana.

In April 1983, in coordination with the IMF, the PNDC launched an economic recovery program, perhaps the most stringent and consistent of its day in Africa, aimed at reopening infrastructural bottlenecks and reviving moribund productive sectors--agriculture, mining, and timber. The largely distorted exchange rate and prices were realigned to encourage production and exports. Increased fiscal and monetary discipline was imposed to curb inflation and to focus on priorities. Through November 1987, the cedi was devalued by more than 6,300%, and widespread direct price controls were substantially reduced.

The economy's response to these reforms was initially hampered by the absorption of one million returnees from Nigeria, the onset of the worst drought since independence, which brought on widespread bushfires and forced closure of the aluminum smelter and severe power cuts for industry and decline in foreign aid. In 1985, the country absorbed an additional 100,000 expellees from Nigeria. In 1987, cocoa prices began declining again; however, initial infrastructural repairs, improved weather, and producer incentives and support revived output in the early 1990s. During 1984-88 the economy experienced solid growth for the first time since 1978. Renewed exports, aid inflows, and a foreign exchange auction have eased hard currency constraints.

Since an initial August 1983 IMF standby agreement, the economic recovery program has been supported by three IMF standbys and two other credits totaling $611 million, $1.1 billion from the World Bank, and hundreds of millions of dollars more from other donors. In November 1987, the IMF approved a $318-million, 3-year extended fund facility. The second phase (1987-90) of the recovery program concentrated on economic restructuring and revitalizing social services. The third phase, focused on financial transparency and macroeconomic stability is scheduled for March 1998.

Ghana intends to achieve its goals of accelerated economic growth, improved quality of life for all Ghanaians, and reduced poverty through macroeconomic stability, higher private investment, broad-based social and rural development, as well as direct poverty-alleviation efforts. These plans are fully supported by the international donor community and have been forcefully reiterated in the 1995 government report, *Ghana: Vision 2020*. Privatization of state-owned enterprises continues, with about two-thirds of 300 parastatal enterprises sold to private owners. Other reforms adopted under the government's structural adjustment program include the elimination of exchange rate controls and the lifting of virtually all restrictions on imports. The establishment of an interbank foreign exchange market has greatly expanded access to foreign exchange.

The medium-term macroeconomic forecast assumes political stability, successful economic stabilization, and the implementation of a policy agenda for private sector growth, and adequate public spending on social services and rural infrastructure. The ninth Consultative Group Meeting for Ghana ended November 5, 1997 after deliberations in Paris. Twenty-four countries and donor entities were represented at this meeting called by the World Bank on behalf of the Ghanaian Government. The World Bank announced that, of the targeted disbursement level of $1.6 billion sought from the donor community for 1998-99, they foresaw only a $150 million shortfall in commitments, and that this shortfall would be easily realized should Ghana rapidly enact its macroeconomic program.

The government repealed a 17.% value-added tax (VAT) shortly after its introduction in 1995, which resulted in wide-spread public protests. The government reverted to several previously imposed taxes, including a sales tax. The government has set in motion a program to reintroduce a VAT bill, with implementation in 1998 after an extensive public education campaign.

FOREIGN RELATIONS

Ghana is active in the United Nations and many of its specialized agencies (including the World Trade Organization), the Nonaligned Movement, the Organization of African Unity (OAU), and the Economic Community of West African States. Generally, it follows the consensus of the Nonaligned Movement and the OAU on economic and political issues not directly affecting its own interests. Ghana has been extremely active in international peacekeeping activities under UN auspices in Lebanon, Afghanistan, Rwanda, the Balkans, and Pakistan, in addition to an eight-year sub-regional initiative with its ECOWAS partners to develop and then enforce a cease-fire in Liberia. Ghana maintains friendly relations with all states, regardless of ideology.

U.S.-GHANAIAN RELATIONS

The United States has enjoyed good relations with Ghana at the nonofficial, personal level since Ghana's independence. Thousands of Ghanaians have been educated in the United States. Close relations are maintained between educational and scientific institutions, and cultural links, particularly between Ghanaians and African-Americans, are strong.

After a period of strained relations in the mid-1980s, U.S.-Ghanaian official relations are stronger than at any other time in recent memory. Ghanaian parliamentarians and other government officials have through the U.S. International Visitor Program acquainted themselves with U.S. Congressional and state legislative practices and participated in programs designed to address other issues of interest. The U.S. and Ghanaian militaries have cooperated in numerous joint training exercises, culminating with Ghanaian participation in the African Crisis Response Initiative, an international activity in which the U.S. is facilitating the development of an interoperable peacekeeping capacity among African nations. In addition, there is an active bilateral international military and educational training program. The Office of the President of Ghana worked closely with the U.S. Embassy in Accra to establish an American Chamber of Commerce to continue to develop closer economic ties in the private sector.

The United States is among Ghana's principal trading partners. The American privately owned VALCO aluminum smelter imports many of its supplies from, and exports almost all the aluminum ingots to, the United States. With a replacement value of more than $600 million, U.S. investments in Ghana form one of the largest stocks of foreign capital. VALCO--90% owned by Kaiser, and 10% by Reynolds--is by far the biggest investment, but other important U.S. companies operating in the country include Mobil, Coca Cola, S.C. Johnson, Ralston Purina, Star-Kist, A.H. Robins, Sterling, Pfizer, IBM, Carson Products, 3M, Pioneer Gold, Stewart & Stevenson, Price Waterhouse, Great Lakes Shipping, and National Cash Register (NCR). Several U.S. firms recently made or are considering investments in Ghana, primarily in gold mining, wood products, and petroleum. In late 1997, Nuevo Petroleum concluded an oil exploration agreement accounting for the last of Ghana's offshore mineral rights zones. Two other U.S. oil companies, Sante Fe and Hunt, are also engaged in offshore exploration.

U.S. development assistance to Ghana in fiscal year 1997 totaled $52 million, divided between small business enterprise, health, education, and democracy/governance programs. Ghana was the first country in the world to accept Peace Corps volunteers, and the program remains one of the largest. Currently, there are more than 150 volunteers in Ghana. Almost half work in education, and the others in various fields such as agroforestry, small business development, health education and water sanitation, as well as youth development.

PRINCIPAL U.S. OFFICIALS

Ambassador-- Robert Porter Jackson

Robert Porter Jackson serves as U.S Ambassador to Ghana. Ambassador Jackson has served as the U.S. Department of State's Principal Deputy Assistant Secretary for African Affairs since October 2013. From 2010 to 2013 he was the U.S. Ambassador to the Republic of Cameroon.

Deputy Chief of Mission--Julie Furuta-Toy
Director, USAID--Cheryl Anderson
Defense Attaché--LTC Jason Turner
Senior Commercial Officer--Heather Byrnes
Public Affairs Officer--Mary Scholl
Political Chief--Brian Shukan
Economic Chief--Philip Cummings
Management Counselor--Jacqueline Holland-Craig
Consul--Michael Evans
Deputy Consul--Kevin Lewis

The U.S. Embassy is located on Ring Road East, near Danquah Circle, Accra (tel. 233-21-775347/8/9). The mailing address is P.O. Box 194, Accra, Ghana. For American citizen services and visa questions, the Embassy Consular Section telephone number is 233-21-776602.

TRAVEL AND BUSINESS INFORMATION

The U.S. Department of State's Consular Information Program provides Travel Warnings and Consular Information Sheets.

Travel Warnings are issued when the State Department recommends that Americans avoid travel to a certain country.

Consular Information Sheets exist for all countries and include information on immigration practices, currency regulations, health conditions, areas of instability, crime and security, political disturbances, and the addresses of the U.S. posts in the country.

Public Announcements are issued as a means to disseminate information quickly about terrorist threats and other relatively short-term conditions overseas which pose significant risks to the security of American travelers. Free copies of this information are available by calling the Bureau of Consular Affairs at 202-647-5225 or via the fax-on-demand system: 202-647-3000. Travel Warnings and Consular Information Sheets also are available on the Consular Affairs Internet home page: http://travel.state.gov and the

Consular Affairs Bulletin Board (CABB).To access CABB, dial the modem number: (301-946-4400 (it will accommodate up to 33,600 bps), set terminal communications program to N-8-1 (no parity, 8 bits, 1 stop bit); and terminal emulation to VT100. The login is **travel** and the password is **info** (Note: Lower case is required). The CABB also carries international security information from the Overseas Security Advisory Council and Department's Bureau of Diplomatic Security. Consular Affairs Trips for Travelers publication series, which contain information on obtaining passports and planning a safe trip abroad, can be purchased from the Superintendent of Documents, U.S. Government Printing Office, P.O. Box 371954, Pittsburgh, PA 15250-7954; telephone: 202-512-1800; fax 202-512-2250.

Emergency information concerning Americans traveling abroad may be obtained from the Office of Overseas Citizens Services at (202) 647-5225. For after-hours emergencies, Sundays and holidays, call 202-647-4000.

Passport Services information can be obtained by calling the 24-hour, 7-day a week automated system ($.35 per minute) or live operators 8 a.m. to 8 p.m. (EST) Monday-Friday ($1.05 per minute). The number is 1-900-225-5674 (TDD: 1-900-225-7778). Major credit card users (for a flat rate of $4.95) may call 1-888-362-8668 (TDD: 1-888-498-3648)

Travelers can check the **latest health information** with the U.S. Centers for Disease Control and Prevention in Atlanta, Georgia. A hotline at (404) 332-4559 gives the most recent health advisories, immunization recommendations or requirements, and advice on food and drinking water safety for regions and countries. A booklet entitled *Health Information for International Travel* (HHS publication number CDC-95-8280) is available from the U.S. Government Printing Office, Washington, DC 20402, tel. (202) 512-1800.

Information on **travel conditions, visa requirements, currency and customs regulations, legal holidays, and other items of interest to travelers** also may be obtained before your departure from a country's embassy and/or consulates in the U.S. (for this country, see "Principal Government Officials" listing in this publication).

U.S. citizens who are long-term visitors or traveling in dangerous areas are encouraged to register at the U.S. embassy upon arrival in a country (see "Principal U.S. Embassy Officials" listing in this publication). This may help family members contact you in case of an emergency.

MINING AND ENERGY RESOURCES IN GHANA: IMPORTANT INFORMATION

The contribution of Ghana's mining sector to the country's gross domestic product increased from 1.3% in 1991 to an average of about 5% in recent years. Export earnings from minerals averaged 35%, and the sector was one of the largest contributors to Government revenues through the payment of mineral royalties, employee income taxes, and corporate taxes. In 2005, gold production accounted for about 95% of total mining export proceeds.

GOVERNMENT POLICIES AND PROGRAMS

The Ministry of Mines and Energy overses all aspects of Ghana's mineral sector and was responsible for granting mining and exploration licenses. Within the Ministry, the Minerals Commission has responsibility for administering the Mining Act, recommending mineral policy, promoting mineral development, advising the Government on mineral matters, and serving as a liaison between industry and the Government. The Ghana Geological Survey Department conducts geologic studies. Ghana National Petroleum Corp. (GNPC) is the Government entity responsible for petroleum exploration and production. The Precious Minerals Marketing Corp. (PMMC) is the Government entity responsible for promoting the development of small-scale gold and diamond mining in Ghana and for purchasing the output of such mining, either directly or through licensed buyers. The Mines Department has authority in mine safety matters. All mine accidents and other safety problems also must be reported to the Ghana Chamber of Mines, which is the private association of operating mining companies. The Chamber also provides information on Ghana's mining laws to the public and negotiates with the mine labor unions on behalf of its member companies.

The overall legislative framework for the mining sector in Ghana is provided by the Minerals and Mining Law of 1986 (PNDCL 153), as amended in 1994 and 2005. Under the Minerals and Mining Law, mining companies must pay royalties; companies may also pay corporate taxes at standard rates. The 1986 mining law had been instrumental in attracting more than $5 billion in foreign investment to the Ghanaian mining industry between 1986 and 2002. The 1994 amendments reduced the 45% general mining corporate tax rate to 35%, which is the same as that imposed on other industries. The 2005 amendments included changes to royalty rates and the establishment of the period of duration of a mining lease.

Other legislation that affects mining and mineral exploration in Ghana includes the Minerals Commission Law of 1986 (PNDCL 154); the Small-Scale Gold Mining Law of 1989; the Investment Promotion Act, 1994 (Act 478); the Additional Profits Tax Law, 1985 (PNDCL 122); the Minerals (Royalties) Regulations, 1987 (LI 1349); the Environmental Protection Agency Act, 1994 (Act 490); and the Environmental Assessment Regulations, 1999, and as amended, 2002. The Petroleum (Exploration and Production) Law, 1984 (PNDCL 84), sets out the policy framework and describes the role of the Ministry of Mines and Energy, which regulates the industry. Ghana National Petroleum Corp. (GNPC), which is empowered to undertake petroleum exploration and production on behalf of the Government, is authorized to enter joint ventures and production-sharing agreements with commercial organizations; GNPC was established under the GNPC Law of 1983 (PNDCL 64). The regulation of artisanal gold mining is set forth in the Small-Scale Gold Mining Law, 1989 (PNDCL 218). The Precious Minerals Marketing Corporation Law, 1989 (PNDCL 219), set up the Precious Minerals Marketing Corporation (PMMC) to promote the development of small-scale gold and diamond mining in Ghana and to purchase the output of such mining, either directly or through licensed buyers.

PRODUCTION

In 2006, bauxite production increased by 38.7% to 842,000 metric tons (t) compared with 607,000 t in 2005. Diamond and silver production decreased by 4% and 12% to 973,000 carats (195 kg) and 3,142 kilograms, respectively. Gold production decreased to 66,205 kilograms (kg) compared with 66,852 in 2005.

INDUSTRY STRUCTURE

In the gold sector, Gold Fields Limited of South Africa held a 71.1% interest in the Tarkwa and the Damang gold mines in a joint venture with Toronto-based IAMGOLD Corp. (18.9%), and the Government of Ghana (10%) (U.S. Securities and Exchange Commission, 2005, p. 41). AngloGold Ashanti Ltd. of South Africa operated the Bibiani and the Iduapriem open pit gold mines and the Obuasi underground gold mine. The Bibiani and the Obuasi Mines were 100% owned by AngloGold Ashanti and the Iduapriem Mine was 80% owned by AngloGold Ashanti and 20% by the International Finance Corporation (AngloGold Ashanti Ltd., 2006a-c). Golden Star Resources Ltd. held a 90% interest in the Bogoso/Prestea and the Wassa open pit mines and a 90% interest in the idled Prestea underground mine. Newmont Mining Corp. of the United States held a 100% interest in the Ahafo gold property and an 85% interest in the Akyem gold property. Companies exploring for gold in Ghana included Adamus Resources Ltd., African Gold plc, Moydow Mines International Inc., and Pelangio Mines Inc.

In the bauxite and alumina sector, Alcoa Inc. of the United States held a 10% interest in Volta Aluminum Company Ltd. (Valco); the remaining equity was owned by the Government. Alcan Aluminum Ltd. of Canada held an 80% interest in Ghana Bauxite Company Ltd.; the Government held the remaining 20% interest.

COMMODITIES

ALUMINUM, BAUXITE, AND ALUMINA

In January 2005, Alcoa signed a memorandum of understanding (MOU) with the Government to develop an integrated aluminum industry in Ghana that would include bauxite mining, alumina refining, aluminum production, and rail transportation infrastructure upgrades. The MOU called for the restart of three of the five existing potlines at the idled Valco smelter, which would produce about 120,000 metric tons per year (t/yr) of aluminum; the designed capacity of the plant is 200,000 t/yr. The Government and Alcoa planned to restart the Valco smelter as soon as an interim power rate agreement is reached with the Volta River Authority. The Government (90%) was to be the managing owner of the smelter and Alcoa (10%), through its subsidiary, Alcoa World Alumina and Chemicals [a joint venture between Alcoa Inc. (60%) and Alcoa Limited of Australia (40%)] was to supply alumina and serve as the distributor of export sales of aluminum. The Government had acquired Kaiser Aluminum Corp.'s 90% interest in Valco in 2004. Kaiser closed the Valco plant in 2003 after struggling with fluctuating operating levels for several years and dealing with restricted power allocations from the Volta River Authority.

Canada-based Alcan Inc. and Alcoa Inc. of the United States were the two companies that operated in the bauxite and alumina sector. During 2006, Alcoa continued to study the possibility of developing an integrated aluminum industry in Ghana that would include bauxite mining, alumina refining, aluminum production, and rail transportation infrastructure upgrades. Alcan, on the other hand, signed a Memorandum of Understanding with the Government for the creation of a joint venture to explore the feasibility of developing a bauxite mine and a 1.5- to 2.0-million-metric-ton-per-year (Mt/yr) alumina refinery in Ghana.

GOLD

More than 90 percent of gold production in the early 1990s came from underground mines in western Ashanti Region, with the remainder coming from river beds in Ashanti Region and Central Region. During the early 1990s, AGC (Ghana's largest gold producer) saw its overall share of the domestic gold market decline from 80 percent to 60 percent as other operators entered the industry.

In 1992, Ghana's gold production surpassed 1 million fine ounces, up from 327,000 fine ounces in 1987. In March 1994, the Ghanaian government announced that it would sell half of its 55 percent stake in AGC for an estimated US$250 million, which would then be spent on development projects. The authorities also plan to use some of the capital from the stock sale to promote local business and to boost national reserves. The minister of mines and energy dispelled fears that the stock sale would result in foreign ownership of the country's gold mines by saying that the government would have final say in all major stock acquisitions.

In the gold sector, Red Back Mining Inc. of Canada, [through its subsidiary Chirano Gold Mines Ltd. (CGML)] operated the Chirano gold mine; AngloGold Ashanti Ltd. of South Africa operated the Bibiani, the Iduapriem, and the Obuasi gold mines; Golden Star Resources Ltd. of Canada operated the Bogoso/Prestea, the Prestea Underground, and the Wassa gold mines; Gold Fields Ltd. of South A Africa operated the Damang gold mine; and Denver-based Newmont Mining Corp. held interest in the Ahafo and the Akyem gold properties.

In October 2005, Red Back Mining Inc. of Canada [through its subsidiary Chirano Gold Mines Limited (CGML)] commissioned a new mine in Ghana. The mine, known as the Chirano gold mine, was an open pit operation located about 21 kilometers (km) to the south of AngloGold Ashanti's Bibiani gold mine in western Ghana. The Chirano gold mine produced 941 kilograms (kg) (reported as 30,247 troy ounces) in 2005 and was 100% owned by Red Back; the Government had the option to exercise its right to back into a 10% ownership in CGML. Chirano was scheduled to produce an average of about 3,800 kg (reported as 123,000 troy ounces) per year during a period of 8½ years. The designed capacity of the processing plant was 2.1 million metric tons per year (Mt/yr). A revised resource and reserve estimate for the Chirano Mine was underway in 2005. The economic potential of the Akwaaba deposit, a high-grade deposit within the Chirano mining concession, was being evaluated in 2005, and a resource estimate of the deposit was scheduled for completion in October 2006.

In 2005, gold production at the Bibiani Mine came from the processing of ore from the mine's remaining pits, stockpiled ore, and tailings. Satellite pits were depleted in December 2005, and AngloGold Ashanti expected stockpiled ore to be depleted by January 2006. Beginning in February, the mill was to process only old tailings. The Bibiani Mine, which had operated between 1903 and 1968 as an underground mine, was reopened in 1998 as an open pit mine with a carbon-in-leach (CIL) plant. The mine included old tailings dumps, which were reclaimed in December 2004. These tailings were expected to yield about 3.9 million metric tons (Mt) of ore at an estimated recovery grade of 0.60 gram per metric ton (g/t) gold during a period of 18 months. The company was studying the viability of restarting production from its main pit to a depth of about 60 meters below.

the current pit floor. Underground exploration was suspended in July 2005 and the underground mine continued to be on care-and-maintenance status. Gold production was expected to decrease to 1 1,700 kg in 2006 from 3,580 kg (reported as 11 115,000 troy ounces) in 2005.

Gold production at the Iduapriem open pit mine increased to 6,380 kg in 2005 (reported as 205,000 troy ounces) from 4,570 kg in 2004 owing to an increase in throughput at the processing plant. AngloGold Ashanti held an 80% interest in the Iduapriem Mine; the remaining 20% was held by the International Finance Corporation. The company also held a 90% interest in the Teberebie Mine, which is adjacent to the Iduapriem Mine; the Government held the remaining 10% interest.

In 2005, gold production at the Obuasi underground mine was hindered by a breakdown at the main processing plant during the first quarter of 2005 and the failure of a primary crusher during the third quarter; production, however, increased to 12,200 kg (reported as 391,000 troy ounces) from 7,930 kg in 2004 mostly owing to the start of mining from the Kubi surface oxide deposit. In terms of growth prospects, the company planned to develop the deep-level ore deposits at Obuasi known as the Obuasi Deeps, which were expected to extend the project's mine life to 2040. The development of Obuasi Deeps will require an initial investment of $44 million during the next 4 years to conduct further exploration and feasibility studies. The total capital expenditure for the development of the Obuasi Deeps was estimated to be about $570 million. AngloGold Ashanti held a 100% interest in the Obuasi Mine.

The Wassa open pit gold mine produced 2,149 kg of gold in 2005. The mine, which is located about 150 km west of Accra, was owned by Golden Star (90%) and the Government (10%). The mine had been in operation as an open pit heap-leach mine in the 1990s but was closed in 2001. Golden Star acquired the mine in 2002 after determining that conventional CIL processing was economically feasible. Plant feed in 2005 was a mixture of newly mined ore from the Wassa pit blended with material from the heap-leach pads left by the previous operation. Golden Star's planned to increase production at Wassa to about 3,700 kg (reported as 120,000 troy ounces) in 2006 and to produce about 4,000 kg (reported as 130,000 troy ounces) in 2007 as higher grade ores are reached at deeper levels. As of December 31, 2005, total probable mineral reserves at Wassa were reported to be 21.9 Mt at a grade of 1.34 g/t gold.

In addition to the Wassa Mine, Golden Star operated the Bogoso/Prestea open pit mine, which is located about 300 km west of Accra. Bogoso/Prestea produced 4,103 kg of gold in 2005. Golden Star held a 90% interest in the property, and the Government of Ghana held the remaining 10%. About 75% of the remaining ore reserve at Bogoso/Prestea is sulfide. Because this type of ore cannot be processed using the company's existing CIL plant, the company decided in June 2005 to build a new 3.5-Mt/yr processing plant which will use biooxidation to treat the remaining sulfide ore. The new processing plant was scheduled to be completed in late 2006.

The Prestea Underground gold mine, which is also 90% owned by Golden Star, remained idle during the year. Prestea Underground was closed in early 2002 owing to low gold prices. During 2005, a total of 8,096 meters of underground exploration drilling was completed at the mine; drilling was to continue in 2006. Golden Star planned to complete a prefeasibility study by the end of 2006 to evaluate the economic potential of restarting production at Prestea Underground. As of December 31, 2005, inferred mineral resources at the mine were estimated to be 6.1 Mt at an average grade of 8.1 g/t.

In 2005, N Newmont announced the company was advancing the Ahafo and the Akyem gold properties to production. The Ahafo property, which is located about 300 km northwest of Accra between the towns of Kenyase and Ntotoroso, was expected to begin production during the second half of 2006. Production of gold was expected to be about 17,100 kilograms per year (kg/yr) (reported as 550,000 troy ounces), with a mine life estimated to be more than 20 years. The company was awaiting the issuance of a mining license for the development of the Akyem property, which is located in Ghana's eastern region, about 130 km northwest of Accra between the towns of New Abirem and Ntronang. Newmont expected to begin production at Akyem in 2008 and to produce about 15,500 kg/yr of gold (reported as 500,000 troy ounces).

About 19.6 Mt of ore was processed at Tarkwa in 2005 from which 21,051 kg of gold was produced (Gold Fields Limited, 2006§). In November 2005, a new semiautogenous grinding (SAG) mill and CIL plant were commissioned at the Tarkwa Mine. The Tarkwa Mine, which is located in southwestern Ghana about 300 km west of Accra, consists of several open pit operations, one CIL plant, and two heap-leach facilities. Some underground mining had been conducted in the past, but underground operations ended in 1999. As of June 30, 2005, proven and probable reserves at Tarkwa were estimated to be about 417,000 kg of gold (reported as 13.4 million troy ounces) and to last until 2025 at current production rates.

The Damang Mine, which is located in the Wassa West District in southwestern Ghana about 360 km west of Accra and 30 km northeast of Tarkwa Mine, consists of an open pit operation, a SAG mill, and a CIL plant. The mine processed about 5.2 Mt of ore in 2005 and produced about 7,700 kg of gold. Owing to the depletion of the high-grade ore in the main Damang pit, an exploration program to seek for alternative ore sources was launched during the year. The exploration program resulted in the establishment of the Amoanda, the Rex, and the Tomento pits, and the extension of an old pit at Kwesie-Lima. Gold Fields and its partners reported that production from the new pits was to be processed along with stockpiles of lower grade ore. Mining of the Tomento pit began in July 2005 and mining of the Amoanda pit began during the fourth quarter of 2005; production from the Rex pit was scheduled to begin in 2007. As of June 30, 2005, proven and probable reserves at Damang were estimated to be about 40,000 kg of gold (reported as 1.3 million troy ounces) and were projected to last until 2010 at current production rates.

MANGANESE

Of the 1.6 million metric tons (Mt) of manganese ore produced in 2006, about 52%, or 832,000 t, was shipped to Ukraine; 37%, or 584,000 t, was shipped to China; and the remaining 184,000 t was shipped to Norway. Manganese carbonate ore exported from Ghana has traditionally been used in China as raw material in the production of silico-manganese. Less than 100,000 metric tons per year (t/yr) of this ore material was used to produce electrolytic manganese metal in China, but China's demand for manganese metal was projected to increase to 300,000 t in 2007. China's other supplier of manganese ore was Mexico. Privat Group of Ukraine, which also used manganese ore from Ghana, imported about 832,000 t in 2006. Privat Group acquired the right to manage Ghana Manganese Co. and, as its first order of business, indicated that it intended to amend all existing manganese contracts.

Ghana is one of the world's leading exporters of manganese; however, only 279,000 tons were produced in 1992, compared with the all-time high of 638,000 tons in 1974-75. Ghana has reserves exceeding 60 million tons, and considerable rehabilitation of the sector took place in the 1980s. Ghana National Manganese Corporation's mine and the surrounding infrastructure were repaired, helping to raise production from a low of 159,000 tons in 1983 to 284,000 tons in 1989 and 247,000 tons in 1990. The corporation earned US$20 million from its exports in 1991, up from US$11.6 million in 1989 and US$14.2 million in 1990. Approximately US$85 million was also invested by private investors at the newly explored Kwesikrom deposit.

DIAMOND

Diamond was recovered by artisanal miners from alluvial and in situ diamond deposits near A Akwatia in the Birim V Valley. The only formal commercial production came from a diamond placer mine in A Akwatia, which was operated by Government-owned Ghana Consolidated Diamonds Ltd. (GCD).

At least one company, Paramount Mining Corporation Ltd., explored for diamond at two properties in Ghana in 2006. In February 2006, the company entered into a joint-venture agreement with Leo Shield Exploration Ghana Ltd. to earn interest in the Osenase project, which covers an area of 330 square kilometers (km²) located about 25 kilometers (km) south of the Akwatia Diamond Project. Field work began in March 2006. A number of pits were dug in both alluvial and hard rock deposits. A total of 83 diamonds, which together weighed more than 3.3 carats (660 mg) and the largest of which was 0.56 carats (110 mg), were recovered from the gravel of alluvial deposits. The project area also contained gold and columbite-tantalite minerals in the alluvial material. The other property, which was known as Ochinso, covers an area of 37 km² within the Birim Diamond Field of southern Ghana. Paramount, through a farm-in arrangement with Aurion Resources Ltd. of Ghana, would be entitled to acquire 85% of the equity interest in the concession. At least 72 diamonds and 325 small gold grains from 20 small test pits were recovered from the property in 2006. The pits were situated in a number of different river systems throughout the Ochinso project area. Most of the diamonds recovered were reportedly of commercial size ranging between 1 to 2 millimeters (mm), with an average stone size of 0.036 carats (7.2 mg).

The government also is trying to expand Ghana's diamond mining industry, which has produced primarily industrial grade gems from alluvial gravels since the 1920s. More than 11 million carats of proven and probable reserves are located about seventy miles northwest of Accra. The main producer is the state-owned Ghana Consolidated Diamonds (GCD), which operates in the Birim River Basin. In the 1960s, the company mined 2 million carats of diamonds a year, but annual production in 1991 amounted to only 146,000 carats (29 kg). This downturn resulted from technical problems and GCD's weak financial position. Production from all mines came to 688,000 carats (138 kg) in 1991 and to 694,000 carats (139 kg) in 1992.

Diamond production was recovered by artisanal miners from alluvial and in situ diamond deposits near Akwatia in the Birim Valley. The only formal commercial production came from a diamond placer mine in Akwatia, which was operated by Government-owned Ghana Consolidated Diamonds Ltd. (GCD).

According to a 2004 report by Partnership Africa Canada and Global Witness Publishing Inc. (2004, p. 3-4), prior to the creation of the PMMC in 1989, as much as 70% of Ghana's diamond was smuggled out of the country. Following the creation of PMMC, diamond was initially shipped to a PMMC office in Antwerp, Belgium, for sale; currently, an open market has been established in Ghana in which registered buyers can operate from offices within the country and in which licensed diamond traders are allowed to operate. All buyers (exclusively Ghanian nationals) must transfer U.S. dollars through the Central Bank in advance for the purchase of diamond. Only about 200 of the 1,000 registered buyers were thought to be active during 2004. Purchased diamond was kept under lock in the custody of the PMMC and subject to inspection before being exported. According to the report, Ghana was fully implementing the Kimberley Process but the country lacked the resources to monitor and control illicit diamond mining and buying, especially from the artisanal mining areas. In Akwatia, for example, an informal diamond market existed where no paperwork was required to buy or sell diamond; this market was known locally as the "Belgian market." The report also indicated the possibility of diamond being smuggled from Côte d'Ivoire, especially following the sanctions on diamond exports imposed on this country in 2004 (Partnership Africa Canada and Global Witness Publishing Inc., 2004, p. 3-5).

It was reported that while annual diamond production from GCD continued to decline, diamond production from artisanal miners was increasing and that there was a possibility for the privatization of GCD. Foreign companies (not identified) were said to be interested in the Akwatia alluvial diamond field in the upper Birim River catchment area.

CEMENT

The Building and Road Institute of the Council for Scientific and Industrial Research of Ghana was conducting laboratory tests to evaluate the possibility of producing pozzolana cement from bauxite mining waste (known as red mud or clay). The two companies that produced cement in Ghana, Ghana Cement Works Ltd. and Diamond Cement Ghana Limited used imported clinker, gypsum, and limestone for the manufacturing of cement. About 2 Mt of clinker was imported in 2003 for the production of portland cement.

PETROLEUM

Petroleum exploration activities have been conducted in Ghana since the late 1800s; no significant commercially sustainable deposits of petroleum or natural gas have been discovered to date, with the exception of the Saltpond oilfield, which produced a total of 294,430 barrels when it reopened in 2002 to its closing in 2004. Gas flared at Saltpond averaged 2 million cubic feet per day. The Tema Oil Refinery refined all the crude petroleum imported into the country, with the exception of consignments going to the Takoradi thermal powerplant.

At least two companies were exploring for petroleum in the country in 2006. These included Dallas-based Kosmos Energy LLC, which was conducting exploration offshore at West Cape Three Points Block, and Vanco Energy Co. of the United States, which explored for petroleum at the Cape Three Points Deepwater Block (CTPD) in the Tano-Ivorian Basin.

Dallas-based Kosmos Energy LLC held an 86.5% working interest in the West Cape Three Points (WCTP) Block in the Gulf of Guinea's Tano Basin. In 2005, the company conducted a 1,075-km2 three-dimensional (3-D) survey to evaluate the potential of the block. The WCTP Block is located about 8 km from the Ghanian coastline and 95 km southwest of the city of Takoradi. The remaining interest in WCTP was held by GNPC (10%) and E.O. Group of Ghana (3.5%).

Final environmental impact assessment permits were granted in Benin, Ghana, and Togo for the West African Gas Pipeline (WAGP) between March and April 2005. The West Gas Pipeline Company Limited (WAGPCo) was granted a license to construct the pipeline in April, and the first shipload of about 8,000 pipes was delivered to the Tema Port in May. In September, Chevron Corporation, which is the WAGP project manager, announced that WAGPCo had begun the installation of the 569 km main offshore segment of the pipeline. The WAGP was expected to be operational by December 2006 and to deliver gas to powerplants and industries in Benin, Ghana, Nigeria, and Togo.

Vanco Energy Company explored for petroleum at the Cape Three Points Deepwater Block (CTPD), which is located in the Tano-Ivorian Basin. The company had signed an exploration agreement with the Government in 2002 at which time it conducted a two-dimensional (2-D) seismic program to evaluate the block. In 2005, the company carried out a 1,500-km2 3-D seismic program to further define the structural and stratigraphic prospects in the block. The first well in the CTPD Block was planned for 2007.

ENVIRONMENTAL IMPACT

The Ghanian Environmental Protection Agency (EPA) was the Government entity responsible for the formulation of policies on all aspects of the environment. The agency's functions included acting in liaison and cooperating with other Government agencies; collaborating with foreign and international agencies, as necessary; conducting investigations into environmental issues; coordinating the activities of bodies concerned with the technical aspects of the environment for the purpose of controlling the generation, treatment, storage, transportation, and disposal of industrial waste; ensuring compliance with environmental impact assessment procedures; issuing environmental permits and pollution abatement notices; making recommendations to the

Government for the protection of the environment; prescribing standards and guidelines related to the pollution of air, water, and land; protecting and improving the quality of the environment; and securing the control and prevention of discharge waste into the environment among several other functions.

In 2005, the Center for Public Interest Law and the Center for Environmental Law, two Accra-based nongovernmental organizations, sued Bonte Gold Mines Ltd. (an 85% owned subsidiary of Akrokeri-Ashanti Gold Mines Inc. of Canada), Ghana's Minerals Commission, and the EPA for the reclamation of the environment after the cessation of Bonte's gold mining operations along the Jeni River. Bonte closed its operations at Bonteso in the Ashanti region in March 2004, citing problems concerning low-grade ore, equipment unavailability, and a default of its financial obligations during 2003. The company allegedly did not follow the due process for mine decommissioning, such as by failing to post bonds to the EPA for the reclamation of lands, failing to notify workers of its intention to liquidate, not paying up-to-date wages to workers, and leaving a debt of about $18 million owed to various state institutions and private companies. The EPA and the Minerals Commission were accused of failing to ensure Bonte's compliance to operate in a sustainable manner.

Ghana's Obuasi region is known to host arsenopyritic goldbearing ore bodies. According to company reports, during the 1990s, an arsenic precipitation plant was installed at the Pompora Treatment Plant for the commercial recovery of arsenic from the roaster flue gases. At the time, the recovered arsenic trioxide was sold to Europe for commercial applications. As the market for arsenic declined, the treatment plant was shut down in 2000 and about 10,000 metric tons (t) of arsenic was stockpiled in bags at Obuasi. After the introduction of the Biox treatment process, the arsenic trioxide was converted to arsenic pentoxide and deposited in tailings dams. AngloGold Ashanti Ltd. (the company that was formed through the merger of Ashanti Goldfields Ltd. and AngloGold Ltd.) reported that inadequate storage of the stockpiled bags allegedly caused arsenic contamination to the Pompora stream. The problem was identified during the company's due diligence study prior to the merger. AngloGold Ashanti constructed a lined storage dam at the old heap leach site. The company planned to move the arsenic to a new facility where it will be stored and gradually disposed of by blending it into the Biox process circuit where it will be chemically stabilized and deposited as a component of the tailings residue in the new Sansu Tailings Storage Facility. The company estimates that it will take about 6 years to dispose of the arsenic.

HISTORY

Ghana has produced and exported gold for centuries. In precolonial times, present-day Ghana was one source of the gold that reached Europe via trans-Saharan trade routes. In the fifteenth century, Portuguese sailors tried to locate and to control gold mining from the coast but soon turned to more easily obtained slaves for the Atlantic slave trade. Most gold mining before the mid-nineteenth century was alluvial, miners recovering the gold from streams. Modern gold mining that plumbs the rich ore deposits below the earth's surface began about 1860, when European concessionaires imported heavy machinery and began working in the western areas of present-day Ghana. The richest deposit, the Obuasi mine, was discovered by a group of Europeans who sold their rights to E.A. Cade, the founder of Ashanti Goldfields Corporation (AGC). Since the beginning of the twentieth century, modern mining in the Gold Coast has been pursued as a large-scale venture, necessitating significant capital investment from European investors.

Under British colonial rule, the government controlled gold mining to protect the profits of European companies. The colonial government also restricted possession of gold as well as of mercury, essential in recovering gold from the ore in which it is embedded. Following independence, foreign control of the sector was tempered by increasing government involvement under the Nkrumah regime; however, production began to decline in the late 1960s and did not recover for almost twenty years. In the mid-1960s, many mines began to hit poorer gold reefs. Despite the floating of the international gold price in the late 1960s, few investors were willing to invest, and the government failed to provide the capital necessary to expand production into new reefs. Of the two major gold mining enterprises, neither the State Gold Mining Corporation nor AGC (40 percent controlled by the government) expanded or even maintained production.

Under the ERP, the mining sector was targeted as a potential source of foreign exchange, and since 1984, the government has successfully encouraged the rejuvenation of gold mining. To offer incentives to the mining industry, the Minerals and Mining Law was passed in 1986. Among its provisions were generous capital allowances and reduced income taxes. The corporate tax rate was set at 45 percent, and mining companies could write off 75 percent of capital investment against taxes in the first year and 50 percent of the remainder thereafter. The government permitted companies to use offshore bank accounts for service of loans, dividend payments, and expatriate staff remuneration.

Ghana's mineral sector had started to recover by the early 1990s after its severe decline throughout the 1970s. One indicator of the scale of decline was that by 1987, only four gold mines were operating in Ghana, compared with eighty in 1938. Throughout the 1970s, the output of gold, as well as bauxite, manganese, and diamonds, fell steadily. Foreign exchange shortages inhibited mine maintenance, new exploration, and development investment. The overvalued cedi and spiraling inflation exacerbated mining companies' problems, as did smuggling and the deteriorating infrastructure. Energy supplies failed to meet the industry's growing needs; foreign exchange shortages constrained oil imports, and domestically generated hydroelectricity was unable to make up the shortfall.

After 1983, however, the government implemented a series of measures to enhance the sector's appeal. In 1986 new mining legislation for the gold and diamond sectors replaced the previous complex and obsolete regulations, and a generous incentives system was established that allowed for external foreign exchange retention accounts, capital allowances, and a flexible royalties payment system. Since then the sector has benefited from a wave of fresh investment totaling US$540 million since 1986, and by the early 1990s mining was the country's second highest foreign exchange earner.

Under legislation passed after 1983, the government liberalized and regularized the mining industry. For the first time, the government made small claim-holding feasible, with the result that individual miners sold increasing amounts of gold and diamonds to the state-operated Precious Minerals Marketing Company. In 1990 the company bought 490,000 carats (98 kg) of diamonds and 20,000 ounces of gold and earned a total of US$20.4 million through sales, 70 percent of it from diamond sales and 30 percent from gold bought from smallscale operators. Diamond output totaled 688,000 carats (138 kg) in 1991 and 694,000 carats (139 kg) in 1992, while gold production amounted to 843,000 fine ounces in 1991 and 1,004,000 fine ounces in 1992. Furthermore, the government succeeded in attracting significant foreign investment into the sector and, by early 1991, had signed over sixty mining licenses granting prospecting rights to international companies. To forestall domestic criticism of large-scale foreign control of the sector, the government announced in mid-1991 the establishment of a state-controlled holding company to buy shares in mines on behalf of private, that is, foreign, investors.

In the early 1990s, the government announced plans to privatize its diamond-mining operations and to expand production. At Accra's invitation, De Beers of South Africa agreed to undertake an eighteen-month feasibility study to determine the extent of the Birim River Basin diamond reserves. The survey was to cost US$1 million. A De Beers subsidiary will be the operator and manager of GCD, while Lazare Kaplan International, a New York-based diamond polishing and trading company, will produce and market the diamonds.

In 1989 the government established the Precious Minerals Marketing Corporation (PMMC) to purchase minerals from small producers in an effort to stem diamond smuggling. Estimates suggested that as much as 70 percent of Ghana's diamonds were being smuggled out of the country in the mid-1980s. In its first sixteen months of operation, the PMMC bought 382,423 carats (76.485 kg) of diamonds and 20,365 ounces of gold and sold 230,000 carats (46 kg) of diamonds worth US$8 million. The corporation also earned ¢130 million in 1991 on its jewelry operations, up 48 percent from the previous year, and it planned to establish joint marketing ventures with foreign firms to boost sales abroad. Nevertheless, because of new complaints over raw gem sales, the government in March 1992 ordered an investigation into the operations of the state agency and suspended its managing director.

BUYING GHANA GOLD & DIAMOND
The Precious Mineral Marketing Corporation (PMMC) manufactures jewellery mainly in traditional African designs. As leading jewelers, PMMC offers a wide range of other unique services for jewellery bought from the organisation such as: -

GOLD

Procedure For Exportation Of Gold

* The gold to be exported shall be a **minimum** weight of 50 Kgs.

* The mineral to be exported shall be sealed in the premises of PMMC and in the presence of Customs Officials, PMMC representatives and that of the Agent. After sealing, the gold will be kept in the vault of PMMC awaiting export.

* PMMC will supply the agent with assay certificates to determine the purity of gold being exported.

* All Bank of Ghana and Customs, Excise and Preventive Services (CEPS) export documents will be completed by the Agent in conjunction with PMMC (and the agent's Bank where necessary).

* The agent shall nominate a carrier and provide all relevant flight details to PMMC 24 hours before export.
* Transportation of gold will be done from PMMC premises accompanied by the agent's representative and given to the carrier.

* Cost of Insurance and Freight will be borne by the agent.

* The agent will undertake to ensure that the export value of the Gold Dore Bars being exported is repatriated to Ghana according to the London (AM) **Gold Fix on the day the Gold is shipped.**

Funds relating to all transactions will be transferred through PMMC's US Dollar account with the Bank of Ghana.

* The agent is responsible for arranging a market overseas. Marketing contracts to be executed by the agent shall be subject to the approval by the Bank of Ghana (BOG) or the Minerals Commission.

* PMMC will export the Gold using its license to the address given by the agent.

* The agent will incur a fee of not more than 0.5% of the value of the gold for each and every shipment, payable before or on the day of export to PMMC. This excludes smelting and assay charges which are separate.

* PMMC agrees to smelt and or assay gold at the request of the agent. The fees payable for such services are:- Assaying - US$50 per bar
Smelting - US$20 per kg gold

DIAMOND

Characteristics Of Ghana Diamonds
The characteristic feature of diamonds of Ghana is their small size. They are mainly industrial but a moderate proportion of about 10 - 15% of them are gems cuttable and polishable for use in jewellery production. Gem diamonds of sizes 1 carat and above are few and may not be available in commercial quantities. The average size of Ghana diamonds is about 10 stones per carat.

Procedure For Purchase Of Diamond

* Application forms for Licenses to purchase Diamond may be obtained by any foreign company and/individuals from the PMMC. Completed forms must be returned to the Managing Director of PMMC with a non-refundable fee of US$100.

* Processing of application forms requires a confidential status report on the company. Whilst this is being done, a temporary license may be issued not exceeding 6 months. A company so issued with a temporary license may commence purchase of rough diamonds only upon the payment in full of US$1,000 per month for the period approved and an up-front payment transfer of not less than US$250,000 if required. All unutilized funds will be transferable. Fees for permanent Licenses are US$12,000 per annum. This is renewable every year.

* Permanent license holders are required to purchase not less than US$150,000 worth of diamonds per month.

* All buying agents are provided with an office at Diamond House with basic office furnishing for the purpose of buying rough diamonds.

* A temporary or permanent buyer must engage resident valuer(s) to purchase the rough diamonds by negotiating directly with local winners and agents alongside other buyers at competitive prices.

* All purchasing activity must be done in this office at Diamond House and not at the mining sites.

* Rough diamonds purchased by License Buying Agents are kept in a special box at the end of each working day and transferred to PMMC for security safe keeping until required by the agent.

* A commission of not more than 3% on the export value of rough diamonds shipped at the request of the agent to a designated address is paid to PMMC.

* A license will be withdrawn immediately for the following reasons:-

* Inactivity for a period exceeding 21 days without prior notices.

* Buying diamonds outside the premises.
* Infringement or violation of Ghana's Mining Laws.
* An official adverse report on the status of the company.
* Buying malpractices including dealing with solely selected agents/winners.
* Using the office for other purposes other than buying diamonds.

For further enquiries, contact:

The Managing Director
Precious Minerals Marketing Corporation
Diamond House
P.O. Box 108
Accra, Ghana
Tel: 233-21-664931-4
Fax: 233-21-662586

Minerals Commission
P.O. Box M.248
Accra, Ghana
Tel: 233-21-772783/772786
Fax: 233-21-773324

Ashanti gold Fields Corporation
P.O. Box 2665
Accra, Ghana
Tel: 233-21-772190/776224/772235/776501
Fax: 233-21-775947

MINE OFFICE
Ashanti Goldfields Corporation
P.O. Box 10
Obuasi, Ghana
Tel: 233-0582-494-9
Fax: 233-0582-268

Ghana Bauxite Co. Ltd.
Ministry Post Office
Accra, Ghana
Tel: 233-21-664287
Fax: 233-21-669497

Ghana Consolidated Diamond De Beers
P.O. Box 2978
Accra, Ghana
Tel: 233-21-664577-9
Fax: 233-21-664635

Ghana National Manganese Corporation
P.O. Box M.183

Accra, Ghana
Tel: 233-21-666607-8/666563

Trade and Export Agencies

Ghana Trade Fair Company Limited
Ghana Trade fair Company (GTFC) Limited formerly the Ghana Trade Fair Authority (FTFA) is an autonomours self-financing state-owned enterprise, estatblished by PNDC Law (215) 1989. GTFC is administratively responsible to the now Ministry of Trade and Industry. The fairs and exhibitions organised by GTFC are noted for their high standards.

Ghana Export Promotion Council
The Ghana Export Promotion Council (GEPC) has the sole responsibility to develop and promote exports of non-traditional products. These involve the provision of technical assistance at the enterprise level in production, marketing and training and general advisory services as well as participation in export finance committees and other fora aimed at creating an enabling environment for non-traditional export expansion.

For more information visit: www.exportghana.org

Ghana National Procurement Agency Limited
The Ghana National Procurement Agency Limited formerly the Ghana National Procurement Agency (GNPA) was set up in 1976 and is primarily charged with purchasing in bulk either within or outside such goods as may be designated from time to time by the Minister of Trade and Industry. Such items include, rice, sugar, coking oil etc.

GNPA has revised its corporate plan and mission statement as a result of the changing competitive environment of business and will now engage in exports of non-traditional goods, and work towards Export House Status.

For more information visit: www.gnpa-ghana.com

Federation of Association of Ghanaian Exporters (FAGE)
The Federation of Assocaition of Ghanaian Exporters (FAGE) is a private, non-governmental organization of Ghanaian exporters and importers associations. Membership comprises of over 2,500 exporting firms ina range of sectors, including agriculture, seafood, crafts, timber, textiles, minerals, and industrial materials. The primary goal of FAGE is to be the premier provider of technical and information services to facilitate transactions betwwen Ghanaian firms and their global partners.

Association of Ghana Industries (AGI)
The Assocation of Ghana Industries is a non-profit voluntary business association with about 500 members - large, medium and small industries operating in all parts of Ghana. Member companies of the Association, from the private and the public sector, account for the majority of the nation's industrial output.

The AGI's objectives include:

Studies, supports and influences legislative or other measures which are considered favourable for industry and oppose those which are considered inimical to the growth of industry. Considers all issues connected with industry in Ghana and presents the views and suggestions of industry to Government and all stakeholders. Delivers quality services to member-companies, particularly small and medium scale interprises to bring about improvement in their performance.

Ghana National Chamber of Commerce and Industry
The Ghana National Chamber of Commerce and Industry (GNCCI) in its present form, was established on 8th November, 1961 under an act of Parliament (Executive Instrument No. 196) following the amalgmation of the then four existing Chambers of Commerce. The Executive Instrument was amended by Legislative Instrument No 611 of 1968 to streamline some of the internal structurs of the chamber. The Ghana National Chamber of Commerce and Industry is an association of business operators,firms and industries set up to promote commercial and industrial interests in the country.

Private Enterprise Foundation (PEF)
The Private Enterprise Foundation is an unbrella private sector body devoted to the orderly and healthy development of the private sector in Ghana through advocay and promotion. In the discharge of this responsibility PEF is involved in policy dialogue to ensure that policies favour the smooth growth of the private sector.

For further ensquries contact: The Private Enterprise Foundation E-

Timber Export Development Board
The Timber Export Development Board (TEDB) now Timber Export Development Division (TEDD) of the Forestry Commission was established under PNDC Law 123, 1985 to undertake export promotion and development, compilation and dissemination of market information and publication of jounals as well as periodicals for the timber industry in Ghana.

For further enquiries contact:
Timber Export Development Board
P. O. Box 515 Takoradi
Tel: +233-31-29216
Fax: +233-31-2336/ 2339

OR
Forestry Commission
P. O. Box M 434, Accra, Ghana
Tel: 233-21-675736/ 221315
Fax: 233-21-7012405

Precious Minerals Marketing Company Limited
The Precious Minerals Marketing Company (PMMC) Limited buys and sells precious minerals such as diamonds and gold. To develope and add value to the jewellery industry in ghana, the PMMC does manufacture jewllery mainly in Traditional African designs.

Send an E-mail to pmmc@ghana.com for more information

Ghana Cocoa Board
The Ghana Cocoa Board, Cocobod, is a statutory public board. It is central administrative body of the institutions and organizations concerned with various operating and servicing aspects of the Ghana cocoa industry. Cocobod has been one of the most useful public organisations ever to be set up by government and people of Ghana, as far as the recorede histrory of the nation.

Visit www.cocobod.org for more information

The Minerals Commission

The Minerals Commission (MINCOM) is the main promotional and regulatory agency in the minerals sector in Ghana. Under the Constitution and Act 450, MINCOM is responsible for the regulation and management of the mineral resources of Ghana and the coordination of policies in relation to minerals. Commission Law (1986) For information visit www.mincomgh.org

GHANA ENERGY POLICY AND RESOURCES: IMPORTANT INFORMATION

STRATEGY AND GOALS

Ghana is well endowed with a variety of energy resources including biomass, hydrocarbons, hydropower, solar and wind. It has the capacity to produce modern bio-fuels and is exploring options to develop nuclear Energy. The energy sector's vision is to

- develop an Energy Economy
- secure a reliable supply of high quality energy services for all sectors of the Ghanaian economy by 2012 and
- become a major exporter of oil and powerand 2015 respectively

The vision of the energy sector is to ensure availability of and universal access to energy services and export by 2020. The achievement of the vision raises the following challenges:

1. Development of infrastructure for the production and supply of adequate energy services to meet national requirement and for export:
2. Developing the requisite infrastructure to ensure universal access as well as the efficient and reliable supply of energy services:
3. Ensuring that energy is produced and supplied in a form that has no adverse health, safety and environmental impact; and
4. Ensuring that energy is produced, transported and used in an efficient manner. Addressing these challenges requires the development of an effective strategy, as well as programmes and projects that are achievable.

NATIONAL GOAL

Within the context of energy sector vision, the goal of the energy sector is to make energy services universally accessible and readily available in an environmentally sustainable manner.

Energy Sector Objectives

The policy objectives to achieve this goal are to:

Secure long term fuel supplies for the thermal power plants;

Reduce technical and commercial losses in power supply; Information from Energy Commission

Support the modernisation and expansion of energy infrastructure to meet growing demands and ensure reliability;

Increase access to modern forms of energy;

Improve the overall management, regulatory environment and operation of the energy sector;

Minimise the environmental impacts of energy supply and consumption through increased production and use of renewable energy and make energy delivery efficient;

Ensure cost recovery for energy supply and delivery;

Ensure the productive and efficient use of energy;

Promote and encourage private sector participation in the energy sector; and

Diversify the national energy mix by promoting renewable energy sources nuclear and coal;

PETROLEUM SECTOR

The Petroleum Upstream sub-sector consists of

- Activities which involves exploration, development and production of oil and gas from oil or gas fields, and
- Activities, which consist of the transportation of oil and gas to the oil refinery or gas processing plant, respectively referred to as midstream activities.

UPSTREAM SUB - SECTOR

The objectives of the Upstream Sub–sector is to ensure the effective management of the oil and gas resources of the country and also accelerate exploitation of and development of new hydrocarbon resources for the overall benefit and welfare of all Ghanaians, present and future. Government is further committed to attracting increased local value-added investments in the oil and gas sector and the indigenization of knowledge, expertise and technology. The main objectives of the upstream sub sector are:

- Manage oil and gas revenues transparently and ensure equity for the benefit of the present and future generation of Ghanaians. This will be achieved through institutional reforms and transparent regulation for the management of the oil revenue through legislative guidelines for the creation of a Future Generation Fund.

- Encourage investments along the oil and gas industry value chain through fiscal incentives and "even- handed" regulation

- Maximise the benefits of oil and gas wealth generation through the use of local goods and services, people, businesses and financing in all aspects of the oil and gas industry value chain and retaining the benefit within Ghana

- Ensure security for oil and gas industry installations and operations through the development of dedicated institutional arrangement for national oil and gas security matters and legislation of oil and gas safety requirements.

- Develop a viable domestic petrochemical industry based on natural gas.

- Support capacity building at all levels in the country's technical, vocational and tertiary institutions.

DOWNSTREAM SUB - SECTOR

The objectives of the petroleum downstream Sub –sector are to rehabilitate and expand petroleum refining, storage, distribution and marketing infrastructure; ensure fair distribution of petroleum products to all parts of the country and reduce heavy burden of oil imports on the country's economy by accelerating the exploitation of indigenous hydrocarbon resources. These objectives will be achieved by:

- Continuing to finance the development of rural kerosene storage and supply infrastructure nationwide. The Ministry of Energy is giving further impetus to the Rural Kerosene Promotion Programme.
- Expanding the petroleum product storage capacity nationwide. BOST is currently expanding existing bulk petroleum products storage capacity.
- Expanding marine related facilities on the Volta Lake for bulk transportation to ensure year-round supply of petroleum products to Northern Ghana.
- Facilitating the availability of more petroleum product distribution outlets in deprived areas to increase access density (number of persons per sale outlet).
- Promote a more efficient licensing regime for sales outlets to ensure optimal economic benefits to both investors and consumers.

MANDATE OF THE PETROLEUM DIRECTORATE

The mandate of the petroleum directorate is to supervise and formulate policies for the petroleum sub-sector, as well as, to monitor and evaluate the implementation of petroleum sub-sector policies and programme.

RENEWABLE ENERGY RESOURCE POTENTIALS IN GHANA

The development of wind energy resource for commercial power generation in Ghana is steadily taking centre stage of national discourse. Preliminary wind resource assessments results in selected sites along the coasts and high elevations showed moderate to excellent wind potentials. Especially, sites with good wind regimes are those along the east coastlines. The gross wind electric potential is about 5,600 MW representing some 1,128km2. Infrastructure such as road, grid network and load centres coincide with most areas where these wind potentials exist. The table shows a summary of gross wind electric potential for Ghana.

GROSS WIND RESOURCE POTENTIAL OF GHANA

Wind Resource Utility Scale	Wind Class	Wind Power at 50 m W/m2	Wind Speed at 50 m m/s	Total Area km2	Percent Windy Land	Total Capacity Installed MW
Moderate	3	300 – 400	6.4 – 7.0	715	0.3	3,575
Good	4	400 – 500	7.0 – 7.5	268	0.1	1,340
Excellent	5	500 – 600	7.5 – 8.0	82	<0.1	410
Excellent	6	600 – 800	8.0 – 8.8	63	<0.1	315
Total				1,128	0.5	5,640

SOLAR ENERGY RESOURCE POTENTIAL

Ghana is endowed with enormous solar energy resource spread across the entire country. Daily solar irradiation level ranges from 4kWh/m2 to 6kWh/m2. Areas of highest irradiation levels are spread across the entire northern belt which represents over 60% of the total national land mass. The annual sunshine duration ranges between 1800 to 3000 hours offering very high potential for grid connected and off-grid applications. Over 6,000 solar systems with an installed capacity of 3.2MW have been installed in the country mainly for off-grid applications.

HYDROPOWER RESOURCE POTENTIAL

The potential exploitable hydro resource for Ghana is about 2500MW. Already, 1,180MW of this potential have been developed and operational at Akosombo and Kpong. An additional 400MW is under construction, bringing the total exploited capacity to 1,580MW or about 60%. The remaining 840MW capacity is located at about 21 sites with capacities ranging from medium (95MW) to small (17MW) hydropower potentials. The Directorate focuses on promoting and developing the country's small hydropower (SHP) potential considered below 40MW.

BIOENERGY RESOURCE POTENTIAL

Ghana has appreciable bioenergy potential with biomass energy in the form of woodfuel and charcoal consumption accounting for about 72% of total energy consumption. Two-thirds of the country or 18.3 Mha is under tree cover. The climatic and soil conditions are very suitable for large scale agriculture, energy crops and sustainable woodfuel productions. It is estimated that with annual rainfall of 1,300 – 2,200mm, about 243PJ/yr or 65,000GWh/yr of woodfuel could be obtained from the existing tropical forests.

Contact
ren.moen@gmail.com
t. (233 0302) 667152/668048
f. (233 0302) 683980

ELECTRICITY SECTOR

Electricity is the dominant modern energy form used in the industrial and service sectors accounting for 69% of modern energy used in the two sectors of the national economy. The generation and supply of electricity provides employment for a significant number of Ghanaian professionals. It is also an important source of foreign exchange earnings in the country as Ghana exports power to neighbouring countries, including Togo, Benin, and Burkina Faso The Ghana electricity supply industry is unbundled with separate jurisdictions and entities regarding activities of electricity generation, transmission and distribution.

Electricity generation is undertaken by the state- owned Volta River Authority (VRA), which operates the Akosombo Hydro Power Station, Kpong Hydro Power Station and the Takoradi Thermal Power Plant (TAPCO) at Aboadze. VRA is also a minority joint partner with TAQA, a private sector company which owns and operates the Takoradi International Power Company (TICO) thermal power plant also located at Aboadze. Bui Power Authority (BPA), another state-owned entity, is charged with the implementation of the Bui Hydro electric Power Project. In addition, independent power producers have been licensed to build, own and operate power plants. The IPP projects are at various stages of development.

The National Interconnected Transmission System (NITS) for electricity is owned and operated by the Ghana Grid Company (GRIDCO).GRIDCO is a state-owned company. The distribution of electricity is done by the Electricity Company of Ghana (ECG), a state-owned company, and the Northern Electricity Department (NED), a subsidiary of the Volta River Authority(VRA). The Energy Commission (EC) and the Public Utilities and Regulatory Commission (PURC) regulate the electricity supply industry.

The Energy Commission, in addition to being responsible for technical regulations in the power sector, also advises the Minister for Energy on matters relating to energy planning and policy. The PURC on the other hand is an independent regulatory agency responsible for the economic regulation of the power sector with the mandate to approve rates for electricity sold by electricity distribution utilities.

The Ministry of Energy is responsible for formulating, monitoring and evaluating policies, programmes and projects in the energy sector. It is also the institution charged with the implementation of the National Electrification Scheme (NES) which seeks to extend the reach of electricity to all communities in the long term.

Ghana has an installed capacity of 1960MW made up of hydro and thermal facilities. Electricity demand which is currently 1400MW is growing at about 10% per annum. It is estimated that Ghana requires capacity additions of about 200MW to catch up with increasing demand in the medium to long term. The existing power plants are unable to attain full generation capacity as a result of limitations in fuel supply owing to rising fuel prices and uncertainty in rainfall and water inflows into the hydroelectric power facilities.

Ghana has an extensive transmission system which covers all the regions of the country. Transmission infrastructure has, however, deteriorated over the years, resulting in transmission bottlenecks, overloaded transformer sub stations and high system losses.

The electricity distribution infrastructure is extensive providing access to about 66% of the population. However, it is old and obsolete, leading to frequent interruptions in power supply and relatively high system losses. While national access is about 66%, access in the three northern regions is about 30%.

In 1994, Ghana's total generating capacity was about 1,187 megawatts, and annual production totaled approximately 4,490 million kilowatts. The main source of supply is theVolta River Authority with six 127-megawatt turbines. The authority's power plant at Akosombo Dam provides the bulk of all electricity consumed in Ghana, some 60 percent of which is purchased by Valco for its smelter. The power plant also meets most of the energy needs of Togo and Benin, which amounted to an estimated equivalent of 180,000 tons of oil in 1991.

The balance of Ghana's electricity is produced by diesel units owned by the Electricity Corporation of Ghana, by mining companies, and by a 160-megawatt hydroelectric plant at Kpong, about 40 kilometers downstream from Akosombo.

A third dam at Bui on the Black Volta River has been under study for some time, with the aim of increasing power supplies in northern Ghana or of selling power to Côte d'Ivoire and Burkina Faso (Burkina, formerly Upper Volta). There have been difficulties, however, in raising the funds needed for the 450-megawatt generating plant. Other sites with the potential for power generation, on the Pra River (Ghana), the Tano River, the White Volta River, and the Ankobra River, would also require substantial investment.

Ghana has attempted to increase distribution of its electricity throughout the country. One program, funded by the World Bank's International Development Association, will provide reliable and widespread electricity in the urban and southern parts of the country. In addition, the extension of the national grid to the Northern Region was commissioned in 1989. The extension links northern Ghana to the power generated from the Akosombo Dam.

The second phase of the extension will connect major towns in Upper East Region with the regional capital, Bolgatanga, at a cost of US$100 million. The final phase will see exports of electricity across the northern border to Burkina. In early 1991, furthermore, the International Development Association announced a loan to the Electricity Corporation of Ghana to finance the supply and expansion of electricity networks in the northwestern areas of Accra. The corporation aims to extend the supply of electricity to all isolated centers where diesel is the main source of power.

Plans were also afoot to increase the supply of electricity by utilization of thermal energy. Construction was anticipated by late 1994 on the country's first thermal power generating plant near Takoradi. Scheduled for completion in 1997, the plant will contribute 300 megawatts of electricity to the national grid.

NUCLEAR ENERGY IN GHANA

Ghana Atomic Energy Commission
P. O. Box LG80, Legon-Accra,
Ghana
Telephone: (+233) 30 2400310
Fax: (+233) 30 2400807

There are currently no nuclear power plants in Ghana, although there are several nuclear research reactors in Ghana and plans to build to a power plant.

The Ghana Atomic Energy Commission has been investigating the use of nuclear power and is a member of the International Nuclear Library Network. The commission is working with the International Atomic Energy Agency to implement nuclear power in Ghana as part of a wider project, Sustainable Energy Development for Sub-Saharan Africa. Ghana also has a National Nuclear Research Institute which trains undergraduate and postgraduate students in the techniques of nuclear science application in such areas as agriculture, medicine, and research. Both of these organizations focus more on research and the two research reactors located in Ghana than nuclear power, as the country has no nuclear power plants.

The government of Ghana plans to commission the building of a nuclear power plant by 2018. President John Agyekum Kufuor supported the future building of nuclear power plants, seeing it as part of a solution to the country's energy problems. He initiated a Nuclear Power Committee to study the issue. In 2011, the director of the National Nuclear Research Institute, Benjamin Nyarko, also said he believed nuclear power could prevent future energy crises

NUCLEAR RESEARCH

Ghana has a National Nuclear Research Institute which trains undergraduate and postgraduate students in the techniques of nuclear science application in such areas as agriculture, medicine, and research. In 1994 a research reactor was constructed at Kwabenyan, near Accra. In addition, a second nuclear physics center is to be established inKumasi on the recommendation of the Ghana Atomic Energy Commission

THE NUCLEAR OPTION FOR GHANA[1]

All countries, particularly the industrially developing ones, share a common concern over energy. In today's economic environment, inflated energy prices are still on the rise and oil sources are growing more tenuous. So many industrially developing countries, having fuelled their progress by importing oil, now face additional challenges to maintaining or increasing their growth. In the early 1970s oil supply problems and dramatic oil price increases became facts of everyday life; which then led industry and research institutions to increase their efforts in the development and improvement of energy conservation techniques and energy supply alternatives.

Today, the panic of previous years concerning oil seems to have given way to a mood of optimism. However, world forecasts of energy supplies and demands up to the year 2000 indicate that this new optimism is unjustified. By adopting various scenarios and speculating from alternative assumptions about relevant factors (such as population and economic growth), projections for world energy requirements in the year 2000 stood at roughly 400 to 100 quod.1 All the recoverable non-renewable energy resources of the world put together stand at 161,000 quods, of which crude oil accounts for only six percent and natural gas for five percent.2Many analysts believe that conservation and greater reliance on non-fossil and renewable energy resources is the key to bringing under control our insatiable appetite for oil. Fortunately, several energy resources that make it possible to do this are found all around us. Solar energy is above; wind and biomass surround us; nuclear potential lies below; and buried even more deeply beneath the surface of the earth lies the enormous reserve of thermal energy associated with the earth's hot interior.

On November 25, 1964, Dr. Kwame Nkrumah, the first president of the Republic of Ghana, declared:

> We have been compelled to enter the field of Atomic Energy, because this already promises to yield the *greatest economic source of power* [emphasis mine] since the beginning of man. Our success in this field will enable us to solve the many-sided problems which face us all, in all the spheres of our development in Ghana and Africa.3

It was clear that Nkrumah had decided to lead the country along the path of the nuclear alternative.

Several events probably drew him to make that decision. Firstly, a general awareness of the enormous potentials of atomic energy had begun to grow in the country with the initial experiments involving the application of radio-isotopes at the University of Ghana (Legon) in the early 1950s. Secondly, around 1958 a nuclear fallout monitoring service was undertaken by the University of Ghana on behalf of the Defense Ministry, whose administrators had become concerned over potential public hazards from radioactive fallout arising from nuclear weapon tests. Out of these efforts came a proposal from the Physics Department of the University for the establishment of a Radioisotope and Health Physics Unit under the aegis of the National Research Council. The activities of the Unit included the provision of health protection monitoring services for users of X-rays and other penetrating radiations, monitoring of radioactive fallout and the establishment of specialized facilities and research equipment for work in atomic physics.4

THE GHANA NUCLEAR REACTOR PROJECT

[1] by J.K.A. AMUZU

In 1961 came the decision by the government to initiate the Kwabenya Nuclear Reactor Project, "to introduce nuclear science and technology into the country and to exploit nuclear energy in its peaceful applications [for] the solution of problems of national development."5 Viewed in contrast to the modest activities initiated at the University, this decision represented a huge leap. Among the initial tasks was to set up the Ghana Atomic Energy Committee in order to implement the Project. This committee was later replaced through an Act of Parliament, by the Ghana Atomic Energy Commission (GAEC) in 1963. It is mildly surprising that the initial agenda of the GAEC included building a nuclear research reactor, since the training of staff had only just begun. As it turned out, the bilateral agreement with the former USSR under which the Project was to be executed provided that scientists and technicians from the former Soviet Union were to man the initial stages of the project. It was no wonder, therefore, that when the First Republic fell the coup-makers suspended the project, for they disliked President Nkrumah's close ties with the East. Indeed, at the time that the change of government occurred, work on the physical structures had reached such an advanced stage that the whole project would have been completed and commissioned by the end of 1966.

At this point, Sir John Cockcroft, the renowned British physicist, undertook a review of the nuclear project for the new government. He concluded that a reactor was not necessary for the research envisaged, and that the operation of a reactor would require too large a proportion (about one-third) of the total number of physicists and chemists in the country. Further, in his view the capacity of a recently commissioned hydroelectric power plant was so great that a nuclear power plant would not be needed for some twenty years.6 Consequently, the Project was scaled down to the establishment of a National Center for Radioisotope Applications. The Radioisotope and Health Physics Unit at the University at Legon was subsequently transferred to the new Center at Kwabenya. These reorganizations led to the departure of a number of the scientific and technical staff specifically trained for the Reactor Project.

There is some irony in the fact that it was another group of coup-makers who decided to reactivate the Ghana Reactor Project in 1973, following another review. A new management committee and a Reactor Technical Committee were appointed, and once again the site of the Project bristled with feverish activity. Setting aside Sir Cockroft's earlier advice, arrangements were again initiated to acquire a research reactor. This time the management turned to the former Federal Republic of Germany (FRG). A one megawatt reactor belonging to Frankfurt University was to be donated by the state of Hessen to the government and people of Ghana.7Fortunately, the newly elected government, which succeeded the military regime that had reactivated the Project, fully supported these fresh moves towards acquiring a reactor. The government therefore signed all papers and made payments towards the dismantling of the donated reactor in Germany, its shipment to Ghana and subsequent assembly at the Project site at Kwabenya, outside Accra. But before any of these things could happen, a fresh set of coup-makers arrived and the government of the former FRG cancelled all the arrangements.

By this time, in 1981, the National Nuclear Research Institute (NNRI) had already been established and therefore was obliged to carry on without a reactor. Its research activities and services included radiation protection, nuclear medicine, sterilization of medical and pharmaceutical products, environmental monitoring, food preservation, pest control and planting-material conservation. Meanwhile, the ambition to acquire a reactor remained undiminished. With massive support from the International Atomic Energy Agency, a Chinese 30-kilowatt miniature neutron source research reactor was installed and became operational in December 1994.

Since the NNRI now has only a small research reactor, the prospects for harnessing nuclear energy to generate electricity for the whole country are on hold. Furthermore, no commitment to nuclear power has been expressed by the government of Ghana since the idea was proposed by President Nkrumah back in 1964. Consequently, it would be useful to discuss here whether the nuclear option for generating electricity nationwide is indeed a viable proposition for Ghana at this time. In this analysis we shall endeavor to avoid the selective and politicized approach which is sometimes apparent in writings on the various facets of the nuclear debate.

NUCLEAR POWER IN INDUSTRIALLY DEVELOPING COUNTRIES

As indicated earlier, rapid escalation of the world's energy requirements and doubts about the sustainability of conventional energy sources have led many to focus on nuclear power's promise of cheap electricity: one pound of nuclear fuel (uranium 235) the size of a golf ball can create as much energy as 1,500 tons of coal.8

However, nuclear power is now counted among the most controversial items on the world scene. It is something that divides people—you are either for it or against it. This is partly because it is a radically new energy source involving forces that have never been released on Earth before. The reasons are also historical; since the Hiroshima and Nagasaki crises, many people have grown to dread anything at all that is labeled 'nuclear'. Some observers claim that important yet unresolved practical questions stem from the use of nuclear power, e.g. the problem of safe nuclear waste disposal. Others see this form of energy production as a grotesquely extreme form of mega-technology.

For industrially developing countries, except for a few of the largest and most technically advanced, the advantages promised by nuclear power are largely illusory. The very high capital cost and the difficulties with international agreements and restrictions on fuel supply may be the main obstacles. There is also the fact that currently the smallest available power-generating reactor is quite large in relation to the system size for most of these countries, and this consideration proves to be unhelpful in negotiations for funding. Hence it is argued that perhaps only India, Brazil, Pakistan, Israel, Argentina, Egypt, Korea, Mexico, The Philippines and Thailand could economically utilize the power plants that are now commercially available.9 Of these, none except the last four have ratified the Nuclear Non-Proliferation Treaty (NPT). As such, these countries would face additional obstacles in negotiating agreements for the supply of critical components of a plant.

THE PROSPECTS FOR A NUCLEAR POWER PLANT IN GHANA

Unanimously, scientists at the NNRI agree that nuclear power is a viable option for the formulation of a coherent, rational energy plan which will enable the country to meet the consumption levels required for sustaining her socio-economic development and for protecting the environment. They base their support on several considerations. With about a third of the total electricity production from the country's hydroelectric plants exported to countries in this sub-region of West Africa — 45 percent taken by the smeltering plant of the Volta Aluminum Company (VALCO) — only about 20 percent is available for domestic consumption. An oil-fired thermal plant is nearing completion, and this will provide an additional 100-megawatts of electricity; this same plant will be upgraded to 300 megawatts by 1999.

Further, it is hoped that the large reserves of gas which the country appears to possess may eventually make it possible to replace oil with gas at this thermal plant in the near future. On the other hand it is argued that the drive to curb the use of fuelwood, in a bid to preserve the environment, may be undermined by such a development since this could mean the diversion of gas from its use as domestic fuel. Although about 1,000 megawatts of power remain to be tapped from the country's hydroelectric energy potential, this can only be achieved with many relatively small dams. The environmental impact of several small dams may be as unacceptable as that of coal-fired plants. Large tracks of arable land will have to be sacrificed to build these small dams. Also, subtle changes in the local climate and the risk of water-borne diseases becoming endemic are troubling consequences that could come with these dams.

These are only some of the arguments that have convinced the researchers at the NNRI that the energy future of the country may be considered secure only if nuclear power becomes a serious option. The NNRI scientists report that GAEC:

> . . . has embarked on the training of a core team of engineers and economists in the area of energy and nuclear power planning, in the hope of building up the country's expertise to plan effectively for the future role of nuclear power in meeting the country's energy requirements beyond the year 2020.10

The Safety of a Nuclear Power Plant in Ghana

Certainly a decision by the government to build a nuclear power plant in Ghana would take full cognizance of the rigor required in the safety regimes of its operation. But just as clearly, the country's track record in the mitigation and management of disaster indicates that there is cause for concern. An accident at a nuclear power plant is not like any other accident. This is why after Chernobyl, people a world away from the site of the accident could not consume beef without the legitimate worry that they might be feeding themselves poison. Eleven years after the Chernobyl disaster, an area of radius up to 30 km from the site remains an exclusion zone; more than 100,000 people who were initially evacuated cannot return.

The release of radioactivity into the atmosphere during normal operation of nuclear power plants is only a small fraction (less than 1 percent) of the release from other sources such as nuclear weapon test fallout, cosmic rays and medical diagnoses. Nonetheless, there are many who believe that so long as the effects of small doses received over a long period of time remain undetermined, nuclear plants must be viewed with suspicion.

It is generally agreed that commercial nuclear power plants that have accumulated more than 800 reactor-years of operation in the United States have an excellent safety record. However, it has been suggested that the decision always to locate nuclear reactors in isolated places manifestly contradicts the claim that the chance of accidents at nuclear plants is no greater than the risk of accidents at oil refineries. Thus it is troubling that not all the compliance actions had been taken by the NNRI several months after the research reactor became operational. For example, the fire protection system had not been completed and communication infrastructure was inadequate. Even more troubling is the fact that although the scientists at the Institute knew exactly what to do they were constrained by lack of funds, telecommunication system, and other logistics. There is little comfort in the realization that some of those government officials and policy-makers that might be responsible for taking future decisions in the running of a nuclear power plant may be wholly unaware that nuclear technology and its safety precautions admit of neither budgeting short cuts nor any half measures.

Broader Issues

There are several more general issues that drive the nuclear power debate. Firstly, the problem of nuclear weapon proliferation is real. Militarily useful weapons with yields in the kiloton range can be constructed using reactor-grade plutonium separated from the spent fuel elements of a reactor.11 This is why so much attention and anxiety have been focussed on the possibility that non-nuclear weapon states with civil nuclear programs might acquire nuclear weapons, especially those having access to reprocessing technology. The Non-Proliferation Treaty has remained contentious among 'Third World' leaders who resent the injustice they perceive in endorsing nuclear weapons for the world's most powerful nations while outlawing them for the industrially developing nations. Hence 'Third World' countries — including those (like Ghana) that have ratified the Treaty — are forced to contend with obstacles erected by the nuclear-empowered states within the international agreements required to develop civil nuclear programs.

Secondly, although there is a lot of uranium in the ground, less than one percent of it is the key isotope, uranium 235, upon whose fission nearly every reactor in the world today is based. It would appear that if present projections about the expansion of nuclear power are correct, and if the mining of various grades of uranium ore (mostly uranium 238) remain economically viable, then one can predict that conventional reactors will exhaust all the economically recoverable uranium 235 in some 40 or 50 years. However, the emerging technology of the breeder reactor can change this outcome. Breeder reactors are designed to produce electricity and, at the same time, to 'breed' more fuel than they consume to generate electric power. They are able to utilize the abundant but otherwise useless uranium 238 in the artificial production of the fissionable plutonium 239. This way the breeder reactor can stretch uranium resources by a factor of about 100.12 If this were to be the case, then — like the sun and like fusion fuel — using uranium in breeder reactors would mean essentially having an inexhaustible source of energy. However, because it is conceivable that a breeder reactor core could explode like a poorly designed atom bomb (nuclear explosion cannot occur in a conventional reactor) its future is legitimately shrouded in intense debate and is largely uncertain.

Also, there are many who fear other problems that are uneliminable not only at reactor sites but also at processing and reprocessing plants, waste disposal sites and during transportation of nuclear materials. The ever-present possibilities of theft or sabotage increase the security worries of a world already troubled by acts of terrorism if rapid expansion of the nuclear plant industry is encouraged.

DOES GHANA NEED NUCLEAR POWER?

Most arguments for expanding and diversifying the energy infrastructure of a country have been based on tho assumption that the pace of economic development may be seriously retarded if adequate and cheap supplies of energy are not available at the right time, in the right place and in the appropriate form. The OPEC embargo of the early 1970s caused serious dislocations in the economic activities of several countries. That embargo also demonstrated that it is possible for some countries to get along with much less electric power than they now consume, or at least with a much lower expansion rate. For example, in the United States electricity demand grew by about seven percent annually from 1900 to 1973. Following the 1973 embargo the growth in demand fell to only one percent in 1974 and two percent in 1975; since that time the rate has hovered around three percent.

A survey concluded that "the United States can do well, indeed can prosper, on much less energy than has been commonly supposed;" and that "achieving low energy growth will not be easy nor cheap, but it will be far easier and less costly than achieving high energy growth."13 Another analysis indicates that conservation can greatly reduce the need for both nuclear and coal power during the remainder of this century, and that the renewable sources can be phased in fast enough to provide a significant fraction of our needs by the year 2000.14

It would appear, therefore, that given the uncertainties regarding the future technology for generating nuclear power, the decision to build these plants must not be taken in a hurry. Meanwhile, the NNRI is doing marvelous work in its varied applications of nuclear energy in the fields of agriculture, health-care delivery and industry. Radiation disinfestation is being used in the preservation of a wide range of foodstuffs, in an economic environment where food distribution and marketing are otherwise severely constrained by shortfalls in preservation technology. There is a project to eradicate the tsetsefly by radiation sterilization of large numbers of the male insects and releasing them into the environment. Research into new and improved varieties of crops (with such characteristics as higher yields per acre, early maturation, pest-resistance and disease-immunity) promises to make a significant impact on the country's food production. In the field of health-care delivery, the Health Physics Unit carries out routine checks of radiation levels and leakage on every X-ray machine in all of the country's hospitals as well as other sources of ionizing radiations. Scientists of the Unit also assist doctors in the diagnosis of several diseases including cancer. The analysis of geological samples (as an aid to the search for minerals and for the determination of the elemental composition of atmospheric pollutants) is carried out by the X-ray fluorescence laboratory of the Institute. The acquisition of the small research reactor has extended the range of public and private service activities of the Institute's various sections; it also facilitates training scientists and engineers in several aspects of nuclear technology.

It may well be that these very useful activities involving the presently installed small research reactor should be continued and expanded at this time when nuclear power is still intensely controversial and its future prospects are so uncertain. A political decision to build a nuclear power plant may only serve to deflect the attention of the nation's scientists away from their current crucial contributions to agriculture, medicine and industry. Additionally, over the years of their policy making, governments in Ghana have tended to view the delicate considerations concerning technical feasibility as arbitrary matters of superficial opinion or academic hair-splitting. There is a real danger that the future development of a nuclear power policy may focus too much on political and economic issues and too little on crucial technical concerns.

It is possible that Ghana's efforts at industrial development can be seriously derailed if other sources of electrical power are not developed soon. Otherwise there may not be enough time to phase in the renewable sources. The relevant question then becomes: how do the problems of nuclear power compare with problems inherent in using other sources of energy? (This concern should replace the simple-minded question of whether nuclear power carries any problems.) However, it is crucial that there be a clearly demonstrated ability to frame such comparisons in a sober, rational and technically-driven atmosphere. At some point in the future most of the controversy and highly publicized anxieties about nuclear energy will be finally resolved. If at that time Ghana finds that she can get along without having to join the ranks of the nuclear elite, I suspect there are many who will think that is a better option.

NATIONAL ENERGY STRATEGY

ENERGY SECTOR STRATEGY AND DEVELOPMENT PLAN

THE ENERGY SECTOR VISION

The vision for the energy sector is to ensure availability of and universal access to energy services and for export by 2020.

The achievement of the vision raises the following challenges:

(i) Developing infrastructure for the production and supply of adequate energy services to meet national requirement and for export;

(ii) Developing the requisite infrastructure to ensure universal access as well as the efficient and reliable supply of energy services;

(iii) Ensuring that energy is produced and supplied in a form that has no adverse health, safety and environmental impact; and

(iv) Ensuring that energy is produced, transported and used in an efficient manner.

Addressing these challenges requires the development of an effective strategy, as well as programmes and projects that are achievable.

The Power Sub-sector covers activities related to Electricity Generation, Transmission, Distribution and Efficiency and Conservation.

The Petroleum Sub-sector covers Upstream, Midstream and Downstream.

The Renewable Energy Sub-sector relates to renewable energy resource exploitation, development and use.

The document also contains funding sources and verifiable indicators to facilitate effective monitoring and evaluation of the programmes and projects.

1. ENERGY SECTOR INSTITUTIONS

Table 1.1 shows the major institutions involved in the energy sector and their responsibilities.

Table 1 .1 Major Players in the Energy Sector

AGENCY	RESPONSIBILITIES
POWER SUB-SECTOR:	* Power generation
* Volta River Authority (VRA)	* Power generation

* Bui Power Authority * Independent Power Producers (IPPs) * Ghana Grid Company (GRIDCo) * Electricity Company of Ghana (ECG) * Northern Electricity Department (NED)	* Power generation * Power transmission • Power distribution in Southern Ghana • Power distribution in Northern Ghana
PETROLEUM SUB-SECTOR: * Ghana National Petroleum Corporation * Tema Oil Refinery (TOR) * Bulk Oil Traders * Bulk Oil Storage and Transportation Company (BOST) * Oil Marketing Companies (OMCs) * Ghana Cylinder Manufacturing Company	* Oil and gas exploration development and production * Crude oil refining and sale of petroleum products * Petroleum products importation and sale * Bulk petroleum products transportation and storage * Petroleum products distribution * LPG cylinder manufacturing
REGULATORY AGENCIES: * Public Utilities Regulatory Commission (PURC) * Energy Commission (EC) * National Petroleum Authority (NPA)	* Electricity tariffs approval, monitoring quality of service and consumer protection * Licensing of operators in the power sector and setting technical standards for their performance, sector planning and policy advice to Minister of Energy * Licensing of operators in the petroleum sector and setting of technical standards and enforcement

2. POWER SUB-SECTOR DEVELOPMENT

Electricity and National Economy

Electricity accounted for 8.4% of total national energy consumption in 2008. It is largely used in the residential sector, accounting for about 47% of total electricity consumed in the country. Electricity is also the dominant modern energy form used in the industrial and service sectors accounting for 65.6% of modern energy used in the two sectors of the national economy. In addition, the generation and supply of electricity provides employment for a significant number of Ghanaian professionals.

Electricity exports have provided an important source of foreign exchange earnings for the country as Ghana exports power to the neighbouring countries including Togo, Benin, and Burkina Faso. On the other hand Ghana imports power from La Cote D'Ivoire when necessary. Becoming a major exporter of electricity is a key objective of the energy sector vision and the opportunity exists for Ghana to expand its electricity exports under the West African Power Pool (WAPP) Project.

STRUCTURE OF THE POWER SUB-SECTOR

The Ministry of Energy is responsible for formulating, monitoring and evaluating policies, programmes and projects for the power sub-sector and the energy sector in general. The Ministry is also implementing the Government's National Electrification Scheme. .

The Electricity Supply Industry (ESI) has an unbundled structure with separate operational functions in respect of power generation, transmission and distribution.

The state-owned Volta River Authority (VRA) is involved in power generation in the country. It owns and operates the Akosombo Hydro Power Station, Kpong Hydro Power Station and the Takoradi Thermal Power Plant (TAPCO) situated at Aboadze. VRA is also a minority joint partner with TAQA, a private sector company, which owns and operates the Takoradi International Power Company (TICO) thermal plant, also located at Aboadze.

Bui Power Authority, another state-owned agency, is implementing the Bui Hydroelectric Power Project, while a number of private Independent Power Producer (IPPs) projects have been licensed and are at various stages of development.

The National Interconnected Transmission System (NITS) for electricity is owned and operated by the Ghana Grid Company Ltd (GRIDCo), which is state-owned.

The distribution of electricity is mainly done by two state-owned enterprises, namely the Electricity Company of Ghana (ECG) and Northern Electricity Department (NED), which is a subsidiary of VRA. ECG distributes electricity in the southern part of the country; NED distributes power in the northern part of the country, while Enclave Power provides power to the Free Zones.

The Electricity Supply Industry is regulated by the Energy Commission (EC) and the Public Utilities Regulatory Commission (PURC). The EC is responsible for technical regulation of the power sub-sector, including licensing of operators. In addition, EC also advises the Minister of Energy on matters relating to energy planning and policy. The PURC is an independent regulatory agency, and is responsible for economic regulation of the power sector, specifically approving rates for electricity sold by distribution utilities to the public. Its functions also include monitoring of quality of electricity services delivered to consumers.

STRATEGY CHALLENGES AND OPPORTUNITIES IN THE POWER SUB-SECTOR

Challenges

The power sub-sector faces the following challenges:

(i) inadequate power supply infrastructure requiring huge investments;

(ii) inadequate access to electricity;

(iii) high cost of fuel for electricity generation;

(iv) inadequate regulatory capacity and enforcement; and

(v) operational and management difficulties in utility companies

(vi) vulnerability to climate change

Opportunities

The following opportunities provide a strong basis for growth of the power sub-sector in the medium to long term:

(i) Strong growth in the national economy will increase the demand for electricity and thus, open up the power market for further development.

(ii) Enhanced sub-regional cooperation in energy will open up the sub-regional market for electricity trading. Ghana can take advantage of this opening to achieve the vision of becoming a major exporter of power by 2015.

(iii) Strong Government commitment to private-sector led economic development will provide an incentive for private sector to increase their participation in the power sub-sector.

(iv) Evolution of the regulatory environment in Ghana, though in an early stage of development, has led to modest progress. A transparent and strong regulatory environment will not only provide comfort for private sector investors, but also ensure efficient and optimal operation of the sector.

POWER SUB-SECTOR STRATEGY GOALS

The power sub-sector strategy is intended to roll out initiatives that will guide the development of the power sub-sector in the medium term and seeks also to achieve the following policy goals:

(i) Ensure adequate, reliable and improved supply of electricity to meet national requirement and for export through consolidation, rehabilitation and expansion of electricity generation, transmission and distribution infrastructure;

(ii) Increase access to electricity from the current 66% to at least 80% by 2015;

(iii) Secure sources of cost-effective and sustainable fuel supply for electricity generation;

(iv) Increase financing for electricity supply infrastructure development from Government sources, Development Partners and the private sector;

(v) Strengthen institutional and management capacity as well as regulatory regime for the smooth development and operation of the power sub-sector; and

(vi) Ensure a cost-effective pricing regime for electricity services.

Power Sub-sector Strategy Issue 1

Power Supply Shortages

Thematic area

Infrastructure Development/Strong Economy for Real Jobs

Diagnostics

Inadequate power supply infrastructure due to failure to sustain power sector investment programmes.

Policy Responses

* Increase generation capacity;

* Reinforce and add capacity at the transmission and distribution levels;

* Open up the sub-sector to Independent Power Producers (IPPs) and private sector participation in generation.

* Continue implementation of Power Sector Reforms initiated in 1995; and

* Strengthen the regulatory environment.

Objectives to be achieved

* Increase generation capacity to 5,000 MW by 2015;

* Achieve gas-based generation for at least 50% of thermal power plant production by 2015;

* Increase participation of IPPs in the Power Sector through transparent procurement;

* Improve and modernise electricity distribution infrastructure to reduce system losses from 25% to 18% by 2015;

* Develop a non-congested electricity transmission network by 2015; and

* Strengthen Regulatory Agencies to perform their functions effectively.

The interventions to achieve the strategy goals are shown in Table 2.1, Table 2.2, Table 2.3 and Table 2.4.

Table 2.1 Strategies to achieve increased electricity generation capacity

Objectives to be achieved	Key Programmes and Projects	Possible Financing Sources	Time-frame	Verifiable Indicators/Milestones	Responsible Agency
Increase generation capacity from 2,000MW to 5,000 MW by 2015	(i) Operationalisation and expansion of the Osagyefo Power Barge Project (125MW)	Private sector	2008-2012	• Report of Technical and Financial Audit available by June 2010 • 125 MW brought on stream in Dec 2010 • Conversion to 185MW combined cycle by 2012	• Ministry of Energy * Ministry of Energy
	(ii) Implementation of the Aboadze TICO Power Plant steam turbine project (to increase total capacity at Aboadze from 550 MW to 660 MW)	Private sector (TAQA)	2009-2012	• MOU signed by June 2010 • 110 MW added capacity available by December 2012	• VRA • VRA
	(iii) Development of Western Rivers Hydropower Project	GoG/Private sector	2009-2014	• Power Purchase Agreement (PPA) signed October 2010 • Construction begin by January 2011 • 625 MW capacity added by December 2014	• Ministry of Energy * Ministry of Energy
	(vi) Development of Juale Hydropower Project	GoG/Gov't of Brazil	2009-2014	• Credit Agreement signed by December 2010 • PPA signed by May 2011 • Construction of Juale commenced by January 2012 • 90 MW available by Dec. 2015	• Ministry of Energy/Ministry of Finance & Economic Planning • Ministry of Energy

Table 2.1 Strategies to increase electricity generation capacity (continued)

Objectives to be achieved	Key Programmes and Projects	Possible Financing Sources	Time-frame	Verifiable Indicators/Milestones	Responsible Agency
Increase power generation capacity to 5,000 MW by 2015	(vi) Completion and expansion of all on-going GoG-Financed Power Projects : (a) Bui Hydropower Project;	GoG/Chinese Gov't GoG GoG GoG/Canadian Gov't	2008-2013 2008-2011 2008 – 2010 2009	• 400 MW added capacity by 2013 • 220 MW operational by 2011 and expanded to 330 MW combine cycle by 2013 • 50MW available by mid 2010	* Bui Power Authority * Ministry of Energy/VRA * Ministry of Energy/VRA * Ministry of Energy

	(b) Kpone Thermal Power Project (c) Tema Thermal 2 Power Plant (TT2PP) (d) Takoradi 3 Power Plant		– 2012	* 132MW available by December 2012	
	(vii) Completion of IPP Projects (a) Completion of Sunon Asogli Power Project (b) Completion of Tema Osonor Power Plant	Private sector Private sector	2009-2015 2008 – 2012	• 200 MW completed in February 2009 and expanded to 560 MW by 2015 • 126 MW of capacity added by 2011	* Sunon Asogli * Ministry of Energy/VRA
	(viii) Development of Wind Power projects.	GoG/Private sector	2009-2014	• MOU signed by June 2010 • 50 MW of Wind Farms added by 2013	• Ministry of Energy/E.C

Table 2.2 Strategies to increase thermal generation from natural gas

Objectives to be achieved	Key Programme and projects	Possible Financing Sources	Time-frame	Verifiable Indicators/Milestones	Responsible Agency
Achieve gas-based generation for 50% of the thermal power plants production	(i) Completion of the West African Gas Pipeline Project to Tema	GoG/Private sector	2009-2011	• Construction of RMS at Tema commenced by December 2009 • Complete RMS by June 2010	• VRA
	(ii) Acceleration of the use of natural gas from WAGPP in place of crude oil at Aboadze,	GoG/VRA	2009-2010	* Commissioning of natural gas utilisation by June 2010	* VRA
	(iii) Construction of pipelines from the Jubilee Field Gas Project to Osagyefo Power Plant at Effasu and the Takoradi Power Plant at Aboadze	GoG/Private sector	2009-2011	• Construction of pipeline to commence by June 2010 • Completion and Commissioning of pipeline by June 2011	• GNPC
	(iv)Intensify Exploration for Gas and Oil	GoG/Private sector	2009 - 2015	• On-going	• GNPC

Table 2.3 Strategies to improve and modernise transmission and distribution infrastructure

Objectives to be achieved	Key Programme and Projects	Possible Financing Sources	Time-frame	Verifiable Indicators/Milestones	Responsible Agency
Develop a non-congested transmission system by 2015	(i) Completion of On-going Substation Projects:-Supply Improvement to Ho; Supply Improvement to Tema, Accra, Takoradi; Akwatia; Supply Improvement to Kumasi, Techiman, Wunneba and Akosombo Substations.	GRIDCo	2009-2011	* Projects completed by December 2010	GRIDCo
	(ii) Grid Extension Projects:- Kintampo Substation; Atebubu Substation; Sunyani-Mim Upgrade; Smelter II Substation; System Reliability Enhancement Project	GRIDCo	2009-2011	* Contracts Awarded by December 2009 * Projects completed by December 2011	GRIDCo
	(iii) Refurbishment of Supervisory Control and Data Acquisition (SCADA) System	GRIDCo	2009-2010	* Project completed by March 2010	GRIDCo
	(iv) Aboadze-Volta 330 kV Project	World Bank	2009-2010	* Project completed by December 2010	GRIDCo
	(v) Accra 3rd Bulk Supply Point project	GoG	2009-2010	* Project contract awarded by December 2009 * Project completed by September 2010	GRIDCo

Table 2.5 Strategies to improve and modernise transmission and distribution infrastructure (continued)

Objectives to be achieved	Key Programme and projects	Possible Financing Sources	Time-frame	* Verifiable Indicators/Milestones	Responsible Agency
Develop a non-congested transmission system by 2015	(vii) Kumasi 2nd Bulk Supply Point	GoG	2009-2011	* Contract awarded by December 2009 * Project completed by December 2011	GRIDCo
	(viii) Buipe Sub-station	Private sector	2009-2011	* Project completed by October 2011	GRIDCo
	(ix)Aboadze-Prestea-Kumasi-Wa 330 kV Project	World Bank	2009-2015	* Contract awarded by February 2010 * Project completed by December 2014	GRIDCo

	(x) Tumu-Han-Wa	World Bank	2009-2015	* Contract awarded by March 2010 * Project completed by December 2014	GRIDCo
	(xi) Development of Electricity Market Rules	Energy Commission/ GRIDCo	2009-2010	* Market Rules available by July 2010 * Stakeholders Workshop completed by October 2010 * Market Rules completed by July 2011	EC

Table 2.4 Strategies to improve and modernise electricity transmission and distribution infrastructure

Objectives to be achieved	Key Programme and projects	Possible Financing Sources	Time-frame	Verifiable Indicators/Milestones	Responsible Agency
Improve and modernise distribution infrastructure for efficient service delivery and reduce system losses to 18% by 2015	(i) Upgrading and Rehabilitation of Electricity Distribution Network	GoG/Development Partners/Private sector	2008-2015	• Distribution system in major cities modernised by 2014 • Technical losses reduced to 9% by 2015	• ECG
	(ii) Commercial Loss Reduction Programme	ECG/Development partners	2009-2015	• Commercial losses of ECG/NED reduced gradually to 9% by 2015	• ECG
	(iii) Prepaid Metering Programme to replace credit metering in residential and commercial sectors	ECG	2008-2015	• Total coverage of customers by 2014 • Improved revenue collection of ECG/NED to over 95% by 2014	• ECG

Power Sub-Sector Strategy Issue 2

Inadequate access to electricity

Thematic area

Infrastructure Development/Strong economy for real jobs

Diagnostics

* Access to electricity is not universal. Electricity access was estimated at 66% in 2009.

* Inadequate distribution infrastructure due to failure to sustain energy development programme.

Policy Responses

* Increase the momentum of the National Electrification Scheme to provide access to electricity progressively to all communities;

* Upgrade and reinforce transmission and distribution network capacity; and

* Open up the sub-sector to private sector participation in power distribution and sale.

Objectives to be achieved

* Achieve universal access by extending electricity to all communities by 2020

* Increase access to at least 80% by 2015

Interventions to achieve the goals are shown in Table 2.6.

Table 2.6 Strategies to achieve universal access to electricity.

Objectives to be achieved	Key Programme and Projects	Possible Financing Sources	Time-frame	Verifiable Indicators/Milestones	Responsible Agency
Achieve universal access by extending electricity to all households by 2020	(i). National Electrification Scheme (Extension of electricity to towns and rural communities)	GoG/Development Partners	1990-2020	• Revised NES Master Plan developed by December 2010 • All communities to be connected to the national electricity grid by 2020	• Ministry of Energy
	(ii) Self Help Electrification Programme (speed up rural electrification through SHEP-Complete SHEP IV and initiate SHEP V, etc)	GoG/Development Partners	2009-2015	• 80% access attained by 2015	• Ministry of Energy
	(iii) Intensification of electricity supply to households in already electrified communities)	GoG/Development Partners/Private sector	2009-2015	• Intensification Programme designed and started by December 2010	• Ministry of Energy
	(iv) Development and use of decentralised electricity	GoG/Development Partners/Private sector	2009-2015	• Detailed National Decentralised Electricity Programme designed by December	• Ministry of Energy

	generation sources for communities remote from national electricity grid			2010	
	(v)Productive Uses of Electricity (PUE) Programme	GoG/Development Partners/Private sector	2009 - 2015	• Five (5) pilot projects completed by 2013 • Comprehensive National PUE Plan completed by Dec 2014 • Commence implementation of PUE Plan by Jan 2015	• Ministry of Energy

Power Sub-Sector Strategy Issue 3

Restoration of financial health of VRA and ECG

Thematic area

Infrastructure Development/Strong economy for real jobs

Diagnostics

Poor financial health of VRA and ECG are reflected in debts and inadequate return on assets. This situation makes it difficult for VRA and ECG to raise financing for projects and operations. The situation has arisen due to long periods of low tariffs coupled with high system losses.

Policy Responses

* Ensure cost-recovery tariffs for electricity production and supply;

* Strengthen the Public Utilities Regulatory Commission (PURC) to determine and implement efficient and cost-reflective tariffs for electricity; and

* Ensure the independence of regulatory agencies.

Objectives to be achieved

* Achieve economically efficient tariffs by 2011.

Table 2.7 shows the interventions to be implemented to achieve the strategy goals.

Table 2.7 Strategies to achieve economically efficient tariffs.

Objectives to be achieved	Key Programme and projects	Possible Financing Sources	Time-frame	Verifiable Indicators/Milestones	Responsible Agency
Achieve	(i) Electricity	GoG/Development	2009-	• RFP issued by	• PURC

economically efficient electricity tariffs by 2011	Tariff Study	Partners (World Bank)	2011	February 2010 • Consultants engaged by June 2010 • Final Report Submitted by September 2010 • Commence implementation of recommendations by January 2011	
	(ii) Financial Recovery Plan for VRA and ECG	GoG/Development Partners (World Bank)	2009-2011	• RFP issued in March 2009 • Consultants engaged in June 2009 • Final Report Submitted by October 2009 • Commence implementation of recommendations by June 2010	• Ministry of Energy • Ministry of Finance & Economic Planning

3. PETROLEUM SUB-SECTOR

The petroleum sub-sector consists of: (i) upstream activities, which involves exploration, development and production of oil and gas from oil or gas fields, (ii) midstream activities, which involves the transportation of oil and gas to the oil refinery or gas processing plant, and (iii) downstream activities, which involves the refining of crude oil and distribution of the petroleum products to consumers.

PETROLEUM UPSTREAM AND MIDSTREAM

Hydrocarbons Resources

In 2007 commercial quantities of oil and gas were discovered in two blocks: Deepwater Cape Three Points and Deepwater Tano. Appraisals conducted indicate that the field contains expected recoverable reserves of about 800 million barrels of light crude oil, with an upside potential of about 3 billion barrels. The discovery provides Ghana an opportunity to reduce foreign exchange requirements for the importation of crude oil and also to increase export earnings significantly.

Strategy Goal

The goal is to sustain exploration, development and production of the oil and gas endowment and also the judicious management of the oil and gas revenue for the overall benefit and welfare of all Ghanaians, present and future as well as attract increased local value-added investments in the oil and gas sector and the indigenization of knowledge, expertise and technology.

Challenges

The major challenges for the upstream petroleum sub-sector are how to:

* develop the oil and gas industry with optimal local content and participation,

* effectively manage the potential revenue from oil and gas production, and ensure security for the industry as a whole.

Strategy Intervention

To address these challenges, Government will pursue the following actions:

Hydrocarbon Resources Development and Management

* Manage Ghana's oil and gas resource endowment to ensure sustainability in reserves and the environment through judicious exploitation and intensive exploration

* Set up the National Petroleum Regulatory Authority to be responsible for the regulation of all activities related to upstream, midstream and downstream oil and gas industry in Ghana

Oil Revenue Management

* Manage oil and gas revenues transparently and ensure equity for the benefit of the present and future generation of Ghanaians. This will be achieved through institutional reforms and transparent regulation for the management the oil revenue through legislative guidelines for the creation of a Future Generation Fund and stabilization fund.

Investment Framework

* Encourage investments along the oil and gas industry value chain through fiscal incentives and "even- handed" regulation

Local Content and Local Participation

* Maximise the benefits of oil and gas wealth generation through the use of local goods and services, people, businesses and financing in all aspects of the oil and gas industry value chain and retaining the benefit within Ghana

Security

* Ensure security for oil and gas industry installations and operations through the development of dedicated institutional arrangement for national oil and gas security matters and legislation of oil and gas safety requirements.

Natural Gas Utilisation and Commercialisation

* Prohibit the flaring or venting of natural gas produced within Ghana to maximise the utilization of natural gas reserves of the country.

* Discourage re-injection of natural gas unless it results in increased benefits to the associated operations.

* Develop a viable domestic petrochemical industry based on natural gas.

Human Resource Development and Technology Transfer

* Support capacity building at all levels in the country's technical, vocational and tertiary institutions.

* Oblige Licensees to provide facilities for training and technology transfer as an integral part of their operations

Petroleum Upstream and Midstream Strategy Issue 1

Inadequate exploration, development and production of oil and gas resources of Ghana

Thematic area

Infrastructure Development/Strong Economy for Real Jobs

Diagnostics

* Low exploration, development and production of oil and gas resources

* Inadequate promotion of oil and gas resources

Policy Responses

* Improve legal framework and fiscal regime for exploration, development and production.

Objectives to be achieved

* Attract requisite private sector investment capital in oil and gas exploration and development as well as ensuring maximum benefits to the people of Ghana

* Ensure adequate funding for the operations of Ghana National Petroleum Corporation (GNPC)

* Facilitate the passing of legislation providing transparent legal and fiscal regimes for oil and gas exploration, development and production

The strategic interventions to address the goals are contained in Table 3.1.

Table 3.1 Strategic interventions to achieve oil and gas exploration, development and production goals.

Objectives to be achieved	Key Programme and projects	Possible Financing Sources	Time-frame	Verifiable Indicators/Milestones	Responsible Agency
Intensify exploration,	(i) Exploration of Voltaian Basin;	GoG/Private sector	2009-2015	• Initial Exploration	• GN

development, production and utilisation of Ghana's oil and gas prospects;				data collected and analysed by December 2010 • Road Show of Voltaian Basin by 2012	PC
	(ii) Development of Jubilee Oil and Gas Field	GNPC/Private sector	2009-2010	• Oil production starts by October 2010	• GN PC
	(iii) Construction of Natural Gas Processing Plant	GNPC/Private sector	2010-2013	• Site selection and EPA certification completed December 2009 • Joint Venture arrangements completed by June 2010 • Construction commences by December 2010 • Gas Plant ready by June 2013	• GN PC
	(iv) Construction of pipeline from Jubilee Field to Gas Processing Plant	GNPC/Private sector	2010-2012	• Pipeline from Jubilee field to processing plant completed by 2012	• GN PC
	(v) Construction of pipeline from processing plant to West African Gas Pipeline (WAGP)	GNPC/Private sector	2010-2012	• WAGP pipeline completed by 2012	• GN PC

Petroleum Upstream and Midstream Strategy Issue 2

Maximise the benefits of exploration, development, production and utilisation of oil and gas to Ghanaians

Thematic area

Infrastructure Development/Strong Economy for Real Jobs/Transparent and Accountable Governance/Investing in People

Diagnostics

* Ghanaians have not benefited adequately, from the exploitation of extractive natural resource such as minerals and timber. This should not occur for oil and gas.

* Some oil producing countries have had unsatisfactory/bad experiences in utilising revenue from oil and gas production

Policy Responses

* Build a transparent regulatory regime for the effective management of revenue from oil and gas development

* Maximise local content in all aspects of the petroleum industry value chain

Objectives to be achieved

* Ensure utilisation of oil revenue in the priority areas of education, health, rural development, infrastructure, water, sanitation and poverty reduction;

* Provide adequate investment for physical and social infrastructure in communities in the oil and gas production areas;

* Set up and provide adequate funding for a Future Generation Fund to ensure sustained national well being into the long term;

* Ensure adequate funding for technical training and scientific research and development;

* Maximise the participation of Ghanaians in the exploration, development, production and utilisation of oil and gas; and

* Develop petrochemical industry.

The strategies to be implemented to achieve the policy goals are contained in Table 3.2 and Table 3.3

Table 3.2 Strategies to achieve petroleum upstream and midstream objectives

Objectives to be achieved	Key Programme and projects	Possible Financing Sources	Time-frame	Verifiable Indicators/Milestones	Responsible Agency
Ensure utilisation of oil revenue in the priority areas of education, health, rural	Develop comprehensive Oil and Gas Master Plan including Local Content and	GoG/Private sector	2009-2015	• Oil and Gas Master Plan completed by July 2010	• Mini stry of Ene

development, infrastructure, water and sanitation to reduce poverty	Participation Implementation Strategy			• Comprehensive Oil and Gas Master Plan approved by August 2010 • Master Plan implementation started by December 2010	rgy
Ensure adequate investment in physical and social infrastructure in communities in the oil and gas production areas	Develop Rolling Strategic Infrastructure Development Plan for Communities in Oil and Gas Production Areas	GNPC/Private sector	2009-2015	• Strategic Plan for Infrastructure Development available by June 2010	• Ministry of Energy
Set up and provide adequate funding for Future Generation Fund to ensure sustained well being into the long term	Develop and promote comprehensive Oil and Gas Revenue Management Law	GoG/GNPC	2009-2010	• Oil and Gas Revenue Management Law passed by Parliament by June 2010	• Ministry of Finance
Ensure adequate funding for technical training and scientific research and development	(i) Collaborate with other Ministries and Agencies to develop and implement curricula for tertiary institutions in petroleum industry related disciplines (ii) Facilitate Middle-Level Skill Training Programme for the Oil and Gas Industry	GoG/GNPC/ Oil and Gas Companies	2009-2015	• Set-up Skill Development Committee put in place by December 2009 • Middle-Levell Skill Development Programme available by December 2009 • 500 middle-level skill trainees by December 2015	• Ministry of Energy

Table 3.3 Strategies to maximise local content and local participation in upstream and midstream oil and gas industry

Objectives to be achieved	Key Programme and projects	Possible Financing Sources	Time-frame	Verifiable Indicators/Milestones	Responsible Agency
Maximise the participation of Ghanaians in the exploration, development, production and utilisation of oil and gas	(i) Support the development of local businesses to build expertise and capacity to participate in the oil and gas industry	GoG/Development Partners/Local Business Associations	2009-2012	• Local Business Development Plan available by June 2010	• Ministry of Energy/AGI/GCC
Develop a viable Petrochemical Industry based on Natural Gas	(i) Develop the Gas-based Industrial Enclave	GoG/Private sector	2009-2015	• Establish Natural Gas Industrial Estates Development Company Limited by Dec 2015	• Ministry of Energy/ MOTI
	(ii) Establish Petrochemical Industry	GoG/Private Sector	2009-2015	• Complete Feasibility Studies for Gas-based Industrial Enclave by Dec 2015	• Ministry of Energy

PETROLEUM DOWNSTREAM

Increasing Domestic Production of Petroleum Products

With only about 60% of the national petroleum product requirement being met from domestic production at the Tema Oil Refinery (TOR), the balance of product requirements is imported. There is also the need for Ghana to build adequate capacity to enable it become not only self sufficient in the production of petroleum products but also the "Petroleum Hub" of the West African Sub-region. This can be achieved by:

* Increasing the capacity of TOR from 45,000 BPSD to 145,000 BPSD Feasibility studies have shown that the expansion of TOR is economically justified; and

* Building new refineries. The Government has already initiated the process of building new refineries. These projects are to be fully developed and financed by the private sector.

Increasing National Access to Petroleum Products

Access to petroleum products in the rural areas is inadequate due to limited infrastructure for storage and equipment for distribution and use. The situation has led to the rural population having to purchase kerosene and LPG at higher prices than the official prices. The medium term strategic objective is to increase access to petroleum products particularly LPG and kerosene in rural areas. This objective will be achieved by:

* Continuing to finance the development of rural kerosene storage and supply infrastructure nationwide. The Ministry of Energy is giving further impetus to the Rural Kerosene Promotion Programme

* Expanding the petroleum product storage capacity nationwide. BOST is currently expanding existing bulk petroleum products storage capacity.

* Expanding marine related facilities on the Volta Lake for bulk transportation to ensure year-round supply of petroleum products to Northern Ghana.

* Facilitating the availability of more petroleum product distribution outlets in deprived areas to increase access density (number of persons per sale outlet).

* Promoting a more efficient licensing regime for sales outlets to ensure optimal economic benefits to both investors and consumers

* Supporting the rehabilitation and expansion of rail infrastructure to enhance the transportation of petroleum products

With regards to LPG, it is intended to increase access from the current level of 6% of households to 50% by 2015. This will be achieved through the development of LPG infrastructure and pricing incentives to encourage distributors to expand their operations to especially the rural and deprived areas. The following measures will be implemented in that regard:

* Speed up the establishment of a Natural Gas Processing Plant to produce LPG from the associated gas to be produced from the Jubilee Oil and Gas Field. It is estimated that 10,000 barrels (1,340 tonnes) a day of LPG could be produced from the gas from the Jubilee Field;

* Re-capitalise GCMC to expand production capacity. The production of cylinders will focus on small sized cylinders that will be affordable to households in rural communities;

* Construct LPG Storage and supply infrastructure in all regional and district capitals in the long term. In the medium term, it is intended to develop district capital LPG infrastructure;

* Increase the LPG distribution margin.

Petroleum Downstream Strategy Issue 1

Limited availability of petroleum products to consumers

Thematic area

Infrastructure Development/Strong Economy for Real Jobs

Diagnostics

* Tema Oil Refinery (TOR) has high levels of debt owing to a combination of factors including under-recovery of costs, inadequate working capital and poor management;

* Inadequate local refining capacity;

* Inadequate storage capacity, bulk transportation and distribution infrastructure for petroleum products including LPG

Policy Responses

* Competitive procurement of crude oil and petroleum products;

* Open up the refining business to both public and private sector participation;

* Ensure strict adherence to implementation of full-cost recovery principles in petroleum pricing; and

* Improve regulatory regime for petroleum products transportation, distribution and sale.

Objectives to be achieved

* Ensure uninterrupted availability and access of petroleum products and eliminate obstacles to access of fishermen to pre-mix fuel;

* Achieve LPG access to at least 50% of households and public institutions by 2015; and

* Eliminate debts incurred by TOR by ensuring full-cost recovery in its operations, strengthening management and the regulatory regime.

The interventions that will be implemented to achieve these goals are contained in Table 3.4 and Table3.5

Table 3.4 Strategies to expand availability of petroleum products to consumers

Objectives	Key Programme and projects	Possible Financing Sources	Time-frame	Verifiable Indicators/Milestones	Responsible Agency
Ensure availability and access of petroleum products	(i) Expansion of TOR by doubling its capacity with private sector involvement	GoG/Private sector	2009-2013	* Engage Project Consultant in 2009 * Financial closure reached by June 2010 * Contract awarded by September 2010 * Construction commenced by March 2011 * Construction	* TOR

			completed by March 2013	
(ii) Development of Private Export-Oriented Refineries	Private sector	2009-2015	* MOUs signed and first refinery completed and commissioned by December 2015	* Ministry of Energy
(iii) Expansion of capacity for bulk storage of petroleum products including LPG	GoG/BOST/Private sector	2009-2011	* Completion of Afram Plains Depot, Akosombo, Savelugu under US Exim Bank financing by December 2011. * Project proposals for Takoradi and Wa Depots prepared by December 2009 * Land acquisition for Takoradi and Wa completed by December 2009 * Financing arrangements concluded by June 2010 * Takoradi Depot construction commence by June 2011	* BOST

Table 3.4 Strategies to expand availability of petroleum products to consumers (continued)

Objectives	Key Programme and projects	Possible Financing Sources	Time-frame	Verifiable Indicators/Milestones	Responsible Agency
	(iv) Petroleum Products Pipeline Transportation Projects to Northern Ghana	GoG/Bilateral Donors	2009 - 2013	* Completion of Accra Plains to Akosombo Pipeline by October 2011	* BOST

				* Completion of Debre – Buipe Pipeline Project by October 2011	
Ensure availability and access of petroleum products	v) Development of Private Export-Oriented Refineries	Private sector	2009-2015	* MOUs signed and first refinery completed and commissioned by December 2015	* Ministry of Energy
	(vi) Establishment of a minimum of 90 days strategic stocks	GoG/Private sector	2009-2010	* Re-introduction of Strategic Stock levy by July 2010	* BOST/ Ministry of Energy
				* Cabinet Memorandum submitted by March 2010	

Table 3.5 Strategies to expand availability of petroleum products to consumers

Objectives	Key Programme and projects	Possible Financing Sources	Time-frame	Verifiable Indicators/Milestones	Responsible Agency
Ensure TOR is able to recover cost of operations	Implementation of strict Cost-Recovery Petroleum Pricing Formula	GoG/NPA	2009-2012	* Preparation of HR Plan by June 2010	* TOR/NPA/ Ministry of Energy
				* Recapitalise TOR by Dec 2010	
	Strengthening Capacity of Board and Management of TOR			* TOR financially stable by December 2010	
Increase access to pre-mix by fishermen	Premix Supply Rationalisation Programme	GoG	2009-2012	* Report of Premix Supply Rationalisation available by June 2010	* Ministry of Energy/ Ministry of Agriculture
				* Commence implementation of Premix Supply Plan by July 2010	
Achieve LPG access to 50%	National LPG Promotion	GoG/Private sector	2009-2015	* Prepare Medium to	* Energy Commissi

of households and Public Institutions by 2015	Programme			Long Term National LPG Promotion Programme by June 2010 * LPG Promotion Fund established by December 2010 * Commence implementation of LPG Programme by May 2011	on/ * Ministry of Energy
Expand local cylinder manufacturing capacity in support of the National LPG Programme	Increasing Capacity Utilisation of Ghana Cylinder Manufacturing Company (GCMC));	GoG/Private sector	2010-2012	* GCMC Financial Recovery Plan ready by December 2009 * Commence implementation of GCMC Financial Recovery Plan by January 2010	* GCMC

4. RENEWABLE ENERGY SUB-SECTOR

Ghana is well endowed with Renewable Energy Resources particularly biomass, solar, wind energy resources, and to a limited extent, and mini-hydro. The development and use of renewable and energy resources have the potential to ensure Ghana's energy security and also mitigate the negative climate change impact of energy production and use as well as solve sanitation problems.

Biomass is Ghana's dominant energy source in terms of endowment and consumption. Biomass resources cover about 20.8 million hectares of the land mass of Ghana and biomass is the source of supply of about 60% of total energy used in the country. The vast arable and degraded land mass of Ghana has the potential for the cultivation of crops and plants that can be converted into a wide range of solid and liquid biofuels.

Solar radiation levels are estimated at about 4-6 kWh/m2. Average wind speed along the eastern coastal areas is estimated at 5m/s at a height of 12 metres. Wind speeds of 9 m/s have been recorded on the mountains along south eastern corner of the country. The wind speed regime along the coastline suggests that wind can be harnessed for power generation as well as for mechanical applications.

Goals

The goals of the Renewable Energy sub-sector are to increase renewable energy in the total national energy mix and ensure its efficient production and use.

Challenge

The major challenge in biomass energy supply is to improve the efficiency of its utilisation and sustain its production and use. A key challenge in the development of mini hydro, solar and wind energy is the higher cost of energy produced from these sources owing to the current state of the technologies.

The focus of the biomass strategy is the (i) regeneration of forest cover through afforestation; and (ii) improvement in the production and efficient use of woodfuels. In the long term, the focus is on fuel substitution to alternative sources of energy. As regards solar and wind, the focus is to assist Ghanaian engineers and scientists to research and develop measures to reduce the cost of renewable energy technologies and provide fiscal, financial and pricing incentives on Renewable Energy Technologies to improve their competitiveness.

Renewable Sub-sector Strategy Objective

In addressing the challenges, Government will:

Woodfuels

* Support sustained regeneration of woody biomass resources through legislation and fiscal incentive;

* Promote the establishment of dedicated woodlots for wood fuel production;

* Promote the production and use of improved and more efficient woodfuel utilisation technologies;

* Promote the use of alternative fuels such as LPG as substitute for fuel wood and charcoal; and

* Promote the production and use of other woodfuel energy resources (waste, biofuels).

Liquid Biomass Fuels

* Balance biofuel development against food security.

* Support development of biofuels as a transportation fuel as well as job creation initiative.

* Support private sector investments in cultivation of biofuel feedstock, extraction of the bio-oil and refining of bio-oil into secondary products by creating appropriate financial and tax incentives.

Solar, Wind and Mini Hydro

* Promote the exploitation and use of mini hydro, solar and wind energy resources.

* Support indigenous research and development aimed at reducing the cost of renewable energy technologies.

* Provide tax incentives for the importation of all equipment used in the development of renewable and waste energy projects.

* Support the use of decentralized off-grid alternative technologies (such as solar PV and wind) where they are competitive.

Cross-cutting issues

* Create favourable regulatory and fiscal regimes as well as attractive pricing incentives.

Renewable Energy Strategy Issue 1

Low level of renewable energy in national electricity supply mix

Thematic area

Infrastructure Development/Strong Economy for Real Jobs/Investing in people.

Diagnostics

* High potential but low exploitation and utilisation of renewable energy. This is due to high cost of renewable energy production.

Policy Responses

* Utilise cost-effective cutting edge technologies to reap the huge potential of renewable energy.

* Provide tax and other financial incentives to attract private sector investments in renewable energy technology.

Objectives to be achieved

* Increase the renewable energy supply in national energy mix to 10% by 2020.

* Establish legislation to encourage development of renewable energy technologies.

Interventions to achieve the strategic goals are contained in Table 4.1.

Table 4.1 Strategies to increase renewable energy in national energy supply mix.

Objectives to be	Key Programme	Possible Financing Sources	Time-frame	Verifiable Indicators/Milestones	Responsible Agency

achieved	and Projects				
Increase the renewable energy supply in national energy mix to 10% by 2020	(i) Grid-connected Solar PV programme for public institutions	ECOWAS Bank for Investment and Development (EBID)	2009-2013	* Finalise proposals with ECOWAS Bank by December 2009	* Ministry of Energy
	(ii) Grid-connected solar PV in estate development	ECOWAS Bank for Investment and Development (EBID)	2009-2013	* Finalise proposals with ECOWAS Bank by December 2009	* Ministry of Energy
	(iii) Wind Farm Project (50 MW at Kpone) Development of wind power projects a). Wind farm project b). 3 Wind Mast	Private sector financing/GOG	2009-2014	* Finalise PPA for project by December 2009 * Commence construction by June 2011 * 3 wind mast installed and monitored by 2013 * 50 MW Wind Project ready by December 2014	* Energy Commission /Ministry of Energy
	(iv) Development of Mini Hydro Demonstration Project	GoG/Development Partners/Concessionary funding	2009-2013	• Prepare detailed Feasibility Studies on 21 mini hydro sites completed by 2010 • Establishme	• Ministry of Energy

				nt of MOU with KNUST by June 2010	
	(v) Bio-fuels Projects	Private sector financing	2009-2010	* Complete Renewable Energy Law (Biofuels) by June 2010 * Complete Biofuels Regulations by August 2010	* Energy Commission

Table 4.1 Strategies to increase renewable energy in national energy supply mix. (Continued)

Objectives to be achieved	Key Programme and Projects	Possible Financing Sources	Time-frame	Verifiable Indicators/Milestones	Responsible Agency
Develop legislation to encourage renewable energy technology development and utilisation	Development of Renewable Energy Law	GoG/Development Partners	2009 - 2010	* Renewable Energy Law passed by June 2010.	* Energy Commission

5. WASTE-TO-ENERGY

Waste-to-Energy projects have become a very important mechanism for the management of the growing sanitation problem facing urban communities as well as a means of contributing to energy supply and security. Significant amounts of wastes are generated in Ghana. These include (i) municipal waste (both solid and liquid), (ii) industrial wastes, and (iii) agricultural wastes.

There are many energy technologies which can convert these waste materials into electricity, heat and fuel. The conversion technologies include (i) combustion, (ii) gasification (iii) pyrolisis (iv) anaerobic digestion (v) fermentation, (vi) esterification.

Some waste-to-energy technologies that have been developed in Ghana are anaerobic fermentation of municipal waste and industrial liquid wastes to produce biogas for heating and electricity generation, combustion of solid wastes to produce electricity in Combined Heat and Power (CHP) systems.

While many waste-to-energy technologies are mature and widely applied in other parts of the world, they are relatively more expensive compared to conventional technologies particularly due to the high cost of waste collection and management.

Policy Goal

The goal is to convert most of the wastes generated in municipal activities, industrial operations and agricultural operations to energy.

Challenge

The major challenge to the development of waste-to-energy technologies in Ghana is the high cost associated with the collection and management of waste materials.

Strategy Framework

The focus is to convert municipal, industrial and agricultural waste into energy as a means of managing the growing sanitation problems and contributing to energy supply security.

Waste-to-Energy Strategy Issue 1

High pollution of the environment by municipal, industrial and agricultural wastes

Thematic area

Infrastructure Development/ Real Jobs/Investing in people.

Diagnostics

Low exploitation of waste-to-energy technologies

Policy Responses

* Maximise energy production from waste

* Divert waste from landfills (prohibit burying of waste and landfills)

* Facilitate access to grid for waste to energy power plants

* Develop infrastructure for waste collection and supply to waste-to-energy facilities

Goals to be achieved

The goal is to convert most of the wastes generated in municipal activities, industrial operations and agricultural operations to energy.

Table 5.1 Strategies to convert wastes to energy

Objectives to be achieved	Key Programme and Projects	Possible Financing Sources	Time-frame	Verifiable Indicators/Milestones	Responsible Agency
Management of municipal,	(i)Metropolitan waste-to-power	GoG/Private sector/DPs	2010-2015	Framework for Metropolitan waste-to-	MoEn/EC

industrial, and agricultural wastes through energy production.	project			power project ready by January 2011	
	(ii)Institutional biogas project (Universities, Polytechnics and Senior High Schools)	GoG/Private	2010-2015	Framework for Institutional biogas project ready by January 2011	MoEn/MoE/Private sector
	(iii)Combined heat and power system for industries	GoG/Private sector	2010-2015	Framework for combined heat and power systems ready by January 2011	MoEn/MoTI/Private sector

6. ENERGY EFFICIENCY AND CONSERVATION

The annual growth in the demand for fuelwood and charcoal is estimated at 3% per annum. Electricity demand, on the other hand, is growing between 6% and 7% annually while consumption of petroleum products is estimated to increase at about 5% per annum. Energy efficiency and conservation can help mitigate these high growth rates.

The losses in the production, transportation and use of energy are also high. System losses in electricity distribution are about 25%, with wastage in the end-use of electricity also estimated at about 30%. Reduction of losses in energy supply and more efficient use of energy would contribute to reduction in the demand for energy.

Strategic Goal

The strategic goal is to ensure efficient production and transportation, as well as end-use efficiency and conservation of energy.

Government intends to reduce the end-use electrical wastage by implementing a comprehensive Demand-Side Management (DSM) Programme. The key objectives of the DSM Programme are to:

(i) Encourage efficiency in energy use in all sectors of the national economy;

(ii) Improve the productivity and competitiveness of Ghanaian industries through the use of more efficient technologies;

(iii) Improve system reliability by reducing demand; and

(iv) Reduce and manage power system demand through load shifting

Challenge

The challenge is to promote and finance the implementation of energy efficiency and conservation measures.

Strategy Framework

The focus will be on removing the obstacles that have constrained the promotion and implementation of energy efficiency and conservation measures. This will be achieved through the application of fiscal and financial incentives, awareness creation and institutional intermediation.

General

* Establish appropriate pricing regime for energy services that would encourage (provide incentive) domestic and industrial consumers to voluntarily manage their energy consumption;

* Develop and implement programmes and measures to help consumers optimize their energy use; and

* Support a sustained and comprehensive public education and awareness building campaign on the methods and benefits of energy conservation.

Electricity

* Discontinue, through legislation, the local production, importation and use of inefficient electricity consuming equipment and appliances.

Petroleum Products

* Establish petroleum products lifting zones in the country;

* Encourage the development and use of efficient fuels; and

* Implement fiscal measures to discourage the importation and use of vehicles which are not fuel efficient.

Energy Efficiency and Conservation Strategy Issue 1

Substantial electricity wastage through inefficient distribution and consumption

Thematic area

Infrastructure Development

Diagnostics

* High losses in the distribution system.

* About 30% of electricity supplied to consumers is wasted as a result of inefficient electrical equipment, poor attitude towards energy conservation, and theft.

Policy Responses

* Reduce the system losses in electricity distribution ;

* Ban the importation and use of inefficient electrical appliances; and

* Provide fiscal and financial incentives to promote the use of efficient electrical equipment and appliances.

Objectives to be achieved

* Achieve 10% savings in electricity consumption through implementation of comprehensive electrical power efficiency and conservation measures

Strategic actions that will be implemented towards the achievement of the goal are contained in Table 6.1

Table 6.1 Strategies to reduce wastage and ensure more efficient use of electricity

Objectives to be achieved	Key Programme and projects	Possible Financing Sources	Time-frame	Verifiable Indicators/Milestones	Responsible Agency
Achieve 10% savings in electricity consumption through electric power efficiency and conservation measures.	(i) Power Factor Correction Programme in Public Institutions, Commercial and Industrial Entities	GoG (Electricity Demand Management Fund)/Private sector	2009-2012	• Equipment installed in first 25 Public institutions by Dec 2010 • Equipment installed in all 100 public and commercial and industrial businesses by 2012	• Energy Commission
	(ii) Public Awareness Campaign Programme on Energy Efficiency and Conservation	GoG/ECG/VRA/Independent Power Producers	2009-2012	• Public Awareness Programme submitted and approved by EC by March 2010 • Commence implementation by April 2010	• Energy Commission/ Energy Foundation
	(iii) Implementation of Legislation on Ban of Importation and Use of Inefficient Electrical Appliances	Energy Fund	2009-2012	• Importation of inefficient electrical appliances eliminated by Dec 2010 to December 2012	• Energy Commission/ Ministry of Energy/CEPS/GSB

Energy Efficiency and Conservation Strategy Issue 2

Losses and wastage in the transportation, distribution and utilisation of petroleum products

Thematic area

Infrastructure Development

Diagnostics

* Perceptible losses in the production, transportation and distribution of petroleum products;

* High influx of over-aged and inefficient vehicles.

Policy Responses

* Reduce the losses in petroleum product transportation, distribution and consumption;

* Ban the importation of high-fuel consuming vehicles;

* Encourage the use of fuel enhancing additives.

Objectives to be achieved

* Achieve 15% savings in petroleum product transportation, distribution and consumption.

Interventions being implemented in the medium term to achieve the above goal are contained in Table 6.2.

Table 6.2 Strategies to reduce wastage and ensure more efficient use of petroleum products

Objectives to be achieved	Key Programme and projects	Possible Financing Sources	Time-frame	Verifiable Indicators/Milestones	Responsible Agency
Achieve 15% savings in petroleum products consumption	(i) Strict Implementation of Petroleum Products Lifting Zoning Mechanisms	GoG (Petroleum Demand Management Fund)/ OMCs/NPA/Private sector	2009-2012	• Letter to Re-introduce Zoning issued by Minister of Energy by January 2010 • Programme commences December 2009	• BOST/Ministry of Energy/TOR
	(ii)Prohibition of Importation of Over-aged Vehicles above 10 years	GoG	2009-2011	• Bill available by June 2010 • Parliamentary approval by December 2010	• Ministry of Energy/ Energy Commission
	(iii) Public Awareness Campaign	GoG/NPA/BOST/OMCs	2009-2014	• Public Awareness Programme approved by Ministry	• Energy Commission/ Energy

	Programme on Fuel Efficiency and Conservation in transportation			of Energy/EC by March 2010 • Programme under implementation	Foundation
	(iv) Promotion of the use of improved fuel performance additives.	OMCs/NPA	2009-2012	• Sale of new petroleum products formulations for transportation by 2015	• Ministry of Energy
	(v) Establishment of Centre for Research in Petroleum Efficiency and Conservation	GoG/Development Partners/OMCs/NPA/Private sector	2009 – 2012	• Feasibility studies completed by June 2010 • Recommendations approved by cabinet by August 2012	• Ministry of Energy

7. ENERGY AND ENVIRONMENT

The production and use of energy impact on the environment and global climate in varying degrees. The exploitation of biomass for energy purposes results in deforestation, while the use of fossil-based fuels contributes to climate change. The use of inferior cooking equipment also has negative health impact. The production, transportation of crude oil, flaring of natural gas associated with petroleum production and the production of petroleum products have associated environmental risks.

Strategic Goal

The goal is to ensure that energy is produced, supplied and used in an environmentally sustainable manner.

Challenge

The challenge is to mainstream environmental issues in all energy projects and to implement and enforce adherence to environmental mitigation plans associated with energy project development.

Strategy Framework

The strategies will focus on the conduct of Strategic Environmental Assessment (SEA) and Environmental Impact Assessment (EIA) Studies and Social Impact Assessment (SIA) Studies of all energy projects, with associated adaptation and mitigation plans for environment and climate change.

Energy and Environment Strategy Issue 1

Energy production and supply produce emissions that have undesirable health and global climate change implications

Thematic area

Infrastructure Development

Diagnostics

* Poor working environment and health conditions in the production and utilisation of energy;

* Perceptible global warming conditions

Policy Responses

* Produce and use environmentally friendly energy forms;

* Deploy mechanisms to limit the emission of environmentally undesirable substances from energy production;

* Use fiscal and financial incentives to promote the production and use of environmentally friendly energy forms.

Objectives to be achieved

* Ensure that in the production and use of energy adverse environmental impacts are minimized;

* Ensure environmental and social impact assessments are a major part of all energy projects.

Interventions to be pursued to achieve the above goals are contained in the

Table 7.1 shows the strategies to mainstream environmental concern in the energy sector.

Table 7.1 Strategies to mainstream environmental concerns in energy development projects.

Objectives to be achieved	Key Programme and projects	Possible Financing Sources	Time-frame	Verifiable Indicators/Milestones	Responsible Agency
Ensure production that in the production and use of energy adverse environmental impacts are minimized	(i) Environmental and Social Impact Assessment review of existing Energy Projects	GoG/VRA/ECG/NPA/ GNPC/BOST/TOR/Private sector operators	2009-2010	• Prepare TOR for Consultancy services by June 2010 • Engage Consultant by August 2010 • Environmental and Social Impact Assessment review Report available by December 2010	• Ministry of Energy

	(ii) Creation and funding of Environmental and Social Impacts Assessment Unit in the Ministry of Energy	GoG/VRA/ECG/NPA/ GNPC/BOST/TOR/Private sector operators/Development Partners	2009-2015	* Design of Organogram for the Unit by June 2010 Staff recruitment completed by December 2010	• Ministry of Energy
Ensure environmental and social impact assessments are a major part of all energy projects	(i) Development of Environmental and Social Impact Assessment Guidelines for Energy projects	GoG/VRA/ECG/NPA/ GNPC/BOST/TOR/Private sector operators/Development Partners	2009-2010	• TOR for consultancy services available by June 2010 • Consultant engaged by August 2010 • Guidelines available by December 2010	• Ministry of Energy
Maximise the benefits of Environmental Credit (Carbon Credits) mechanisms for energy projects/Adaptation fund	(i) Establishment and Implementation of Environmental Credit Facility for development of energy project	GoG/Energy Fund	2009-2015	• Develop Concept Paper by June 2010 • Complete studies by December 2010	• Energy Commission

8.0 ENERGY AND GENDER

Energy issues are of concern to all. However, women are the most important actors in the energy sector, in terms of their contact, use and management of renewable energy sources, which in their very crude or primary form are used mostly by women. Biomass (primarily wood fuel and charcoal) constituted 67% of the total energy consumed in Ghana. Women in Ghana bear the brunt in the use of the wood fuel based energy economy in the country. The health impacts of indoor air pollution from traditional biomass fuels and their negative impacts on women, girls and babies remain a critical issue.

Strategic Goal

The goal is to mainstream gender concerns in the energy sector

Challenge

* Unequal access of men and women to modern forms of energy
* Limited involvement of women in the planning and management of Energy services

Strategy Framework

The strategies will focus on minimizing the adverse health effects of energy use on women by promoting the use of modern forms of energy in households; and ensuring participation of women in the formulation and implementation of energy interventions

Energy and Gender Strategy Issue 1

The health impacts of indoor air pollution from traditional biomass fuels and their negative impacts on women, girls and babies remain a critical issue.

Thematic area

Infrastructure Development

Diagnostics

High exposure to women to indoor pollution from the use of wood fuels.

Policy Responses

Promote the use of modern forms of energy in households

Objectives to be achieved

Minimize the adverse health effects of the use of wood fuels on women

Energy and Gender Strategy Issue 2

Concerns of women in the policies in the energy sector.

Thematic area

Infrastructure Development

Diagnostics

Women's influence in decision making in the energy sector

Policy Responses

* Ensure participation of women in the formulation and implementation of energy interventions

* Build capacity of women in the energy Sector

Objectives to be achieved

Address the concerns of women in energy policy formulation and implementation

Table 8.1 Strategies to mainstream Gender in Energy Sector Programmes and Project

Objectives to be achieved	Key Programmes and Projects	Possible Financing Sources	Time-frame	Verifiable Indicators/Milestones	Responsible Agency

Minimize the adverse health effects of the use of wood fuels on women	Women in LPG Promotion Programme	GoG/ Private Sector	2010-2012	Number of women in LPG promotion programme	MoEn
	Women in Energy Efficiency and Conservation Programmes	GOG	2010-2012	Number of women in Energy Efficiency and Conservation Programmes	MoEn
Address the concerns of women in energy policy formulation and implementation	Capacity building for Women in Energy	GOG/ Private Sector	2010-2012	Number of female professionals in the energy sector	MoEn/ Energy sector agencies
	Establishment of Gender Desk at the Ministry of Energy	GoG	2010-2012	Gender desk established in the Ministry of Energy	

9. FINANCING THE ENERGY SECTOR

Strategy Goal

The strategy focuses on enhancing private sector investment in partnership with the public sector.

Financing the Power Sub-Sector

The strategy to mobilize financing for the development of the power sub-sector will focus on:

* Restoring the financial and economic soundness of utility companies. In the past the power sector companies have posted negative net revenues, leading to negative returns. This situation is as a result of inadequate tariffs and poor revenue collection rate. The unhealthy financial positions of the utility companies have limited their ability to adequately maintain and expand the power system infrastructure, leading to deterioration in supply quality. Resolving this concern will require efforts by Government and PURC in managing the tariff setting process and may require introduction of new and innovative pricing mechanisms in the tariff setting framework.

* Securing private sector investments in re-capitalisation of power sector institutions, Owing to the poor financial health of the companies and the inability of Government to inject funds into the sector, the most viable option is to secure private sector capital to finance the power sector infrastructure.

* Increasing public financial support for investments in the power sub-sector.

Policy Direction

Restoring the financial health of Utility Companies.

The following measures will be pursued in the medium term:

* Support revision of electricity rates such that utility companies are allowed cost recovery in the immediate term to achieve ROR of 10% by 2011.

* Enhance managerial efficiency in order to improve cooperate governance and profitability of the utilities

* Raise revenue for critical power sector projects, with the approval of Parliament, by the imposition of levies on electricity consumption.

* Review the rationale for setting up of various funds in order to ensure that they accrue the appropriate amount of funding and also that they are used judiciously for the purposes for which they were established. Currently, there are a number of Funds into which levies on energy consumption are paid to finance specific development activities in the power sector. These include: (i) Rural Electrification Levy which is paid into the National Electrification Fund, (ii) Street Lighting Levy, and (iii) the Power Factor Surcharge Levy which is paid into the Electricity Demand Management Fund.

Securing increased private sector involvement.

The strategic actions and measures to be pursued in the medium term are:

* Support PPAs between distribution utility companies and prospective IPPs

* Examine the possibility of private sector capital injection in Government-owned power plants.

* Complete the necessary legal, institutional and regulatory framework that will provide comfort to the private sector. Energy Commission Act 541 provides for a number of regulations that are intended to support private sector participation in the power sector. The related legislative instrument would be completed by June 2010.

Financing the Petroleum Sub-Sector

Financing of the petroleum sub-sector has, in recent times, posed a major challenge. Government has recognised this challenge and steps are being taken to address this challenge. To this end, the implementation of the cost recovery pricing regime is expected to improve financial health of the players in the sub-sector. This will enable them to improve their financial health, generate adequate internal financial resources and also secure commercial loans on their own to implement their infrastructure development projects.

Strategy Focus

Government intends to take the following actions:

* Maintain the existing pricing regime and ensure that the full costs of petroleum products production and importation are fully recovered;

* Support private sector participation and investment in refining as well as oil and gas exploration, development and production activities;

* Increase funding from Government sources to GNPC in order to accelerate exploration of indigenous hydrocarbon resources. In that regard, Government will revise the exploration levy to cover the full budget for exploration activities; and

* Continue to source funding from commercial loans and capital market to support exploration, development and production activities of GNPC.

Financing of Renewable Energy Sub-Sector

In the past, Government has collaborated with Development Partners to fund renewable energy activities in Ghana. Investment fund have come from the consolidated national budget, while loans and grants from bilateral and multilateral donor agencies have been used for basic research and pilot projects. Direct private sector funding and investment has not been significant.

It is the intention of Government, as a priority medium term objective, to reach out to and encourage the private sector to play a lead role in the development of the renewable energy sector.

Strategic Actions

The following actions will be implemented to create the necessary environment for the mobilization of financing for renewable energy projects:

* Increase Government funding for non-grid connected renewable energy technologies for agriculture and social services including schools, health centres, provision of potable drinking water, etc.;

* Provide fiscal incentives to attract private sector investment in the development of renewable energy technologies (RETs);

* Fund the collection of primary data on renewable energy resources and conduct Pre-Feasibility Studies for RETs with promising prospects for development. This is intended to reduce the up-front investment by private sector, and thus speed up private sector involvement in the implementation of renewable energy projects;

* Seek bilateral and multilateral financing sources including CDM facility for development of RETs projects;

* Establish LPG fund to support LPG promotion; and

* Allocate a significant portion of the Rural Electrification Fund (to be established) to support implementation of renewable energy programmes.

Financing of R & D

In the past, Government had collaborated with Development Partners to fund R&D activities in energy sector. Government funds came from the Energy Fund while grants from bilateral and multilateral donor agencies have been used for basic research and pilot projects. Direct private sector investment has been negligible.

Strategic Actions

Government proposes, as a priority medium term objective, to pursue the following actions:

* Allocate at least 20% of the Energy Fund annually for R&D activities relating to policy, renewable energy, energy conservation and institutional development;

* Allocate at least 10% of the Exploration Levy annually for R&D activities relating to petroleum sub-sector;

* Allocate at least 10% of Electricity Demand Management Fund annually for R&D activities related to Energy Conservation and Efficiency;

* Secure donor grants for energy R&D activities;

* Encourage private sector and industry to support energy R&D and also the local manufacture of energy technologies. Government will provide fiscal and financial incentives for industries which support energy R&D; and

10. COMMUNICATION STRATEGY

The implementation of the Medium Term Strategy will require a robust communication plan backed by a sustainable strategy to ensure ownership and support for the Medium Term Plan.

Objectives to be achieved

The goal of the Communication Strategy is to create awareness and acceptance among all stakeholders and the general public about the Energy Policy and Programmes of Government of Ghana

Strategic Actions

To ensure an effective communication programme to reach all stakeholders and the general public:

Table 9.1 contains the programmes to be implemented to roll-out the communication strategy.

Table 10.1 Communications strategies and programmes

Objectives to be achieved	Key Programme and projects	Possible Financing Sources	Implementation Time-frame	Verifiable Indicators/Milestones	Responsible Agency
Increase public awareness on Energy Policy and Programmes of Government	(i) National Energy Sector Development Communication Plan	GoG/VRA/ECG/NPA/GNPC/ BOST/TOR/Private sector operators in energy	2009-2015	• Engage Communication Expert by March 2010 • Communication Plan available June 2010 • Commence full implementation of Communication Plan by July 2010	• Ministry of Energy

11. CONCLUSIONS

While this document intends to achieve a vibrant energy sector, the successful implementation of the energy sector policy will require the support and cooperation of all stakeholders, including the Development Partners.

NATIONAL ENERGY POLICY

This Energy Policy outlines the Government of Ghana's policy direction regarding the current challenges facing the energy sector. The document provides a concise outline of the Government's policy direction in order to contribute to a better understanding of Ghana's Energy Policy framework. It is hoped that the document will facilitate the effective management and development of the energy sector as well as provide the public with information about the Government's policy goals. The document is, therefore, intended to serve as a:

- Decision-making platform for the effective management and development of Ghana's Energy Sector;

- Guide to key stakeholders and institutions in the energy sector highlighting the definition and implementation of key activities in respect of their mandates;

- Guide for coordinating the implementation and monitoring of energy sector policies; and

- Platform for dialogue on investment opportunities with Ghana's development partners and the private sector.

The document is divided into nine (9) sections.
Section One (1) a brief account of the various policy directions in the energy sector.

Section Two (2) acknowledges the concerns relating to power and identifies appropriate measures to address them.

Section Three (3) indicates the state of affairs in the energy sector with respect to petroleum issues and the necessary Government interventions required to support and enhance the growth of this sector.

Section Four (4) highlights Government's efforts to increase the amount of renewable energy in the national energy mix.

Section Five (5) gives a brief account of the measures being taken to tackle the waste management problem in the country. The focus is to convert all wastes to energy.

Section Six (6) outlines Government's attempt to ensure that energy is supplied and used efficiently with the least possible wastage.

Section Seven (7) focuses on the course being pursued to limit the adverse effects of energy production and usage on the integrity of the environment.

Section Eight (8) highlights the steps being taken by Government to mainstream gender concerns in the energy sector.

Section Nine (9) explicates Government plans to develop the sector to play its role as a fulcrum of the national economy.

EXECUTIVE SUMMARY

Ghana's Development Challenge

Ghana has huge potential to grow and transform its economy through industrialization, creating jobs and ensuring the equitable distribution of wealth. The fundamental goal of the Government of Ghana's development agenda is to achieve macro-economic stability and grow the economy to a middle income status by 2020.

The Energy Challenge

Ghana's total energy supply has to grow significantly to help achieve the development agenda goal. The challenge is how to increase the energy supply and also expand the energy infrastructure in the country in a way that is sustainable.

The Energy Resources and Vision

Ghana is well endowed with a variety of energy resources including biomass, hydrocarbons, hydropower, solar and wind. It has the capacity to produce modern bio-fuels and is exploring options to develop nuclear energy.

The energy sector vision is to develop an "Energy Economy" to secure a reliable supply of high quality energy services for all sectors of the Ghanaian economy and also to become a major exporter of oil and power by 2012 and 2015 respectively.

Energy Policy Platform

This National Energy Policy outlines the energy sector goals, challenges and actions. In general, these goals are ambitious but they are also feasible.

The Policy covers the broad spectrum of issues and challenges relating to the following areas:

(i) Power Sub-sector;

(ii) Petroleum Sub-sector;

(iii) Renewable Energy Sub-sector;

(iv) Waste-to-Energy;

(v) Energy Efficiency and Conservation;

(vi) Energy and Environment;

(vii) Energy and Gender; and

(viii) Managing the future of the sector.

A summary of the sub-sector policy framework is provided below.

Power Sub-sector

The goals of the power sub-sector are to increase installed power generation capacity quickly from about 2,000 MW today to 5,000 megawatts (MW) by 2015, and increase electricity access from the current level of 66% to universal access by 2020.

The challenge is how to attract investments to build the necessary infrastructure for the generation, transmission and distribution of electricity throughout the country. This is key to ensuring the sustainable development of the sector.

Apart from financing, the policy focuses on institutional and human resource capacity strengthening as well as regulatory reforms required to create a competitive electricity market. Creating the right

environment for private-public partnerships in the development of new power plants is essential to the growth of the power sector. The biggest obstacle to achieving this is the issue of cost-recovery, a challenge that this policy tries to directly address.

Petroleum Sub-sector

The goals of the petroleum sub-sector are to ensure the sustainable exploration, development and production of the country's oil and gas endowment; the judicious management of the oil and gas revenue for the overall benefit and welfare of all Ghanaians; and the indigenisation of related knowledge, expertise and technology.

The major challenges regarding the sector, especially the upstream petroleum sub-sector, are how to sustainably develop the oil and gas industry and judiciously manage the revenue received from the industry.

In view of these goals and challenges, the policy focuses on the regulation of the petroleum industry with respect to licensing and operation of the oil and gas companies; improving Ghana's institutional and human resource capacity; enhancing local content; and fiscal incentives that will ensure maximum benefits to the people of Ghana. The policy seeks also to ensure transparency in the use and distribution of the oil revenue.

Renewable Energy Sub-sector

The Renewable Energy sub-sector covers biomass, mini hydro, solar and wind resources.

The goals of the renewable energy sub-sector are to increase the proportion of renewable energy in the total national energy mix and ensure its efficient production and use.

The major challenges facing the Renewable Energy sub-sector are to:

* Sustain exploitation of woodfuel by improving efficiency;
* Reduce the high costs of solar and wind energy technologies, which make them uncompetitive; and
* Reduce the high cost of waste collection and management for waste-to-energy technologies

The renewable energy policy actions shall focus on:

* Improving production and promoting the efficient use of biomass in the short term, while increasing regeneration;

* Switching from the use of biomass to alternative sources of energy;

* Engaging Ghanaian engineers and scientists to cooperate with international experts to bring down the cost of solar and wind energy technologies; and

* Creating fiscal and pricing incentives to enhance the development and use of renewable energy.

Waste-to-Energy

The policy is to convert most of the wastes generated in municipal activities, industrial operations and agricultural operations to energy. This comprehensive waste management approach will enable Ghana to generate reasonable amount of energy from its wastes. The major challenge is to reduce the high cost of waste collection and management.

Energy Efficiency and Conservation

Energy production, transportation and utilisaton result in losses and wastage. Reducing these losses will lead to significant benefits for the national economy. The challenge is to reduce the wastage in all aspects of the energy sector.

The policy will focus on removing the obstacles that have constrained the promotion and implementation of energy efficiency and conservation measures. The policy measures required to promote energy efficiency and conservation are fiscal incentives, awareness creation, institutional and human resource capacity development, and financial intermediation.

Energy and Gender

Energy issues are of concern to all. However, women are one of the most important actors in the energy sector, in terms of their contact, use and management of renewable energy sources, which in their very crude or primary form are used mostly by women. Biomass (primarily wood fuel and charcoal) constitutes 66% of the total energy consumed in Ghana. The negative health impacts of indoor air pollution from traditional biomass fuels on women, girls and babies remain a critical issue.

The goal is to mainstream these gender concerns in the energy sector and align them with proper health, safety and environmental standards.

Managing the future

Policy actions addressing regulation of the sector, mobilisation of investments for the sector, strengthening of human capacity, research and development are addressed in the document.

This document also contains information regarding the regulations governing operations within the energy sector, as well as information pertaining to strengthening the various regulatory agencies to enhance their effectiveness.

1.0 INTRODUCTION

1.1 Ghana's Development Challenge

Ghana has a huge potential to grow and transform its economy through industrialization with a view to creating jobs and ensuring equitable distribution of wealth. The fundamental goal of the Government of Ghana's development agenda is to achieve macro-economic stability and grow the economy to a middle income status by 2020.

Ghana's total energy supply must increase significantly if the development agenda is to be achieved.

1.2 ENERGY CONSUMPTION AND SUPPLY PROFILE

In 20081, Ghana's biomass energy consumption was 11.7 million tonnes, while petroleum products and electricity consumption were 2.01 million tonnes and 8,059 GWh, respectively. In terms of total energy equivalents, biomass (fuelwood and charcoal) constituted 65.6%, with petroleum products and electricity accounting for 26.0% and 8.4%, respectively.

1 Information from Energy Commission

1.3 THE ENERGY SECTOR VISION

The energy sector vision is to develop an "Energy Economy" that would ensure secure and reliable supply of high quality energy services for all sectors of the Ghanaian economy, and to become a net exporter of oil and power by 2012 and 2015, respectively.

1.4 Challenges

The challenges facing the energy sector are:

(i) inadequate infrastructure requiring huge investments;

(ii) inadequate access to energy services;

(iii) high cost of fuel for electricity generation;

(iv) inadequate regulatory capacity and enforcement; and

(v) operational and management difficulties in utility companies

(vi) vulnerability to climate change and environmental impacts

(vii) inefficiency in the production, transportation and use of energy

1.5 THE ENERGY SECTOR GOAL

Within the context of energy sector vision, the goal of the energy sector is to make energy services universally accessible and readily available in an environmentally sustainable manner.

1.6 Energy Sector Objectives

The policy objectives to achieve this goal are to:

(i) Secure long term fuel supplies for the thermal power plants;

(ii) Reduce technical and commercial losses in power supply;

(iii) Support the modernisation and expansion of energy infrastructure to meet growing demands and ensure reliability;

(iv) Increase access to modern forms of energy;

(v) Improve the overall management, regulatory environment and operation of the energy sector;

(vi) Minimise the environmental impacts of energy supply and consumption through increased production and use of renewable energy and make energy delivery efficient;

(vii) Ensure cost recovery for energy supply and delivery;

(viii) Ensure the productive and efficient use of energy;

(ix) Promote and encourage private sector participation in the energy sector; and

(x) Diversify the national energy mix by promoting renewable energy sources nuclear and coal ;

2.0 POWER SUB SECTOR

2.1 OVERVIEW

Electricity is the dominant modern energy form used in the industrial and service sectors accounting for 69% of modern energy used in the two sectors of the national economy. The generation and supply of electricity provides employment for a significant number of Ghanaian professionals. It is also an important source of foreign exchange earnings in the country as Ghana exports power to neighbouring countries, including Togo, Benin, and Burkina Faso

The Ghana electricity supply industry is unbundled with separate jurisdictions and entities regarding activities of electricity generation, transmission and distribution.

Electricity generation is undertaken by the state- owned Volta River Authority (VRA), which operates the Akosombo Hydro Power Station, Kpong Hydro Power Station and the Takoradi Thermal Power Plant (TAPCO) at Aboadze. VRA is also a minority joint partner with TAQA, a private sector company which owns and operates the Takoradi International Power Company (TICO) thermal power plant also located at Aboadze. Bui Power Authority (BPA), another state-owned entity, is charged with the implementation of the Bui Hydro electric Power Project. In addition, independent power producers have been licensed to build, own and operate power plants. The IPP projects are at various stages of development.

The National Interconnected Transmission System (NITS) for electricity is owned and operated by the Ghana Grid Company (GRIDCO).GRIDCO is a state-owned company.

The distribution of electricity is done by the Electricity Company of Ghana (ECG), a state-owned company, and the Northern Electricity Department (NED), a subsidiary of the Volta River Authority (VRA).

The Energy Commission (EC) and the Public Utilities and Regulatory Commission (PURC) regulate the electricity supply industry. The Energy Commission, in addition to being responsible for technical regulations in the power sector, also advises the Minister for Energy on matters relating to energy planning and policy. The PURC on the other hand is an independent regulatory agency responsible for the economic regulation of the power sector with the mandate to approve rates for electricity sold by electricity distribution utilities.

The Ministry of Energy is responsible for formulating, monitoring and evaluating policies, programmes and projects in the energy sector. It is also the institution charged with the implementation of the National Electrification Scheme (NES) which seeks to extend the reach of electricity to all communities in the long term.

Ghana has an installed capacity of 1960MW made up of hydro and thermal facilities. Electricity demand which is currently 1400MW is growing at about 10% per annum. It is estimated that Ghana requires capacity additions of about 200MW to catch up with increasing demand in the medium to long term. The existing power plants are unable to attain full generation capacity as a result of limitations in fuel supply owing to rising fuel prices and uncertainty in rainfall and water inflows into the hydroelectric power facilities.

Ghana has an extensive transmission system which covers all the regions of the country. Transmission infrastructure has, however, deteriorated over the years, resulting in transmission bottlenecks, overloaded transformer sub stations and high system losses.

The electricity distribution infrastructure is extensive providing access to about 66% of the population. However, it is old and obsolete, leading to frequent interruptions in power supply and relatively high system losses. While national access is about 66%, access in the three northern regions is about 30%.

2.2 SUB-SECTOR GOAL

The goal is to become a major exporter of power in the sub-region by 2015. This will be achieved through capacity addition; modernisation of transmission and distribution infrastructure.

2.3 CHALLENGES

The challenges facing the power sub-sector are to:

* Sustain power generation capacity expansion, as well as rehabilitate and reinforce the transmission and distribution infrastructure to meet the projected growth in power demand of 10% per year in the medium term2;

* Secure long term reliable and cheaper fuel for the operation of the thermal power plants;

* Increase access to electricity of consumers, especially in the rural areas;

* Achieve cost recovery for electricity services in spite of relatively low incomes; and

* Reduce power system losses and waste in electricity supply and consumption.

2 The medium term refers to a period of 5 years up to 2015.

3 This refers to installed capacity in 2009 and includes the Emergency Power Units of 126 Megawatts (MW).

2.4 EXPANSION OF POWER SUPPLY INFRASTRUCTURE

The first step towards the delivery of reliable power supply services and becoming a net exporter of power by 2015 will be to increase power supply infrastructure.

Policy Direction

The policy direction is to attract private investments to support the public sector to improve and expand the capacity of the existing infrastructure.

a) Power Generation Capacity

The policy objective is to increase installed generation capacity from about 2,0003 MW to 5,000 MW in the medium term. To achieve this objective, Government will pursue the following policy actions:

Thermal Power Plants

* Seek financing from the private sector for the rehabilitation and expansion of existing power plants

* Complete the construction of on-going power projects

* Encourage private sector investment in the construction and ownership of additional power plants.

Hydro Power Resources Development

* Complete the development of the Bui Hydropower Project on the Black Volta; and

* Support the development of small and medium4 scale hydro power projects on other rivers, including the Western Rivers (Ankobra, Tano and Pra), River Oti, and the White Volta.

4 Small scale hydropower project refers to a hydropower project with generating capacity between 1 MW and 10 MW. Medium scale hydropower project refer to a hydropower project with generating capacity between 10 MW and 100 MW.

5 Currently total system losses are estimated at 25%, consisting of technical losses of 11% and commercial losses of 14%.

b) Transmission Infrastructure

The policy objective is to provide adequate, safe and reliable electricity transmission network. To achieve this, Government will:

* Support the mobilisation of commercial and domestic capital resources to supplement external funding for transmission infrastructure development;

* Enforce technical regulations and operational standards; and

* Provide support for the maintenance of existing transmission infrastructure

c) Distribution Infrastructure

Policy Direction

The policy direction will be to seek adequate investment to improve the electricity distribution network and thereby reduce high system losses5 and improve the poor quality of electricity supply. Accordingly, Government will:

* Assist distribution utilities in regaining their financial heath;

* Encourage distribution utilities to seek commercial loan financing to modernise their infrastructure;

* Encourage the injection of investment capital from private sources and from the domestic capital market in the medium to long term; and

* Support management in the restructuring of the distribution utilities' operations towards achieving improved operational performance.

2.5 Securing fuel supply for power generation

Policy Direction

In order to secure future fuel supplies, efforts will be made to increase and diversify the fuel mix in power generation. The following policy actions will be pursued:

Infrastructure for new fuel supply sources

* Support the strategic exploitation of domestic natural gas discoveries through fiscal incentives, financial support, and creation of a favourable and effective regulatory environment; and

* Encourage public-private partnership financing of natural gas infrastructure.

Nuclear Power Development

* Develop nuclear power as an option for electricity generation in the long term.

Coal Power Development

* Develop coal as an option for electricity generation in the long term.

Regional Integration of Energy Resources

* Support regional initiatives for integrating energy infrastructure to expand and accelerate cross-border energy trade and investments.

* Secure supplies of cheaper fuels such as natural gas from Ghana's domestic natural gas resources and the West Africa Gas Pipeline Project for power generation.

* Harmonise the legal, regulatory and institutional regimes in conformity with the ECOWAS Energy Protocols.

2.6 Increasing Access to Electricity Supply

Policy Direction

The policy objective is to achieve universal access to electricity by extending the reach of electricity infrastructure to all communities by 2020. To meet this objective, Government will pursue the following policy actions:

Infrastructure Development

* Increase funding from Government and other multilateral and bilateral sources for the National Electrification Scheme

* Support private sector co-financing with Government for grid-extension to designated franchised zones;

* Establish a sustainable internally generated funding mechanism for rural electrification;

* Support new service connections for electricity in rural areas;

* Address institutional and market constraints that hamper increasing electricity access to the poor; and

* Promote productive uses of electricity as an integral part of the Rural Electrification Programme.

Street Lighting Access and Infrastructure

* Provide street lighting infrastructure in all Regional Capitals and subsequently in all District Capitals

* Develop sustainable mechanisms to finance the operation and maintenance of street lighting infrastructure.

2.7 Electricity Pricing

Policy Direction

The objective is to ensure that electricity pricing is efficient and competitive while providing rates that are affordable. Government will pursue the following measures with respect to pricing and the setting of rates for electricity:

* Uniform electricity tariffs throughout the country;

* Support the implementation of cost recovery pricing in electricity supply

* provide special rates for the needy in society (lifeline tariffs)

* Base wholesale dispatching of generating units on Economic-Merit-Order Dispatch principles.

* Electricity generated from Akosombo and Kpong Hydro Power plants shall not be the subject of a bilateral contract; and

* Regulate pricing of transmission and distribution services to achieve financial sustainability of the utility companies as well as ensure consumer protection.

2.8 Power Sector Reforms

Power sector reforms were initiated in 1995 to ensure an efficient and effective power sector and also to allow increased private sector investment and participation. In implementing the Power Sector Reform Programme, Government will continue to pursue the following actions:

* Promote competition in the generation of electricity through the development of a Wholesale Electricity Market (WEM), ;

* Create the environment for retail competition in the electricity market;

* Facilitate the entry of Independent Power Producers (IPPs); and

* Ensure improved performance of electricity utility companies.

3.0 PETROLEUM SUB SECTOR

3.1 Overview

The petroleum industry is segmented into upstream, midstream and downstream which covers activities from exploration and production of petroleum through transportation to the marketing of the final products.

Ghana has five sedimentary basins that are considered to have prospects for oil and gas: the Tano Basin, Saltpond Basin, Accra/Keta Basin, Cape Three Points Basin which are all off-shore and are fairly well explored; and the Voltaian Basin which is on-shore and is hardly explored.

In July 2007, Ghana National Petroleum Corporation and its partners discovered oil in commercial quantities in the Jubilee field in the offshore Tano/Cape Three Points Basin of the

Ghanaian continental shelf. Appraisal work conducted on the field has estimated reserves of oil at about 800 million with an upside estimate of 3 billion barrels. The field has substantial associated natural gas reserves.

In addition to the Jubilee Field, there have been more discoveries in the Mahogany Deep, Odum, Tweneboa and Sankofa. Exploration activities are being intensified, and it is expected that more discoveries will be made both offshore and on-shore. With the significant potential economic prospects offered by the discovery of oil and gas a key pre-occupation of government is to ensure judicious exploitation and maximum benefits to Ghanaians of the oil and gas resources.

It is expected that the development of the oil and gas industry will stimulate accelerated economic growth, job creation, poverty reduction and general prosperity to the people of Ghana. . To satisfy this expectation, there is the need to build the necessary human, financial and technological capacity of Ghanaians to be able to participate fully in the petroleum industry. This can be achieved through a well formulated Ghanaian local content and participation policy and regulatory environment.

The petroleum products marketed in Ghana are (i) Premium Gasoline; (ii) Kerosene; (iii) Gas oil; (iv) Residual Fuel Oil; (v) LPG; and (vi) Premix. Approximately 70%of products is produced by Tema Oil Refinery (TOR) and the remaining 30% from imports. The country imports all of its crude oil requirements which is refined at TOR. The TOR, whose capacity is 45,000 Barrels-Per-Stream-Day (BSPD), is wholly owned by the Government of Ghana.

Bulk supply petroleum products are fairly reliable and are done through an extensive infrastructural network comprising of storage depots located at strategic parts of the country, pipelines for the movement of petroleum products, Bulk Road Vehicles (BRVs) and also barges located on the Volta Lake. Secondary distribution and retail activities comprise (i) transportation of refined products from the bulk storage depots by road and (ii) retailing of the products at the pump.

It is projected that the requirement for the major petroleum products -gasoline, kerosene, gas oil and LPG- will increase significantly from 1.62 million tonnes in 2005 to 2.49 million tonnes by 2015 representing an average annual growth rate of 5.3% over the period. The consumption of these products could grow faster if the strong economic growth experienced in the past decade should continue. On the basis of these projections, Ghana will continue to import refined products to meet national consumption requirements.

Access to petroleum products in Ghana is satisfactory but has to be improved as the population grows. There are presently a total of 1,700 petroleum products retail outlets of which 37% are Service Stations6 (SS), 20% are Filling Stations (FS) and 43% are Reseller Outlets (RO). The total number of retail outlets represents an access ratio of 71 retail outlets per one million people. There are also vendors who sell mainly kerosene, in all rural communities thereby increasing the accessibility of petroleum products in most parts of the country. In addition to the service stations and reseller outlets, the Ministry of Energy,

6 The Service Stations and Filling Station are big retail outlets located mainly in the cities and large towns while the Reseller Outlets are small outlets serving mainly the rural areas.

under the Rural Kerosene Distribution Improvement Project (RKDIP), has extended the reach of kerosene retail outlets to 1,540 rural communities by installing 5,000 litre capacity surface tanks for the retailing of kerosene.

3.2 Sub sector Goal

The goal is to sustain and optimise the exploitation and utilisation of Ghana's oil and gas endowment for the overall benefit and welfare of all Ghanaians, present and future. .

Upstream and Midstream

3.3 Challenges

The major challenges in meeting the goal for the upstream and midstream activities are:

(i) Sustain interest in exploration activities;

(ii) Security of the oil and gas installations;

(iii) Environmental sustainability;

(iv) Maximise local content and participation in petroleum industry; and

(v) Prudent management of revenue from oil and gas exploitation;

Policy Direction

In addressing the challenges Government seeks to pursue the following actions:

Hydrocarbon Resources Development and Management

* Manage Ghana's oil and gas resource endowment to ensure the sustainability of the reserves and of the environment.

Regulation

* Strengthen the regulatory agency for the regulation of all activities related to upstream, midstream and downstream oil and gas industry in Ghana.

Oil Revenue Management

* Manage oil and gas revenues transparently and ensure equity for the benefit of present and future generations of Ghanaians; and

* Facilitate the use of revenue from the oil and gas sector to other sectors of the economy.

Investments Framework

* Encourage investments along the oil and gas industry value chain; and

* Facilitate periodic reviews of the terms and conditions in the Model Petroleum Agreement and other relevant regulations to sustain interest in exploration and production.

Local Content, Local Participation and Local Capacity Development

* Maximise the benefits of oil and gas wealth generation on a comprehensive local content platform by optimising the use of local expertise, goods and services, job creation for people,

businesses and financing in all aspects of the oil and gas industry value chain, and retention of the benefit within Ghana;

* Develop local capacity in all aspects of the oil and gas value chain through education, skills and expertise development, transfer of technology and know-how;

* Achieve maximum practicable influence over development initiatives for local/domestic stakeholders;

* Maximise local content and local participation in all aspects of oil and gas industry value chain within a decade;

* Increase the capacity and international competitiveness of domestic businesses and industrial sectors; and

* Create supportive industries that will sustain economic development.

Security

* Ensure security for oil and gas industry installations and operations, with an emphasis on engaging National Security Agencies to assist in the provision of protective security for the oil and gas industry installations and activities.

Natural Gas Utilisation and Commercialisation

* Maximise the utilisation of natural gas reserves by prohibiting flaring or venting of natural gas produced within Ghana unless necessary in operations;

* Discourage re-injection of natural gas unless it results in increased benefits to the associated operations;

* Assign to GNPC any natural gas produced in the country either in association with crude oil or not in association with crude oil unless otherwise agreed in the Petroleum Agreement ;

* Support GNPC or some other national entity to secure the required financing, in partnership with private sector, to develop infrastructure for the utilisation of all natural gas produced in the country; and

* Facilitate the utilisation of natural gas for the development of a viable domestic petrochemical industry.

Human Resource Development and Technology Transfer

* Support capacity building at all levels in the country's technical, vocational and tertiary institutions; and

* Oblige Licensees to provide facilities for training and technology transfer as an integral part of their operations.

Downstream

3.5 Policy Goal

The goal is to facilitate the universal access to adequate, reliable and cost effective petroleum products such as Liquefied Petroleum Gas (LPG).

3.6 Challenges

The challenges facing the petroleum sub sector include:

* Inadequate refining infrastructure

* Inadequate infrastructure for the transportation of petroleum products

* Inadequate storage infrastructure

* Inadequate and inefficient distribution of petroleum products

* Inadequate sales outlets

* Ineffective implementation of petroleum pricing mechanism

* weak institutional and regulatory environment

3.7 EXPANSION OF PETROLEUM PRODUCTS SUPPLY INFRASTRUCTURE

Policy Direction

The policy focus for the petroleum downstream sub-sector is therefore to attract investments in order to expand the capacity of the existing infrastructure in the medium to long term. To meet the short to medium term objective, Government will pursue the following:

* Expand the national crude oil refining capacity through public and private sector investment;

* Secure increased private sector investment in partnership with the public sector for the expansion of infrastructure for the supply of petroleum product;

* Allocate adequate resources to meet national strategic petroleum stocks requirement; and

* Support mobilisation of domestic capital markets for petroleum supply infrastructure and operations.

3.8 Increasing Access to Petroleum products

Policy Direction

The policy focus is to extend the reach of petroleum products to all Ghanaians. To meet this objective, Government will pursue the following policy actions:

* Expand petroleum product storage capacity, and extend petroleum products bulk distribution infrastructure to all parts of the country;

* Support expansion of the supply and reach of LPG to homes and small businesses; and

* Address institutional and market constraints that hamper increasing access of petroleum products.

3.9 Petroleum Sector Reforms

Policy Direction

Government's policy actions will focus on:

* Completing the full cycle of the deregulation.

3.10 Petroleum Pricing

Policy Direction

Government will:

* Ensure pricing of petroleum products at cost recovery levels while maintaining uniform national prices for petroleum products;

* Base ex-refinery prices of petroleum products on import parity prices of petroleum products or other cost-effective pricing formula;

* Regulate transportation and distribution charges for petroleum products to ensure reasonable profit margins for transporters and distributors; and

* Apply cross-subsidies between petroleum products to achieve specific national development objectives.

4.0 RENEWABLE ENERGY SUB SECTOR

4.1 Overview

Ghana is well endowed with renewable energy resources, particularly biomass7, solar and wind energy. The development and use of renewable energy and waste- to- energy8 resources have the potential to ensure Ghana's energy security and mitigate the negative climate change impacts. The use of waste-to- energy resources has the potential to act as a significant part of the national sanitation programme.

7 Biomass constitutes woodfuel and charcoal

8 Waste-to-Energy is the conversion of waste material to energy

9 Mini hydro refers to hydropower project with generating capacity of less than 1 MW.

Biomass is Ghana's dominant energy resource in terms of endowment and consumption. Biomass resources cover about 20.8 million hectares of the 23.8 million hectare land mass of Ghana, and is the source of supply of about 60% of the total energy used in the country. The vast arable and degraded land mass of Ghana has the potential for the cultivation of crops and plants that can be converted into a wide range of solid and liquid biofuels.

The production, transportation, sale and pricing of woodfuels are all undertaken by the private sector except for taxes and levies which are regulated by local Government authorities. The woodfuels business will continue to be operated and managed by the private sector.

The development of alternative transportation fuels such as gasohol and other biofuels can provide substitute fuels for the transportation sector and help diversify and secure future energy supplies of Ghana.

By virtue of its geographic location, Ghana is well endowed with solar resources which could be exploited for electricity generation and low heat requirements in homes and industries. Solar energy utilisation has however been limited owing to its comparatively higher cost. Government is committed to improving the cost-effectiveness of solar and wind technologies by addressing the technological difficulties, institutional barriers, as well as market constraints that hamper the deployment of solar and wind technologies.

Even though the overall potential of mini-hydro is limited, 21 potential mini9 hydro sites that could be developed for power generation have been identified in the country. The generating capacities of these sites range between 4kW and 325kW.

4.1 Goal for the sub-sector

The goal of the renewable sub-sector is to increase the proportion of renewable energy, particularly solar, wind, mini hydro and waste-to-energy in the national energy supply mix and to contribute to the mitigation of climate change.

4.2 Challenge

The challenge is to increase renewable energy in the national energy mix in a sustainable manner

4.3 Biomass

Policy Direction

The policy focus is to:

* Support sustained regeneration of woody biomass resources through legislation, fiscal incentives, and attractive pricing;

* Promote the establishment of dedicated woodlots for wood fuel production;

* Promote the production and use of improved and more efficient biomass utilisation technologies.

* Promote the use of alternative fuels such as LPG as substitute for fuel wood and charcoal by addressing the institutional and market constraints that hamper increasing access of LPG in Ghana; and

Biomass Pricing

The policy for pricing woodfuels focuses on:

* Prices based on market forces; and

* Taxes and levies on woodfuels being regulated by the appropriate national agencies or local authorities, as may be necessary.

4.4 Liquid Biomass Fuels

The policy is to:

* Balance biofuel development against food security;

* Support the development of indigenous alternative transportation fuel industry based on bio-energy resources (Biofuels); and

* Support private sector investments in cultivation of biofuel feedstock, extraction of the bio-oil and refining of bio-oil into secondary products by creating appropriate legislation.

4.5 Solar and wind

Policy Direction

The policy focus is to:

* Improve the cost-effectiveness of solar and wind technologies.

* Create favourable regulatory and fiscal regimes;

* Support indigenous research and development to reduce the cost of solar and wind energy technologies; and

* Support the use of decentralised off-grid alternative technologies (such as solar PV and wind) where they are competitive with conventional electricity supply.

4.6 Mini Hydro

Policy Direction

The policy actions are:

* Create appropriate fiscal and regulatory framework; and
* Provide pricing incentives for mini hydropower projects.

5.0 WASTE-TO-ENERGY

5.1 Overview

Waste-to-Energy projects have become a very important mechanism for the management of the growing sanitation problem facing urban communities as well as a means of contributing to energy supply and security. Significant amounts of wastes are generated in Ghana. These include (i) municipal waste (both solid and liquid), (ii) industrial wastes, and (iii) agricultural wastes.

There are many energy technologies which can convert these waste materials into electricity, heat and fuel. The conversion technologies include (i) combustion, (ii) gasification (iii) pyrolisis (iv) anaerobic digestion (v) fermentation, (vi) esterification.

While many waste-to-energy technologies are mature and widely applied in other parts of the world, they are relatively more expensive compared to conventional technologies particularly due to the high cost of waste collection and management.

Some waste-to-energy technologies have been utilised in Ghana in the past. These include (i) anaerobic fermentation of municipal waste and industrial liquid wastes to produce biogas for heating, and (ii) combustion of solid wastes to produce electricity in Combined Heat and Power (CHP) systems in wood and oil palm industries.

5.2 Policy Goal

The goal is to convert most of the wastes generated in municipal activities, industrial operations and agricultural operations to energy.

5.3 Challenge

The major challenge to the development of waste-to-energy technologies in Ghana is the high cost associated with the collection and management of waste materials.

POLICY DIRECTION

THE POLICY FOCUS IS TO CONVERT MUNICIPAL, INDUSTRIAL AND AGRICULTURAL WASTE INTO ENERGY AS A MEANS OF MANAGING THE GROWING SANITATION PROBLEMS WHILE CONTRIBUTING TO ENERGY SUPPLY SECURITY.

IN THAT REGARD THE SPECIFIC POLICY ACTIONS WILL BE TO:

* Maximise energy production from waste
* Divert waste from landfills (prohibit burying of waste and landfills)
* Facilitate access to grid for waste to energy power plants

* Develop infrastructure for waste collection and supply to waste-to-energy facilities

6.0 ENERGY EFFICIENCY AND CONSERVATION

6.1 OVERVIEW

The growth in the demand for fuelwood and charcoal is estimated at 3% per annum. Electricity demand, on the other hand, is growing between 6%-7% annually while consumption of petroleum products is estimated to increase at about 5% per annum. Energy efficiency and conservation can help reduce these high growth rates.

The losses in the production, transportation and use of energy are also high. System losses in electricity distribution are about 25% while wastage in the end-use of electricity is estimated at about 30%. Reduction of losses in energy supply and more efficient use of energy would also reduce the demand for energy and delay investment in energy supply infrastructure.

Efforts, in the past, have been made by the Ministry of Energy and other agencies to promote energy efficiency and conservation in homes and industries. These efforts have however not resulted in sustained adoption of energy efficiency and conservation in the country owing to a number of financial and institutional obstacles. Empirical evidence also suggests that pricing of energy services has been successfully used to encourage consumers to adopt measures to conserve energy and use energy efficiently. To encourage and sustain energy efficiency and conservation in the development of the sector requires new and innovative interventions to deal with the challenges.

6.2 GOAL

The goal is to ensure efficient production and transportation as well as end-use efficiency and conservation of energy.

6.3 CHALLENGE

The challenges are:

* Inefficient energy pricing
* Inadequate financing for energy conservation and efficiency
* Limited awareness of energy conservation measures

Policy Direction

The following policy directions will be pursued by Government to conserve and use energy efficiently:

General

* Establish appropriate pricing regime for energy services that would provide incentives to domestic and industrial consumers to voluntarily manage their energy consumption;

* Develop and implement programmes and measures to help consumers optimise their energy use;

* Support a sustained and comprehensive public education and awareness creation campaign on the methods and benefits of energy conservation;

* Promote the establishment of a Centre for Energy Efficiency; and

* Discontinue, through legislation, the local production, importation and use of high energy consuming vehicles and inefficient electricity consuming equipment and appliances.

Transportation

* Develop and implement measures to reduce petroleum product consumption in transportation;

* Enforce the implementation of the zonal system for lifting of petroleum products from dedicated storage depots;

* Encourage the use of fuel enhancing additives; and

* Reduce electricity transmission and distribution losses.

7.0 ENERGY AND ENVIRONMENT

7.1 OVERVIEW

The impact of the production and use of energy on the environment is undeniable and varying in its degrees. The exploitation of biomass for energy purposes results in deforestation, while the use of fossil-based fuels contributes to carbon dioxide emissions. The use of inferior cooking equipment also has negative health impacts. The production and transportation of crude oil and petroleum products and the flaring of natural gas associated with petroleum production have associated environmental risks.

7.2 GOAL

The goal is to ensure that energy is produced and utilised in an environmentally sound manner.

7.3 CHALLENGE

The challenge is to

* Mitigate the environmental hazards of energy production, transportation and use.

* Build capacity to adapt and mitigate the effects of climate change

* Regulate all activities in the energy sector to protect the environment

Policy Direction

To address the challenge, Government will:

* Promote the use of environmentally friendly energy supply sources such as renewable energy (solar, wind, waste) in the energy supply mix of the country;

* Encourage a shift from oil to gas wherever gas is a technically feasible alternative;

* Promote the use of improved wood fuel burning equipment for cooking in households and other commercial activities;

* Support and actively participate in international efforts and cooperate with international organisations that seek to ensure sustainable delivery of energy to mitigate negative environmental impacts and climate change;

* Encourage and enable all relevant entities engaged in activities in the energy sector to explore and access international environmental financial mechanisms and markets to overcome investment, technology and other relevant barriers;

* Ensure effective disposal of all hazardous substances and materials associated with the production, transportation and use of energy; and

* Facilitate environmental protection awareness programmes.

8.0 ENERGY AND GENDER

8.1 OVERVIEW

Energy issues are of concern to all. However, women are one of the most important actors in the energy sector, in terms of their contact, use and management of energy. With woodfuels constituting the bulk of the energy used for cooking and heating in Ghanaian homes and in other commercial activities, women in Ghana bear the brunt of the pollution and negative health impacts of emissions from these fuels.

Given that majority (57%) of Ghanaians live in rural areas, statistics show that many people, especially women, lack access to electricity and rely on biomass for cooking. The negative health impacts of indoor air pollution from traditional biomass fuels on women, girls and babies remain a critical issue in Ghana's energy development.

8.2 POLICY GOAL

The goal is to mainstream Gender in the Energy Sector

8.3 CHALLENGES

The Energy and Gender challenges include:
* Dominance of women in the collection and use of fuelwood and charcoal
* High Exposure of women to indoor pollution
* Limited involvement of women in the planning and management of energy services
* Limited capacity of women in management positions in the Energy Sector

Policy Direction

In addressing the Energy and Gender challenges Government will:
* Promote the use of modern forms of energy in households;
* Support the capacity development of women in the energy Sector;
* Promote the development of solar and other renewable forms of energy on off grid communities; and

* Ensure participation of women in the formulation and implementation of energy interventions

9.0 MANAGING THE FUTURE

9.1 OVERVIEW

Effective management is critical for the sustainable development of the energy sector. To achieve this requirement requires a transparent regulatory regime and strong institutional and human capacities as well as a vibrant financial platform.

There are three regulatory agencies established by Acts of Parliament to ensure the proper functioning of all players in the energy sector and to create the requisite conducive environment for protection of private investment in the sector. These are Energy Commission, Public Utility Regulatory Commission and National Petroleum Authority.

The Energy Commission (EC) has responsibilities for the licensing of operators and setting technical standards for power sector and natural gas transportation. The EC also advises the Minister for Energy on energy sector policy and planning issues.

The Public Utilities Regulatory Commission (PURC) is responsible for electricity tariffs approval, monitoring quality of service and consumer protection.

The Ministry of Energy has the mandate to regulate upstream petroleum activities including the granting of licenses for petroleum exploration, development and production.

National Petroleum Authority (NPA) combines the responsibilities of the licensing of operators in the downstream petroleum sector and setting of technical standards and enforcement as well as pricing of petroleum products.

These regulatory institutions are limited in their professional capacity and operational effectiveness. This leads to uncertainty in regulation resulting in difficulties in the supply and delivery of energy services. With the recent developments in the petroleum sector, there is also the need to streamline the regulatory environment to avoid duplication and conflict of mandates.

9.2 REGULATORY ENVIRONMENT

Goal

The policy goal is to build a transparent and effective regulatory environment as well as strengthen the regulatory institutions to fulfil their mandate effectively.

Challenges

The challenges are:

* Inadequate financial resources for operational activities

* Inadequate human resources

Policy Direction

The policy actions for the development of the regulatory environment will focus on the following:

* Streamline regulations and institutional arrangements;

* Strengthen human resource capacity of the regulatory institutions;

* Ensure the independence of the national regulatory agencies;

* Implement administrative and regulatory changes that will enhance the financial independence of regulatory institutions; and

* Strengthen the capacity of regulatory agencies to enforce regulations.

9.3 MOBILISATION OF INVESTMENT FOR ENERGY SECTOR DEVELOPMENT

The energy sector requires huge capital investment (16 Billion US Dollars) to develop infrastructure in the energy sector – petroleum, power and renewable energy-in the medium term.

Goal

The goal is to encourage public and private sector investment in the energy sector.

Challenges

The challenges for the sector are to:

* Establish a transparent and effective regulatory environment; and

* Transparent and efficient pricing regime for energy services.

Policy Direction

Government will:

* Provide a conducive legal, fiscal, and regulatory environment to attract investment into the energy sector;

* Encourage the capital markets, including the Ghana Stock Exchange, to raise financing for investments in the energy sector;

* Establish transparent and non-discriminatory practices in the implementation of rules and regulations; and

* Ensure efficient and transparent pricing regime for energy services.

9.4 BUILDING HUMAN RESOURCE CAPACITY AND R&D

The effective development of the energy sector requires Ghana to build the requisite levels of human resource capacity. Effective and well-focused Research and Development (R&D) will also contribute to accelerating the development of the sector.

Goal

The goals are to build adequate Ghanaian human resource capacity in the control and management of the energy sector, and create an enabling environment for effective R&D.

Challenges

The challenges are to:

* Mainstream human resources development and R&D issues in all energy sector operations; and

* Develop requisite educational and institutional capacity to support Ghanaian expertise and skills development in the energy sector

Policy Direction

Government will pursue the following actions:

* Develop comprehensive Ghanaian local content in all aspects of energy sector operations;

* Ensure maximum ownership and management control of all aspects of the energy sector;

* Support the training of Ghanaians in all fields of energy development and management and build capacity in indigenous manufacture of energy technologies;

* Increase the allocation of resources for energy R&D activities;

* Give priority to adaptive R&D in energy technology while promoting basic research;

* Support the transformation of Ghanaian energy research institutions into Centres of Excellence for energy research and development; and

* Collaborate with relevant Government, local and international agencies to develop capacity of tertiary and allied institutions for training and research.

9.5 IMPLEMENTING THE ENERGY POLICY

To make the necessary impact on the national economy will require that the management, operations and monitoring of the energy sector receive adequate focus. Team work and total commitment of all stakeholders should be the primary driving principle to ensure smooth implementation of the National Energy Policy.

To achieve this objective, the following actions will be pursued:

* Develop requisite human resource capacity and logistical support for the implementation and monitoring of the Energy Policy;

* Strengthening the Policy, Planning, Monitoring and Evaluation Divisions of relevant Ministries, Departments and Agencies;

* Regular interaction between the Ministry of Energy and relevant Ministries, Departments and Agencies, Traditional Authorities, Members of Parliament, District Assemblies to discuss issues relating to the National Energy Policy;

* Refine strategies and programmes to achieve the policy goals; and

* Develop comprehensive programme to create awareness and ensure acceptance among policy makers and the general public on the National Energy Policy.

FUNDAMENTAL PETROLEUM POLICY FOR GHANA

POLICY GOAL

To become a net exporter of Oil and Gas and a major player in the global petroleum industry, through the development and management of the nation's petroleum resources and revenue streams in a transparent and environmentally responsible manner for the benefit of every Ghanaian, now and in the future.

EXECUTIVE SUMMARY

In July 2007, light crude oil in commercial quantities was discovered by the National Oil Company, Ghana National Petroleum Corporation (GNPC) and its partners, exploring for oil in the offshore Tano/Cape Three Points Basin of the Ghanaian Continental Shelf. Since these significant discoveries, appraisal work conducted has estimated core reserves of oil at about one billion barrels as of June 2008, with substantial associated natural gas reserves. It has become urgent, therefore, that prior to first oil production targeted for 2010; the Nation takes steps to guide the entire petroleum industry, both direct and ancillary, with policy and legal frameworks. There are three main segments and activity phases in any petroleum industry that a petroleum nation must regulate in order to create a successful petroleum industry: the Upstream, Midstream and Downstream segments.

Currently petroleum activity in Ghana is conducted under the framework of the Petroleum Exploration and Production Law, 1984, (PNDCL 84), the GNPC Law, 1983, (PNDCL 64), and the Petroleum Income Tax Law, 1986 (PNDCL 188). The Ministry of Energy, the ministry in charge of Ghana's petroleum sector, has worked closely with GNPC, the Attorney-General's office (AG) and the Internal Revenue Service (IRS), over the years to develop the existing legal and regulatory framework

Fundamental issues in this policy document focus on basic questions about resource ownership and jurisdiction issues, fundamentals of the fiscal and legal framework; broad relationships among actors in the petroleum sector; broad institutional frameworks; principles of State and national participation.

In terms of scope, the Policy addresses two main areas that Government must concentrate on developing, for the successful regulation and monitoring of petroleum operations. These are: the guiding principles for governmental monitoring of petroleum operations; and the regulatory framework for petroleum operations.

The Policy provides ground-rules for the monitoring of the operations of petroleum companies and the government's role in relation thereto. The cross-cutting governmental activities covered by this Policy are as follows: Development of Petroleum Legal and Contractual Framework; Petroleum Good Governance; Social Impact Management; Sector Organisation; Health, Safety and Environment; National Participation/Local Capacity and Competence; Fiscal Administration; Revenue Management; Resource Management; Data and Information Management; Human Resource Development; and Technology Development.

Highlighted in the policy document are the four main pillars of the regulatory (policy, fiscal and legal) framework for the management of the operational and commercial aspects of Ghana's petroleum sector. These are: A Fundamental Petroleum Policy; Petroleum Legislation; Petroleum Regulations; and a Model Contract.

To address and ensure management transparency, industry predictability and development sustainability, issues of primary concern that are covered by the petroleum regulatory framework include: *pre-licensing; licensing and exploration; development, production and decommissioning; transportation; midstream and downstream value enhancement.*

This policy will be supported by a Master Plan which shall embody Strategies and Action Plans based on the principles and ground-rules for governmental monitoring and management of petroleum operations established.

1. INTRODUCTION

There are three main segments and activity phases in any petroleum industry that a petroleum nation must regulate in order to create a successful petroleum industry: the Upstream, Midstream and Downstream segments. These form the mainframe areas of petroleum operations by oil companies, and include upstream activities such as pre-licensing, licensing and exploration and appraisal, planning for development and production operations, field development, petroleum production and disposal to primary customers. In addition, a government must also regulate the tail-end and decommissioning phases of petroleum production in order to ensure that there are no lasting negative environmental and social issues left behind after petroleum activity ceases.

These upstream activities are complemented by midstream activities including marine transportation and pipelines and downstream activities including refining and processing, downstream marketing and retail activities.

Although the focus of this policy document is on the upstream segments of the petroleum industry value chain, the other phases are critically considered to ensure that effective linkages are established for the overall optimal benefit of the nation. Care has been taken to recognize the fundamental differences in consequences of policy on the upstream, midstream and downstream segments. The policy caters for these differences accordingly, as for example with clarifying the differences in fiscal systems for the upstream as opposed to the midstream and downstream.

The common feature of the upstream petroleum industry is the high risk involved, and for this reason oil companies at this time seek to maximize net present value. Government policy governing this phase of petroleum activity must therefore monitor and guide the industry to ensure that national interests are not subsumed to those of oil companies, to the detriment of the nation, but rather that a balance is ensured between the interests of oil companies and those of the nation.

Midstream and downstream petroleum activities, involving the transporting and selling of petroleum, and the activities of associated industries, are less risky ventures, but should be of equal importance to a government in fundamental policy development as they contribute substantially to maximizing national benefit, and provide enhanced opportunities for local participation and value addition.

It is necessary that well before oil production begins, the Government of Ghana develops ground rules that will guide and monitor the newly developing petroleum industry in Ghana. Although there has been a lot of exploration activity in Ghana, there is minimal production of crude oil from the Saltpond field. Recent significant discoveries in the Tano/Cape Three Points Basin increase the onus on the government to create ground rules to guide Ghana's petroleum industry. The monitoring system must be supported by policy guidelines that link all the activity streams of the industry.

Currently petroleum activity in Ghana is conducted under the framework of the Petroleum Exploration and Production Law, 1984, (PNDCL 84), the GNPC Law, 1983, (PNDCL 64), and the Petroleum Income Tax Law, 1986 (PNDCL 188). The Ministry of Energy, the ministry in charge of Ghana's petroleum sector, has worked closely with the national oil company, Ghana National Petroleum Corporation (GNPC) and the Attorney-General's office over the years to develop the existing legal and regulatory infrastructure. However, recognizing the expected upsurge in petroleum activity that will stem from the significant

petroleum discoveries and the novelty of Ghana becoming a significant petroleum producing country, it will be necessary to review and update what is currently available. This process commenced in 2006 and is ongoing with the assistance of the Commonwealth Secretariat.

It should be noted that the significant quantities of gas associated with the oil discoveries impose challenges for its utilisation. Ghana does not have experience of gas production and utilisation and would thus need to develop a comprehensive framework to govern the development of a vibrant and sustainable indigenous gas industry.

2. THE FUNDAMENTAL ISSUES

The ingredients of a well formulated and lasting policy will include a focus on fundamental issues, coverage and linkage of all aspects of petroleum activity, providing the critical ground rules that will guide the entire upstream value chain from pre-licensing through licensing to the conduct of exploration and production activities, through tail-end activities and decommissioning, and delivery of petroleum to the primary markets.

The fundamental issues are those that address basic questions about the stakeholders in the industry, their relationships with each other and to the resource, and the principles that must guide these relationships and the development of the industry to ensure success. It is important that these issues are addressed at the initial stages of developing the industry, as they serve as the precursor to the establishment of a successful and sustainable petroleum industry. They include:

* *Resource ownership and jurisdiction issues*

* *Fundamentals of the fiscal and legal framework*

* *Broad relationships among actors in the petroleum sector*

* *Broad institutional frameworks*

* *Principles of State and national participation*

RESOURCE OWNERSHIP AND JURISDICTION ISSUES

All petroleum existing in its natural state within the jurisdiction of the Republic of Ghana is the property of the Republic and shall only be explored and exploited pursuant to authorization and supervision by the Government of Ghana. No exploration shall be undertaken in an area where the Ghanaian jurisdiction is unclear due to unresolved boundaries with neighboring states. Efforts shall be made to expeditiously establish such boundaries.

FUNDAMENTALS OF THE FISCAL AND LEGAL FRAMEWORK

The legal frameworks supporting Ghana's petroleum industry shall protect the rights of all participants in the industry and shall be designed to ensure the right balance between national developmental needs and agenda and investor needs, predictability of contract and operations, fiscal responsibility and industry development.

All petroleum activities in Ghana shall be conducted with due diligence and efficiency, making use of the best international techniques and practices prevailing in the petroleum industry and in accordance with the established legal framework. This shall provide predictability, stability and profitability to both investors and the nation.

BROAD RELATIONSHIPS AMONG ACTORS IN THE PETROLEUM SECTOR

All petroleum companies operating in Ghana shall be expected to operate under the control of the Government of Ghana. The government shall cooperate with all licensed petroleum companies in Ghana to serve common interests in accordance with the established laws and regulations of the nation, and the international community where applicable.

BROAD INSTITUTIONAL FRAMEWORKS

The Minister responsible for petroleum shall cooperate with all stakeholder institutions including, but not limited to, the Ministers responsible for finance, the environment, fisheries, local government and, all other relevant institutions to monitor petroleum operations and ensure that the nation benefits from petroleum operations in the achievement of developmental goals and objectives, optimal revenue collection, the highest possible local value addition, and maximum environmental protection.

PRINCIPLES OF STATE AND NATIONAL PARTICIPATION

Petroleum is of strategic importance to the nation and as such, Government shall, in addition to managing the sector by policy and regulation, actively participate in the commercial aspects of the petroleum industry to maximize national benefit and promote local value addition.

3. SCOPE

The Policy addresses two main areas that Government must concentrate on developing for the successful regulation and monitoring of petroleum operations. These are:

* The guiding principles for governmental monitoring of petroleum operations, and

* Regulatory framework for petroleum operations.

3.1 GUIDING PRINCIPLES

Ground-rules to guide Ghana's petroleum industry development must be in the form of Fundamental Policy Guidelines. These guidelines shall form the basis for monitoring and guiding distinctly inter-governmental activities in the management, administration and regulation of operational activities in the petroleum industry and petroleum revenue streams. The guidelines shall protect the rights of Ghanaians, as well as, the rights of petroleum sector investors and strike a balance between the needs of the industry and the rights of citizens to have their environment and social needs protected. The policy shall also provide the foundation that will ensure that as much as possible, Ghanaians shall benefit from the petroleum industry in terms of revenue collection and improvements in human resources, industry and technology.

This Policy is designed to provide for governmental monitoring of pertinent areas of national interest, at all times maintaining linkages among the upstream, midstream and downstream activities of the petroleum industry. It will thus provide government with an overall view of the petroleum industry in Ghana, plus a measure of the industry's impact on the citizenry and nation as a whole. In this way, the Policy will ensure at all times that governmental activity regarding the industry shall always be for the benefit of the nation.

The Policy shall provide ground-rules for the monitoring of the operations of petroleum companies and the government's role in relation thereto. The cross-cutting governmental activities covered by this Policy are as follows.

* *Development of Petroleum Legal and Contractual Framework*

* *Petroleum Good Governance*

* *Social Impact Management*

* *Sector Organisation*

* *Health, Safety and Environment*

* *National Participation/Local Capacity and Competence*

* *Fiscal Administration*

* *Revenue Management*

* *Resource Management*

* *Data and Information Management*

* *Human Resource Development*

* *Technology Development*

* Development of Petroleum Legal and Contractual Framework

The petroleum laws of Ghana shall reflect and expand on the principles stated in this Fundamental Policy document. Whereas this Policy shall serve as a permanent guideline for governmental monitoring of the petroleum industry, the petroleum laws of Ghana shall be amended as and when necessary to reflect changing petroleum industry and societal standards and needs.

Because it is fundamentally important to the survival and success of Ghana's petroleum industry to attract investors, the petroleum legal framework established in Ghana shall be transparent and shall provide predictability in contracting and in operations.

* Petroleum Good Governance, including Principles of Transparency, Accountability and Integrity

Recognizing that general good governance promotes investor confidence, which is essential to the profitability of Ghana's petroleum industry, general principles of good governance shall be applied to the sector in order to entrench transparency, credibility, predictability, accountability and integrity in all activities of the industry.

* Social Impact Management

It is anticipated that petroleum operations and revenues will have various impacts on socio-economic statuses in Ghana, including monetary impact, impacts on national industry, urban development, other livelihoods, employment opportunities and patterns, as well as foreign relations. Government shall establish avenues of lasting benefit to impacted communities and the nation as a whole, to monitor, manage and mitigate anticipated and real time negative social impacts, whilst promoting and entrenching the positive impacts.

* Sector Organisation

Given that the successful management of Ghana's petroleum industry is dependent upon efficient and effective sector organisation, the government of Ghana shall ensure that all relevant institutions shall be organised so as to promote coordination, continuity, impose accountability and create the necessary checks in the management systems for petroleum operations, revenues and resources.

* Health, Safety and the Environment

Petroleum operations have the potential to cause irreparable damage to the environment and compromise the health and safety of the people, thus affecting the sustainable development of the country. It is important that health, safety and environmental issues are integrated into the planning and development of the petroleum sector.

Government shall promote sound and sustainable environmental practices in the management of petroleum operations and ensure compliance with national environmental health and safety regulations and standards.

* National Participation/Local Capacity and Competence

Ghana is severely lacking in local competencies and capacity to permit meaningful involvement of Ghanaians in the development of the petroleum industry. It is therefore of prime importance for Ghanaians to acquire and achieve the high levels of capacity and competencies needed in the industry, over time.

In order to maximize national participation, government shall facilitate a structured and organized collaboration among the petroleum industry, local research and training institutions, other industries with linkages to the petroleum industry, business associations and local communities to this end. All petroleum companies shall be expected to support the nation's efforts to achieve desired levels of expertise and know-how, over time.

* Fiscal Administration

To ensure maximum benefit to the national development agenda from the petroleum sector, government shall establish processes to maximize petroleum revenue collection in a transparent and cost effective manner and without jeopardizing incentives for petroleum investors. Government shall also promote fiscal discipline to ensure that correct petroleum revenues are collected and accounted for, and establish mechanisms to facilitate and simplify fiscal administration.

* Petroleum Revenue Management

Recognizing that revenue management by government will have to undergo significant changes to accommodate the optimum inflows of revenue anticipated from petroleum operations, government will take deliberate steps to establish a transparent and predictable fiscal regime for the collection, verification and utilisation of petroleum revenues.

Government shall ensure that petroleum revenue collected is invested in equitable, sustainable and value oriented national development for current and future generations of Ghanaians.

* Petroleum Resource Management

Given that petroleum resources are finite, all petroleum companies operating in Ghana shall be expected to optimize production, utilizing only the best available technology and field practices to this end. Government shall require resource extraction and production to be in a sustainable manner and at a rate appropriate for the development of Ghana and its economy.

* Data and Information Management

As provided by law, all data derived from petroleum operations shall belong to the state. In view of the importance of data and information management for the long-term successful operation of the petroleum and related industries, all pertinent data, from whatever source derived, whether directly or indirectly related to petroleum operations, must be collected and stored in a responsible and sustainable manner to ensure recovery at all times.

* Human Resource (HR) Development

Given the significance of human capital to the productivity and overall development of the country, the petroleum sector shall perform a catalytic role in enhancing the human resource competence culture within the country.

* Technology Development

Recognising the importance of technology to the advancement of the nation, Government shall encourage the development and utilisation of technological innovation in developing the petroleum industry and the economy as a whole.

3.2 REGULATORY FRAMEWORK

The policy, fiscal and legal framework for the management of Ghana's petroleum sector shall include: A Fundamental Petroleum Policy; Petroleum Legislation; Petroleum Regulations; and a Model Contract. These documents must regulate the operational and commercial aspects of petroleum industry.

Issues of primary concern that must be covered by the petroleum regulatory framework to address and ensure management transparency, industry predictability and development sustainability, include:

* *Pre-licensing*

* *Licensing and Exploration*

* *Development, Production and Decommissioning*

* *Transportation*

* *Midstream and Downstream value enhancement*

3.2.1 PRE-LICENSING ISSUES

Regulation of pre-licensing issues must cover and clarify areas of primary concern both to oil companies that will be investing in petroleum operations and the government. This will enable Government to successfully meet its obligation of expectation management and credible revenue forecasting for the development of an appropriate and beneficial fiscal regime. These areas include:

- Clarification of jurisdiction and boundary
- Assessment of petroleum potential
- Environmental assessment
- Local administration issues
- Expectation management

CLARIFICATION OF JURISDICTION AND BOUNDARY ISSUES

Ghana gives due recognition to previous arrangements with neighbours regarding boundaries. Where discoveries are trans-boundary in nature, Ghana shall cooperate with her neighbours in the joint development of such discoveries.

No exploration shall be undertaken in an area where Ghanaian jurisdiction is unclear due to unresolved boundary issues with neighbouring States. Efforts shall be made to expeditiously resolve such issues.

ASSESSMENT OF PETROLEUM POTENTIAL

Government shall establish mechanisms for verifying petroleum potential, thus ensuring at all times that Government has a well founded assessment of Ghana's petroleum potential.

ENVIRONMENTAL ASSESSMENT

All activities that may be deemed to significantly impact the quality of the environment shall only be conducted subject to national environmental assessment regulations.

LOCAL ADMINISTRATION ISSUES

In the implementation of this policy, due regard shall be taken to coordinate and harmonize with local administrative bodies to achieve national goals and interests, and also with relevant laws.

EXPECTATION MANAGEMENT

In view of the uncertainties and risks associated with petroleum operations, and in order to avoid false expectations, government shall make every effort to pre-empt the dissemination of false and/or unfounded information about petroleum operations, by providing the public with accurate, pro-active and objective information on a timely basis.

3.2.2 LICENSING AND EXPLORATION ISSUES

In order to encourage investment in the petroleum sector and the selection of only the most qualified oil companies to operate in Ghana, it is important that the licensing process remains transparent, and that this be entrenched in legislation. Government shall maintain a policy of healthy competition among licensees in an atmosphere of cooperation for the benefit of the nation. Licensing issues that must be regulated and monitored for transparency encompass:

- Promotion/Announcement of Licensing
- Pre-qualification
- Variety among licensees
- Reconnaissance licenses
- Allocation criteria
- Work Programmes
- Government monitoring of operations & approvals
- Periodic reports on exploration

Promotion/Announcement of Licensing: Open Door/Competitive Bidding

Ghana shall have a mix of open door policy as well as the competitive bidding process where necessary. The Minister responsible for petroleum shall be tasked to oversee the promotion and announcement of licensing rounds under the competitive bidding process.

Licensing rounds shall be on a periodic basis to be consistent with the desired rate of resource exploitation.

Pre-Qualification

All petroleum companies seeking to operate in Ghana under Exploration and Production (E & P) Licenses shall be pre-qualified.

Variety among Licensees

In the interest of enriching the petroleum environment and to promote competition, the licensing of several petroleum companies shall be encouraged. Further, to promote internal controls, a variety of different licensees shall be encouraged to join together and operate within each individual license.

Reconnaissance Licence

The acquisition of substantial data is of prime importance to the petroleum industry and to the nation as a whole, and as such, government will encourage the granting of reconnaissance licenses subject to laws to monitor reconnaissance activities and ensure that they do not interfere with existing petroleum exploration and production activities.

Allocation Criteria

In line with the principles of transparency and equity that underlie this Policy document and subject to any pertinent national procurement laws in effect, allocation criteria shall be published in order to inform oil companies of the basis for allocations.

Work Programmes

Inasmuch as the government of Ghana recognizes the rights of oil companies to make returns on their investments, the benefits of petroleum operations to the nation as a whole shall remain paramount at all times. To this end, government shall consider as a major criterion in determining the quality of a work programme, the added value in terms of services and benefits that it contributes to the development goals and interests of the nation.

Government Monitoring of Operations & Approvals

Government shall establish effective systems for monitoring and auditing petroleum operations to ensure compliance with regulations, law and contract terms, and shall create avenues for open dialogue and cooperation with petroleum companies to attain best solutions for the mutual interests. In spite of the foregoing, government shall promote self-regulation by petroleum companies in conformity with law, national goals and interests.

Periodic Reports on Exploration

In addition to annual budgetary reports on the petroleum sector, the minister responsible for petroleum shall oversee and coordinate periodic briefings to Parliament on petroleum operations throughout each year. These will serve the purpose of ensuring transparency, accountability and the management of expectations.

3.2.3 DEVELOPMENT, PRODUCTION AND DECOMMISSIONING ISSUES

In view of Government's interest in managing petroleum operations to ensure optimal and sustainable production in an environmentally responsible and safe manner, it is important that the government is kept informed of the ideas and solutions developed by operators for field

development. This will enable Government to take the necessary steps to protect national interests, ensure maximum production and influence resource utilization.

Petroleum development and production issues must be covered with legislation and be catered for by the fundamental petroleum policies governing upstream activities. Relevant development and production issues include, primarily, of:

- Discovery, evaluation and delineation
- Monitoring commerciality evaluations
- Unitisation
- Dialogue on field development planning
- Approval of Field Development Plan (FDP)
- Monitoring reservoir performance and under-production
- Tail-end plan approval
- Approval of decommissioning of installations
- End Production and Decommissioning
- Natural gas issues

DISCOVERY, EVALUATION AND DELINEATION

Government shall focus on evaluating all discoveries, either alone or in consultation with petroleum companies or other consultants. This will enable Government to prepare the way forward for the benefit of all stakeholders, determine competence building strategies and also manage expectations.

MONITORING COMMERCIALITY EVALUATIONS

The monitoring of commerciality evaluations is essential for revenue management, including national budgetary assumptions. Government shall, therefore, focus on implementing reliable systems and procedures to monitor the commerciality of evaluations.

Unitisation

To enable fields that straddle multiple licenses to be developed in a coordinated manner and to develop such fields so as to maximise their economic value over time, Government shall encourage and, where necessary, mandate unitization agreements.

Where a field straddles the country's boundaries with its neighbours, Government shall co-operate with its neighbours to ensure efficient and effective development of the field on the basis of best international practices for mutual benefit. In such situations, cross-boundary unitisation shall be encouraged

Dialogue on Field Development Plan (FDP)

Recognizing the importance of a well negotiated FDP as an essential tool for Government in ensuring high recovery of petroleum and entrenching national interest, Government shall encourage professional dialogue with petroleum companies to enable the proper authorities understand the relevant issues upon which the FDP will be based. This will offer Government the opportunity to provide timely and informed input into the development of FDPs and evaluate them to ensure that they address and protect national interest.

Approval of Field Development Plan (FDP)

In addition to ensuring the preparedness of the government for meaningful dialogue on the development of FDPs, Government shall also ensure that relevant local competencies and capacities are developed and enhanced to permit informed governmental approval of FDPs in order to maximize, promote and protect national interests.

Monitoring Reservoir Performance

In view of the fact that reservoir performance may dictate changes to the Field Development Plan, Government shall closely monitor reservoir performance and shall enter into dialogue with petroleum companies, when necessary, on improvements in the Field Development Plan to ensure optimal recovery at all times.

Tail-end Plan Approval

The decision by a contractor that further production is no longer commercial does not necessarily preclude further production under different licenses. Government shall therefore, proactively pursue ways and means of maintaining production in order to maximize resource recovery.

Approval of Decommissioning of Installations

Since decommissioning is of significant environmental importance in the national interest, Government shall, in addition to approving decommissioning plans, monitor the manner in which decommissioning of installations is performed to ensure that legal and environmental obligations to restore the environment are at the least met, and that other interests affected are protected.

End Production and Decommissioning

Given that the proper decommissioning of installations upon cessation of petroleum production is essential for maintaining the integrity of the country's environment and for ensuring public safety, Government shall ensure that petroleum companies seek effective and balanced decommissioning solutions, which are consistent with national environmental legislation and international obligations and have a proper regard for safety, the environment, other legitimate uses of the sea and land, and economic considerations.

Government shall be proactive to ensure that end production and decommissioning plans are addressed at the initial stages of preparing the Field Development Plan, and approved. In order to avoid the possibility of decommissioning becoming a national financial responsibility, Government shall establish mechanisms to monitor and ensure that petroleum companies assume full financial and obligatory responsibility for decommissioning. In this regard Government shall approve decommissioning plans and monitor to ensure that they are implemented in a manner that meets legislative requirements, uses best available engineering and environmental practice, and avoids unnecessary taxpayer exposure.

NATURAL GAS ISSUES

Government shall enact gas specific legislation where existing legislation does not sufficiently provide for the development of gas.

In furtherance of national and global efforts to reduce emissions of greenhouse gases, protect the environment and considering the fact that natural gas is a valuable resource, Government shall maintain a policy of no flaring or venting of natural gas, except for testing, emergencies and for safety reasons.

Recognising the catalytic role that natural gas can play in accelerating local participation in the petroleum sector, Government and petroleum companies operating in Ghana shall identify opportunities for natural gas utilisation.

Natural gas is rapidly growing in global importance both as an energy source and as a feedstock for downstream industry. The processing of natural gas either for export or for further utilisation on land shall be encouraged and Government shall provide appropriate incentives to this end.

3.2.4 TRANSPORTATION ISSUES

Transportation issues in the petroleum sector are closely linked to environmental, safety and metering issues. As with upstream petroleum activities, in addition to legislation, the initial policy framework conditions for this midstream activity must encompass guidelines addressing responsibilities and rights issues associated with the transportation of petroleum, such as:

- Transportation of oil and gas
- Permits and approvals for transportation plans
- Tariffs for use of pipelines
- Treaties with neighbouring countries

TRANSPORTATION OF OIL AND GAS

Government policy on the transportation of petroleum shall be guided by the national interest in ensuring that all transportation infra-structure is optimally designed, utilized and operated so as to maximize production and utilization. The interest of third parties to use the infra-structure shall be secured in a fair and equitable manner and regulated by legislation where necessary.

PERMITS AND APPROVALS FOR TRANSPORTATION PLANS

Development and operation of the minimum infield transportation infrastructure and pipelines for the production and disposal of petroleum to the primary market shall not require separate licenses if developed as part of field development plans. All other infrastructure shall be developed and operated under separate licenses. As part of the policy for gas utilisation, Government shall encourage third party development, ownership and operation of pipelines and transportation infrastructure.

Government shall require optimal and efficient utilisation of infrastructure through sharing of capacity by industry participants. All petroleum infrastructure shall be operated on the basis of fair, equitable and open access principles which shall be detailed in the Laws and regulations from time to time. The legal framework shall provide for the eventual transfer of infrastructure to the State.

TREATIES WITH NEIGHBOURING COUNTRIES

Government shall consult and establish Treaties and Agreements with neighbouring countries to avoid conflict in the event of cross border fields.

3.2.5 MIDSTREAM AND DOWNSTREAM VALUE ENHANCEMENT ISSUES

Midstream and downstream activities, although less risky and of little importance to petroleum producers, provide areas of great significance in the economic development of Ghana. The activities that characterize these sectors involve the processes that petroleum undergoes after production and deal primarily with the marketing and uses petroleum. These sectors are significant for the achievement of Ghana's developmental goals and agenda for poverty reduction and the attainment of middle-income status by the year 2015. This is because they provide most opportunities for government to promote policies for capacity and competencies development and enhancement programmes for Ghanaians.

As with the upstream sector, it is important for Government to develop fundamental policy to serve as the ground-rules to guide governmental oversight of these sectors in addition to establishing regulatory frameworks to direct the development of the sectors and the commercial relationships within them, whilst protecting national interests.

Within the framework of petroleum operations, the midstream and downstream issues that must be catered for by fundamental policy include:

- Regulatory framework for midstream and downstream sectors: Refinement of crude petroleum
- Industrial use of petroleum
- Sale and pricing of crude petroleum
- Product marketing, distribution and storage

- Tariffs for use of infrastructure
- Pricing regulations

Regulatory Framework for Midstream and Downstream Sectors: Refinement of Crude Petroleum

To strike a balance between protecting the national benefits inherent in promoting the relatively low risk investments in the midstream and downstream sectors, and protecting the high risk investments in the upstream sector, Government shall give priority to Ghana's requirements for crude petroleum in a manner that does not jeopardize incentives for investors, and shall regulate same by legislation and by contract.

Additionally, in line with Ghana's policy of full cost recovery for energy, Government shall establish and enhance, where necessary, systems and processes to ensure that all the national share of crude petroleum will be refined to the extent that is economically and technically viable.

INDUSTRIAL USE OF PETROLEUM

To further promote the use of petroleum as a stimulus for economic growth and improved societal value, Government shall carefully consider the availability of petroleum as an opportunity for the growth of other industries and new avenues for employment, and shall encourage and sponsor research and development into value generation opportunities available in the use of petroleum.

SALE AND PRICING OF CRUDE PETROLEUM

GOVERNMENT SHALL PARTICIPATE FULLY IN ALL SALE NEGOTIATIONS FOR CRUDE OIL. CRUDE OIL PRODUCED IN GHANA SHALL BE PRICED ACCORDING TO ITS API AND INDEXED TO EQUIVALENT CRUDE ON THE WORLD MARKET.

Ghana shall have first right of refusal for the purchase of crude oil produced in the country to satisfy local demand as and when Government deems necessary.

PRODUCT MARKETING, DISTRIBUTION AND STORAGE

The institutional and infrastructural aspects of marketing and distribution shall be reviewed periodically in order to absorb and promote the opportunities that will be created by the availability of petroleum to Ghana through its national share of production.

TARIFFS FOR USE OF INFRASTRUCTURE

Government shall, in line with its policy of full cost recovery, monitor the links and relationships of the petroleum sector to determine how to regulate use of the new infrastructure that will develop out of the petroleum sector. Where feasible, tariffs for use of the infrastructure will be left to institutional arrangements.

4. SUPPORT FOR THE FUNDAMENTAL POLICY OF GHANA

This Policy shall be supported by a Master Plan. The Master Plan shall embody Strategy and Action Plans based on the principles and ground-rules for governmental monitoring and management of petroleum operations established in this Policy.

In order to ensure that the strategies and actions to develop Ghana's petroleum industry can evolve easily to cater for changing socio-economic and petroleum industry needs, the supporting documents shall be created separately and apart from the Policy. In this way, as often and as necessary as it may become for the strategies and actions to be changed, the policy will remain consistent for a much longer time period, to continually guide and inform industry development and its desired linkages with national development on a long term basis.

The Government of Ghana shall be responsible to make the necessary and appropriate monetary investments for the successful implementation of this Policy and any supporting plans. It shall be the responsibility of government to regulate and manage petroleum operations in Ghana in a manner that protects and promotes the national interest as a priority, protects petroleum investments and encourages the industry as a catalyst to the country's socio-economic and infrastructure development.

IMPORTANT LAWS REGULATING ENERGY SECTOR

ENERGY EFFICIENCY STANDARDS AND LABELLING (NON-DUCTED AIR CONDITIONERS AND SELF-BALLASTED FLUORESCENT LAMPS) REGULATIONS, 2005

IN exercise of the powers conferred on the Minister responsible for Energy by section 56 of the Energy Commission Act, 1997 (Act 541) these Regulations are made this 2nd day of June 2005.

APPLICATION OF REGULATIONS

1. These Regulations apply to non-ducted air conditioners or self-ballasted fluorescent lamps manufactured in Ghana or imported for use in Ghana.

REQUIREMENT TO COMPLY WITH REGULATIONS

2. (1) A person who manufactures or imports non-ducted air conditioners or self-ballasted fluorescent lamps for use in Ghana shall ensure that,

(a) the air conditioners comply with the standard specification for nonducted air conditioners stipulated in Ghana Standard 362:2001 published in the Ghana *Gazette* of 8th February, 2002;

(b) the lamps comply with the standard specification on self-ballasted fluorescent lamps stipulated in Ghana Standard GS324:2003 published in the Ghana *Gazette* of 30th August, 2003; and

(c) the non-ducted air conditioners and self-ballasted fluorescent lamps comply with the minimum performance and labelling requirements prescribed by these regulations.

(2) A person who manufactures in Ghana or imports

(a) non-ducted air conditioners for use in Ghana in contravention of regulation 2(1) *(a)*, or

(b) self-ballasted fluorescent lamps for use in Ghana in contravention of regulation 2(1) *(b)*;

commits an offence and is liable on summary conviction to a fine not exceeding two hundred and fifty penalty units or imprisonment for a term not exceeding twelve months or both.

MINIMUM PERFORMANCE REQUIREMENTS

3. (1) A non-ducted air conditioner manufactured or imported for use in Ghana shall in accordance with Ghana Standard 362:2001 have a minimum energy efficiency ratio of 2.8.

(2) A self-ballasted fluorescent lamp manufactured or imported for use in Ghana shall in accordance with Ghana Standard GS 324:2003 have;

(a) a minimum rated life of six thousand hours; and

(b) a minimum efficacy measured in lumens per watt matching the lamp configuration (bare or covered with or without reflector) and lamp power (LP) rating as provided for in Schedule I.

INFORMATION ON PACKAGE AND LABELLING REQUIREMENTS FOR NON-DUCTED AIRCONDITIONERS

4. (1) A person shall not store, offer for sale, sell, distribute, import or otherwise dispose of a non-ducted air conditioner unless the air conditioner bears a label that indicates the minimum performance.

(2) The Label on a non-ducted air conditioner shall be in the form provided in Schedule II and shall

(a) where the label is not printed on the packaging but placed or attached to the packaging, be in full colour, and

(b) where the label is printed on the packaging and in "black on white" be in colours that preserve the legibility of the label.

(3) The label shall be in the English language and shall be pasted conspicuously on the packaging of the air conditioner.

(4) A label on an air conditioner shall also provide the following information:

(a) the manufacturer's name or trade mark;

(b) the manufacturer's model identifier and for split and multi-split units, the model identifier of the indoor and of the outdoor elements of the combination to which the figures quoted in the table in Schedule III apply;

(c) the indicative annual energy consumption calculated with the total input power as defined in GS 362:2001 multiplied by an average of 2000 hours per year in cooling mode at full load, determined in accordance with the test procedures of GS 362:2001;

(d) the energy efficiency ratio star rating of the model, determined in accordance with GS 362:2001;

(e) the cooling output defined as the cooling capacity in kW of the appliance in cooling mode at full load, determined in accordance with the test procedures of GS 362:2001;

(f) the Energy Efficiency Ratio (EER) of the appliance in cooling mode at full load determined in accordance with the test procedures of GS 362:2001;

(g) the type of refrigerant; and

(h) a one-star to five-star energy efficiency ratio rating in which the ascending number of stars represents a higher energy efficiency ratio determined in accordance with the table in Schedule III where EER is determined in accordance with the test procedures of GS 362:2001.

(5) The label shall be printed in colour on a water proof material and pasted conspicuously on the appliance.

(6) The background of a label pasted on an appliance shall be gold and all stars on the label shall be black and the text shall be in black, whilst the box enclosing the label shall be in green or red.

(7) A person who contravenes any of the requirements on labelling in this regulation commits an offence and is liable on summary conviction to a fine not exceeding two hundred and fifty penalty units, or a term of imprisonment not exceeding twelve months or to both.

INFORMATION ON PACKAGE AND LABELLING REQUIREMENTS FOR SELF-BALLASTED FLUORESCENT LAMP

5. (1) A person shall not store, offer for sale, sell, distribute, import or otherwise dispose of a self-ballasted lamp unless the lamp bears a label that indicates the minimum performance.

(2) The label on a self- ballasted fluorescent lamp shall be in the form provided in Schedule IV and shall

(a) where the label is not printed on the packaging but placed or attached to the package, be in full colour;

(b) where the label is printed on the packaging, be in "black on white" with the print and background in colours that preserve the legibility of the label;

(c) be in the English language; and

(d) be pasted conspicuously on the package of the self-ballasted fluorescent lamp.

(3) The label shall include the following information

(a) the energy efficiency star rating of the lamp, determined in accordance with the test procedures of GS 323:2003 and as shown in Schedule V;

(b) the luminous flux of the lamp in lumens, measured in accordance with the test procedures of GS 323:2003;

(c) efficacy performance measured in lumens per watt (lm/W) and in accordance with GS 323:2003;

(d) the input power (wattage) of the lamp, measured in accordance with test procedures of GS 323:2003;

(e) the average rated life of the lamp in hours measured in accordance with the test procedures of GS 323:2003;

(f) luminous flux comparison data (Self -ballastedfluorescent lamp versus filament lamp); and

(g) the number of stars corresponding to the star rating class relevant to the information referred to in sub regulation (2) *(b)*, shaded black.

(4) Where no side of the packaging is large enough to contain the label and the blank border, or where the label would cover more than fifty per cent of the surface area of the largest side, the

label and the border together with the border shall be reduced to not less than forty per cent (by length) of the side of the box where it is printed or pasted.

(5) The background of a label pasted on an appliance shall be gold and all stars on the label shall be in black and the text shall be in black whilst the box enclosing the label shall be in green or red.

(6) A person who contravenes any provision of this regulation commits an offence and is liable on summary conviction to a fine not exceeding two hundred and fifty penalty units or a term of imprisonment not exceeding twelve months or to both.

OFFENCES IN RELATION TO REMOVAL OF LABEL

6. (1) A person shall not remove the label on an air conditioner or a lamp package before the first retail purchase of the item.

(2) A person who contravenes sub-regulation (1) commits an offence and is liable on summary conviction to a fine not exceeding two hundred and fifty penalty units or a term of imprisonment not exceeding twelve months or to both.

POWERS OF AN INSPECTOR

7. (1) An inspector appointed under section 52 of the Act may at any reasonable time

(a) enter any premises or place where the inspector has reason to believe that non-ducted air conditioners or self-ballasted fluorescent lamps are being manufactured, imported, offered for sale or otherwise being disposed of; and

(b) examine or if necessary test non-ducted air conditioners or self-ballasted fluorescent lamps,

(i) displayed for sale;

(ii) at the point of import; or

(iii) at a warehouse to ascertain whether the items comply with the provisions of these Regulations.

(2) An inspector or a Customs officer may without prejudice to regulation 10 seize any imported non-ducted air conditioners or self-ballasted fluorescent lamps which contravene any provision of these Regulations or which are improperly labelled or labelled in such a way as to be deceptive, misleading or false.

(3) An inspector or a Customs Officer shall refuse to release to the importer a non-ducted air conditioner or self-ballasted fluorescent lamp imported for use in Ghana which is not labelled in the manner provided for under these Regulations.

(4) Where an inspector or Customs Officer refuses to release a non-ducted air conditioner or self-ballasted fluorescent lamp to the importer under sub-regulation (3), the inspector or Customs Officer shall within forty-eight hours of detention of these goods give notice to the importer to properly label the goods, and the notice shall state that within twenty-eight days after the date of

the notice the goods must be relabelled in the required manner or be re-exported out of the country.

(5) Where an importer is required under sub- regulation (4) to relabel the imported goods the relabelling of the goods shall be done under the supervision of an officer authorized for the purpose by the Energy Commission and the Ghana Standards Board.

(6) Where an importer fails to re-label goods as required under sub-regulation (4), an inspector or a Customs officer shall after the expiration of the period specified, seize the goods.

(7) An inspector or Customs officer who assists a person to contravene these Regulations commits an offence and is liable on summary conviction to a fine not exceeding two hundred and fifty penalty units or imprisonment for a term not exceeding twelve months and shall be liable to dismissal.

PETITION AGAINST DETENTION OR SEIZURE

8. (1) Any person whose air conditioner or self-ballasted fluorescent lamp is detained or seized under regulation 7 may within seven days after the detention or seizure petition the Commission for the release of the seized or detained item.

(2) The Commission shall within seven days of receiving the petition either confirm the seizure or order the seized items to be released to the petitioner.

FORFEITURE OF AIR CONDITIONERS OR SELF-BALLASTED FLUORESCENT LAMPS

9. (1) Subject to regulation 8, an air conditioner or self-ballasted fluorescent lamp found in the country and which does not conform to these Regulations is liable for seizure and forfeiture.

(2) The Minister shall acting on the recommendation of the Commission given in collaboration with the Ghana Standards Board, dispose off or re-export any forfeited air conditioner or self-ballasted fluorescent lamp.

OFFENCES AND PENALTIES

10. A person who obstructs or interferes with an inspector in the performance of the inspector's functions commits an offence and is liable on summary conviction to a fine not exceeding two hundred and fifty penalty units or imprisonment for a term not exceeding twelve months or both.

OFFENCE BY CORPORATE BODIES

11. (1) Where an offence under these Regulations is committed by a body corporate or by a member of a partnership or other firm, every member, director or officer concerned with the management of the firm shall also be guilty of the offence and is liable on summary conviction to a fine not exceeding two hundred and fifty penalty units or a term of imprisonment not exceeding twelve months or to both unless that member, director or officer proves to the court that:

(a) the member, director or officer exercised due diligence to secure compliance with the provisions of these Regulations; and

(b) the offence was committed without that member, director or officer's knowledge, consent or connivance.

INTERPRETATION

12. In these Regulations unless the context otherwise requires, "Act" means the Energy Commission Act, 1997 (Act 541); "air conditioner" means non-ducted room air conditioners; "Commission" means Energy Commission; "energy efficiency ratio (EER) means ratio of the total cooling capacity

to the effective power input in any given set of rating conditions; "GS" means Ghana Standards; "label" means a label relating to a CFL or air conditioner which contains

information on its consumption of energy (whether or not it also contains other information);

"lamp efficacy" means average of the lesser of the lumens per watt

measured in the base up or other specified position; "Minister" means Minister responsible for Energy; "Non-ducted air conditioner" means an assembly or assemblies designed

as a unit primarily for mounting in a window, through a wall or as a console designed primarily to provide free delivery of conditioned air to an enclosed space, room or zone and includes a prime source of refrigeration for cooling;

"self–ballasted fluorescent lamp" means a unit which cannot be dismantled without being permanently damaged, provided with a lamp cap and in corporating a light source and any additional elements necessary for starting and for stable operation of the light source.

SCHEDULE I

Regulation 3 (2)*(b)*

Lamp Configuration	Lamp Power Rating (LP, Watts)	Minimum Efficacy (Lumen/W)
Bare Lamp Covered LampWithout Reflector Lamp with Reflector	Less than 15;More than or equal to 15; Less than 15; More than or equal to 15 but less than 19; More than or equal to 19 but less than 25; More than or equal to 25; Less than 20; More than or equal to 20;	More than or equal to 45 More than or equal to 60 More than or equal to 40 More than or equal to 48 More than or equal to 50 More than or equal to 55 More than or equal to 33 More than or equal to 40

SCHEDULE II

Regulation 4 (2)

SCHEDULE III

Regulation 4 (4)(b)& (h)

ENERGY EFFICIENCY RATING FOR NON DUCTED AIR-CONDITIONERS

Energy Efficiency Star Rating	Non-ducted air cooled air conditioners

5 -star 4 -star 3 – star 2 – star 1 – star	4.00 < EER 4.00 > EER > 3.75 3.75 > EER > 3.45 3.45 > EER > 3.15 3.15 > EER > 2.80

SCHEDULE IV

Regulation 5 (2)

SCHEDULE V

Regulation 5 (3)(a)

ENERGY EFFICIENCY RATING OF SELF-BALLASTING FLUORESCENT LAMPS

1. Lamps shall be classified as 5-star if:

$$W <= 0.24 \sqrt{O} + 0.0103\ O$$

where $_O$ is the lumen output of the lamp and W is the power input into the lamp in watts.

2. If a lamp is not classified as 5-star, a reference wattage W&subR:; shall be

calculated as follows: $W_R = 0.88 \sqrt{O} + 0.049$ when O > 34 lumens 0.2 , when O < = 34 lumens

where O is the lumen output of the lamp.

An energy efficiency index EI is then set as W $E_1 = {}^{W}R$ where, W is the power input into the lamp in watts.

The energy efficiency star ratings are then set in accordance with the following table:

Energy Efficiency Star rating

Energy efficiency class	Energy efficiency index E1
4-star	E1 < 60%
3-star	60% < = E1 < 80%
2-star	80% < = E1 < 110%
1-star	110% < = E1

PRACTICAL INFORMATION FOR INVESTING IN GHANA ENERGY AND MINING SECTOR

PARTNERS AND INFORMATION

»Chamber of Mines: www.chamines.com.gh

»Forestry Commission: www.fcghana.com

»Survey Department: www.survey.gov.gh

»Environmental Protection Agency (EPA): www.epa.gov.gh

»University of Mines and Technology: www.ghanauniversities.com/kust.htm

»University of Ghana, Department of Geology: www.ug.edu.gh/facscience.php

»Ghana Customs Excise and Preventive Service: http://cepsghana.org

»Internal Revenue Service: www.ghana-com.co.uk/bodies.html#IRS

»Ghana Investment Promotion Centre: www.gipc.org.gh

»Attorney General Department: www.ghana.gov.gh/governing/ministries/governance/justice.php

»Federal Institute for Geosciences and Natural Resources of Germany: www.bgr.bund.de

»Geological Survey of Denmark and Greenland: www.geus.dk

»Geological Survey of Finland: www.gsf.fi

»British Geological Survey: www.bgs.ac.uk

»Geological Survey of Sweden: www.sgu.se

»Bureau de recherches géologiques et minières, France: www.brgm.fr

»China Geological Survey: www.cgs.gov.cn/Ev/English.htm

»Council for Geoscience, Republic of South Africa: www.geoscience.org.za

INVESTING IN GHANA

Ghana Investment Promotion Centre
P. O .Box M.193, Accra, Ghana
Tel: (+233)-(21)-665125 - 9; (+233)-(24)-4318254
Fax: (+233)-(21)-663801 ; (+233)-(21)-663655
www.gipcghana.com
Investment opportunities exist for investors to set up manufacturing plants and machinery for the mining industry.

GOLD REFINERY AND VALUE ADDED PRODUCTS

Ghana is already producing over two million ounces of gold per annum. In spite of this level of production, there is no refinery in the country and the bullion is exported for final refining. Feasibility studies have confirmed the viability of refining gold in Ghana. Such a facility will serve other gold producing countries within the sub-region. This is a project that investors with the technical know-how would wish to consider.
Opportunities also exist for setting up downstream production facilities to manufacture key inputs for the mining industry eg mill balls, drill bits, cyanide and activated carbon etc., commemorative coins, jewellery and electronic components. Investors could take advantage of the Industrial Freezone facility to produce such items for the international market.

ACTIVATED CARBON

Activated carbon is employed extensively in the cyanidation process for gold production. The raw material for the manufacture of the commodity – coconut husk-is readily available locally. Investors are invited to consider the establishment of a facility to produce the commodity.

DECORATIVE STONES

Ghana is endowed with extensive deposit of granite of various types. These deposits could be exploited to produce high quality floor tiles. Opportunities exist to produce dimension stones for the country's building industry.

CONTACTS

For further information on any of the opportunities, you may contact:
The Chief Executive
Minerals Commission
P.O. Box M.248
Accra – Ghana
Tel: (233) 21 – 771318 / 773053 / 772783
Fax: (233) 21 – 773324
E-mail: mincom@mc.ghanamining.org / mincom@mincomgh.org

For technical questions, please go to Contact or to the page Agencies. There, you will find the right agency to contact for your particular request.

MINERALS COMMISSION'S VISION & MISSION STATEMENT

BACKGROUND:
In the unpredictable and contantly changing world of mining, where long term, risky mining investment is becoming more and more rare and therefore mining investors are demanding greater security and return on their investments, while Governments are seeking increased revenues from investors, local communities are demanding more "social responsibility" from mining investors, and we all desire to have growth and development as well as a natural environment that is as pleasant as possible:

VISION:
The Commission would strive to make Ghana the leading destination of mining sector investment in Africa through creating a congenial atmosphere in which all stakeholders work as partners in a safe environment to achieve one common goal: sustainable development through mining.

MISSION:
The Commission's primary responsibility is to foster the efficient and effective regulation and management of the utilization of Ghana's mineral resources. This we will accomplish through the deveolpment of a solidly knowledge-based, self-led organization, which recognizes that mining investment would take place and be sustained only if it is under Win-Win circumstances.

POTENTIAL PARTNERS : MINERALS PROCESSING

MN.001 **GHANA CONSOLIDATED DIAMOND LIMITED**
Diamond mining

Investment Information

The company was established and operated by the Consolidated Africa Selection Trust (CAST) owned by Selection Trust of UK from 1924 to 1972 when Ghana Government took 55% majority shares until 1982 when Selection Trust pulled out completely.

The Ghana Government is the sole shareholder with 100% ownership. Almost 80 million carats of diamonds have been recovered over the period 1924 to date with peak production of 2.5 millions carats per annum from 1964-1974. The current reserves inventory is made up of;

The Akwatia diamond concession covering an area of 240 sq km. The Birim reserves have a total of 24 million carats of diamonds and some quantities of gold in the region of 0.1gm per cubic meter of gravel. The diamonds are mainly small and industrial with 20% being of gem quality. There is also the Apinamang Gold Concession which covers an area of 128sq km of which little exploration work has been done. The available business proposal is to raise capital to finance the company to turn it into more viable mining company through acquiring new machinery and efficient management. An initial investment of US$ 5.6m will be required to recapitalize the company.

Company Requirement
Company is seriously looking for a strategic investor who can assist company to raise the required capital of US$5,600,000.00 for its re-capitalization programme. There is a comprehensive business report available for consideration of any interested investor. For any further enquiries you can contact the (MD) direct or through the GIPC

Contact Details
DR MAXWELL KUSI-MENSAH (MD)
P.O.BOX 26, Akwatia
Tel233-882 2662
Or 233-21 771254/771255/ 764343/773615
Fax:233-27 518100
gcdltd@ghana.com
Project Location: Akwatia- Eastern Region

INVESTMENT PROCEDURES

Establishment of Investment Projects
Under the Ghana Investment Promotion Centre Act, 1994 (Act 478), investment in all sectors of the economy, other than mining, petroleum, free zones and portfolio investments, can be established without prior approval by GIPC. Mining and Petroleum sector projects have to be approved or licensed by the **Minerals Commission** and the **Ministry of Mines and Energy**, respectively. Industrial activities in the Export Processing Zone are administered by the **Ghana Free Zones Board** while portfolio investments are handled by the **Ghana Stock Exchange.**

Foreign investors intending to invest in Ghana are by law to register with the Ghana Investment Promotion Centre (GIPC) under the GIPC ACT 478. **The registration will be concluded only when the legal minimum equity contribution has been met.**

The amounts involved are:

- Joint Venture - US$10,000.00
- 100% Foreign-Owned - US$50,000.00
- All Trading Enterprises - US$300,000.00

To satisfy the minimum equity requirement, the investor must follow the following steps:

STEP 1 - Registration with Registrar General's Department
Incorporate a company at the Registrar General's Department. The department has five (5) working days to complete formalities if all documents are in order.

STEP 2 - Minimum Equity Contribution
Foreign investors should comply with the GIPC Act 478 regarding minimum equity requirements either in cash or in kind as follows:

(a) Bank Account - Open two corporate accounts, (i.e. foreign and local) with a local bank of your choice.

(b) By Bank Transfer - Effect a Bank to Bank transfer of minimum equity requirement, which has to be converted into local currency (Cedis). This transaction should be confirmed to the Bank of Ghana by the investor's local authorised dealer bank. Bank of Ghana in turn, confirms this transaction to GIPC for the company's registration purposes.

(c) **By Physical Cash** - Physical cash carried into Ghana by individuals for investment purposes should be declared on Bank of Ghana Form T5 on arrival and subsequently deposited in a bank account within the shortest possible time. This transaction should be confirmed by your dealer Bank and the Bank of Ghana as in (b) above.

Importation of Plant, Machinery and Equipment
Enterprises are free to implement their projects by importing the relevant plant, machinery and equipment. Zero-rated and concessionary duty items should be cleared automatically and directly through CEPS. Essential plant, machinery and equipment, which fall under Section 24 of Act 478 should be cleared with the GIPC.

(d) Equity in Kind - In the case of equity in kind in the form of imported machinery, equipment and goods, all documents covering such imports should be in the name of the registered company and evidenced by the following which should be submitted to GIPC for registration purposes:

- Bill of Lading/Airway Bill (Originals)
- Destination (Ghana) Inspection Certificate
- Customs Bill of Entry (Originals)
- Import Declaration Form (IDF)
- Certified/Final Invoices
- Evidence of Capitalisation – Form 6 from the Registrar General Department.

(e) Registration with relevant Agencies - Registration with the relevant agencies as applicable to the sector of operation.

STEP 3 - Registration with GIPC
The investor then registers with the GIPC (after paying the relevant fees), which has five (5) statutory working days to complete the registration process, provided the registration forms are in order.
GIPC Investor Registration Forms

STEP 4 - Wholly Ghanaian-owned Enterprises
Wholly Ghanaian-owned enterprises do not need to register with GIPC since the minimum foreign capital requirement does not apply to such enterprises.

STEP 5 - Immigrant Quota
All wholly Ghanaian-owned enterprises and enterprises with foreign participation seeking immigrant quota facilities in respect of expatriate personnel (experts) for their businesses should satisfy the relevant minimum capital requirements specified under **Section 30 of Act 478**. Immigrant quota request is by a letter to GIPC.

STEP 6 - Registration with IRS and VAT Secretariat
All enterprises must register directly with the Internal Revenue Service and the Value Added Tax (VAT) Secretariat for purposes of statutory tax, e.g. taxes, rebates and exemptions thereof.

STEP 7 - Environmental Impact Assessment Certificate
Enterprises must register and obtain an environmental permit from the Environmental Protection Agency (EPA).

For all of the above, GIPC may assist as the need arises, either directly or through referral to accredited public sector agencies and/or management, accounting or legal firms.

COST OF DOING BUSINESS IN GHANA

A. Business Registration

(a) Registrar General's Department (RGD)

The Registrar General's Department is the organization that registers all companies (societies and institutions) in Ghana. The Law regulating the formation of companies is the Companies Code, 1963 (Act 179). A Limited Liability company is the most common structure utilized by businesses, particularly foreign investors and others who want to limit their liabilities.

Limited Liability companies are expected to fill out the relevant Application Forms, which serve as the Company 's Regulations. All companies must have an auditor, who must be a member of the Institute of Chartered Accountants, but should not be an officer or servant of the company or be an employee or partner of such persons. When all such forms have been filled satisfactorily and relevant fees paid, a **Certificate of Incorporation** and a **Certificate to Commence Business** are issued. Below are the basic costs and fees applicable at the RGD office:

i. Application Forms ¢65,000.00 (GH¢6.50) (US$8.00)
ii. Stamp Duty 0.5% of Stated/Paid-up Capital
iii. Filing Fees ¢100,000.00 (GH¢10) (US$12.00)
iv. Incorporation Fees¢560,000 (GH¢56) (US$64.00)

v. Auditors' Fees Varied

(b) Ghana Investment Promotion Centre (GIPC)
The GIPC is responsible for registering all (foreign) investment, which qualify under the GIPC Act 1994. This Act does not apply to either mining or petroleum enterprises.

Application Procedure: Investors are required to complete Investor Registration Forms (Form GIPC/R1) in triplicate. Within five (5) days from the date of orderly receipt of these forms (and its attachments) the GIPC will formally register the investment. Below are the relevant fees and costs applicable at GIPC:

CATEGORY	US$	¢	GH ¢
1. REGISTRATION			
a)Wholly Ghanaian Owned Business	Free	Free	Free
b)Joint-venture (ie $10,000)	1,000	9,200,000	920
c) Wholly Foreign (ie $50,000)	2,500	23,000,000	2,300
d)General Trading (ie $300,000)	5,000	46,000,000	4,600
e)Renewal (Every 2 years)	1,500	13,800,000	1,380
f)Certificate Replacement	100	920,000	92
g) Liaison Office	7,500	69,000,000	6,900
h) Tourism • Up to $500,000 investment • $500,000 - $2million investment • above $2million investment	1,000 5,000 10,000	9,200,000 46,000,000 92,000,000	920 4,600 9,200
i)All Strategic Investment (LI 1817 and section 25)	20,000	184,000,000	18,400
2. EXEMPTION			
a)Invoice Value up to $100,000	500	4,600,000	460
b)Invoice Value up to $500,000	1,000	9,200,000	920
c) Invoice Value up to $1,000,000	2,500	23,000,000	2,300
d)Invoice Value greater than $1,000,000	5,000	46,000,000	4,600
3. TECHNOLOGY TRANSFER (Max 10 years)			
a)Transfer Value up to $500,000 per annum	2,500 p.a	23,000,000 p.a	2,300 p.a
b)Transfer Value up to $1,000,000 per annum	5,000 p.a	46,000,000 p.a	4,600 p.a
c) Transfer Value greater than $1,000,000 per annum	15,000 p.a	138,000,000 p.a	13,800 p.a

(c) Ghana Free Zones Board (GFZB)
The GFZB is responsible for the promotion of the processing and manufacturing of commodities through the establishment of export processing zones. It also

encourages the development of commercial and service activities within the ports of Ghana. These activities are regulated by the Free Zone Act, 1995 (Act 504).

Application Procedure: As a basic requirement for commencing business with GFZB, investors are expected to incorporate a company/partnership in Ghana and provide evidence of possession or lease of property or intent to acquire such property.

Depending on the activity to be undertaken in the zone, the applicant should obtain and complete GFZB Form 3, 4 or 5; and submit it with the required attachments to the Secretariat of the Board. The GFZB shall notify the investor of his/her Application for License within 28 working days.

(i) Application Forms (US$100.00)

(ii) Licensing Fees:

Business	Initial	Renewal/Year
Manufacturing	US$2,000.00	US$1,600.00
Commercial	US$5,000.00	US$4,000.00
Service	US$3,000.00	US$2,000.00
Development	US$4,000.00	US$3,000.00

B. Labour Issues/Employment

The Labour Act 651 of 2003 regulates employment and labour issues in Ghana. This Act consolidates all laws relating to labour, employers, trade unions and industrial relations. The result of a collaborative effort among the social partners – Government, Employers and Organized Labour – the Act provides for the protection of employment, general conditions of employment, unfair labour practices, trade unions and employers organizations, occupational health, safety and environment, and labour inspection.

National Labour Commission

An important feature under the Act is the establishment of seven-member National Labour Commission. The Commission consists of two members each nominated by Government, organized labour, and employers' organization. The chairperson is nominated by organized labour and employers.

Mission Statement

"To develop and sustain a peaceful and harmonious industrial relations environment through the use of effective dispute resolution practices, promotion of co-operation among the labour market players and mutual respect for their rights and responsibilities."

Functions

The functions of the Commission are:

a) to facilitate the settlement of industrial disputes;
b) to settle industrial disputes;
c) to investigate labour related complaints, in particular unfair labour practices and take steps as it considers necessary to prevent labour disputes;

d) to maintain a data base of qualified persons to serve as mediators and arbitrators; and

e) to promote effective labour cooperation between labour and management

Independence

In the exercise of its adjudicating and dispute settlement function, the Commission is not subject to the control or direction of any persons or authority.

Powers

In settling industrial disputes the Commission has the powers of the High Court in respect of enforcing the attendance of witnesses and examining them on oath, affirmation or otherwise and compelling the production of documents, among others.

Enforcement of Orders

In enforcing its orders, the Commission makes application to the High Court for an order to compel any person who fails or refuses to comply with its direction or order.

Settlement of Industrial Disputes - Mediation

When the Commission is notified by parties to an industrial dispute that they have failed to settle the dispute by negotiation, the Commission requests the parties to settle the dispute by mediation and the settlement agreement is binding on the parties.

Voluntary Arbitration

When mediation fails and the Commission is notified, it refers the dispute to an arbitrator, selected by the parties, and the decision of the arbitrator is binding on the parties.

Compulsory Arbitration

In industrial disputes that affect workers engaged in essential services, which are prohibited from resorting to lockout or strike, the Commission settles the dispute by compulsory arbitration. The award in a compulsory arbitration is final and binding on the parties unless challenged in the Court of Appeal on questions of law.

The Value of Labour

The National Tripartite Committee, comprising the Minister responsible for Labour, representatives of the Government, employer's organizations and organized labour, determines the national minimum wage. Currently, the daily minimum wage is **¢13,500.00 (US$1.50)**. Another financial obligation of the employer is the payment of a statutory monthly contribution of **12.5%** of employee's basic salary to the Social Security and National Insurance Trust (SSNIT). The following are some other fees and charges expected in the case of the employment expatriates resident in Ghana –

(a) Ghana Immigration Service

(i) Resident Permit/Person (ECOWAS) - ¢250,000 (GH¢25) (US$28.40)
(ii) Resident Permit/Person – Others - ¢500,000 (GH¢50) (US$57.00)
(iii) Re-Entry Permits (Single/Multiple) - US$40.00/100.00

(b) Ghana Investment Promotion Centre

(i) Automatic Quota (per person) - US$500 ¢4,600,000 GH¢460
(ii) Additional Quota (per person) - US$2,500 ¢23,000,000 GH¢2,300
(iii) Replacement of Quota (per person) - US$500 ¢4,600,000 GH¢460
(iv) Short term Quota up to 2 years - US$1000 ¢9,200.000 GH¢920

(c) Ghana Free Zones Board

(i) Resident Permit/Person/Year - US$200.00

C. Taxes

Companies operating in Ghana are liable to pay varied levels of taxes depending on the sector of operation and whether the company is listed on the Ghana Stock Exchange. Taxable profits are based on profits declared in audited accounts subject to adjustments made for capital allowances.

Income tax incentives are provided under the Income tax Decree, 1975 (SMCD5) as modified by the Internal Revenue Act, 2000 (Act 592) and further amended by Act 622 of 2003.

1. Income Tax rates applicable to resident individuals are:

Chargeable Income	**Rate of Tax**
Not exceeding ¢1,500,000 (GH¢150)	Nil
Exceeding ¢60,000,000 (GH¢6,000)	¢10,125,000 (GH¢1,012.50)

The income tax rate applicable to non-resident individuals is 20%.

D. Utilities

(a) Electricity
The Electricity Company of Ghana (ECG) is responsible for the distribution of electricity within all but northern Ghana.

Application Procedure: Investors need to apply by letter to the ECG, which must specify the following, among others:

- Where the company will be located;
- A site plan of the area (as obtained from Town & Country Planning);
- Total load required;
- Processes to be used in the production activity; and
- Number of shifts (if applicable

Following receipt of the letter, the ECG makes a visit to the site to determine the nearest source of supply and to assess the cost of the connection. Before installation can be effected, the investor typically pays 100% of the installation costs. The ECG generally has the required equipment in stock and installation typically occurs immediately thereafter.

Installation costs vary depending on a number of factors and are calculated by the ECG. Rates payable for electricity consumption for both industrial and domestic purposes are approved by the Public Utilities Regulatory Commission (PURC).

For further information, contact:

The Managing Director
Electricity Company of Ghana
P. O. Box 521
Accra – Ghana
Tel: (+233-21) 676747; 676727
Fax: (+233-21) 666262
Email: ecgho@ghana.com

(b)Telecommunications

i. **Landline Telephone Services:** There are two (2) network operators of landline telephone services in Ghana, namely Ghana Telecom Limited and WESTEL. Ghana Telecom is by far the larger of the two operators. WESTEL currently deploys only 3,000 lines as against Ghana Telecom's 400,000 lines.

Application Procedure: Investors are required to apply to and complete a Form requesting telephone services (business/residential) giving his/her particular including site location.

A site survey will be carried out by Ghana Telecom to enable estimation of materials required. The cost of the services is dependent on the location and materials, among others.

The investor is informed of cost and after the payment the service will be provided, almost immediately thereafter.

For further information, contact:
The Managing Director
Ghana Telecommunications Company Limited
Tel: (+233-21) 200200
Fax: (+233-21) 221002
Website: http://www.ghanatel.net/

ii. **Mobile Telephone Services:** Currently, there are four (4) cellular phone service providers, namely SCANCOM, MILLICOM, Ghana TELECOM (GT) and KASAPA (formerly CELLTEL).

Connecting to mobile operators is through dealers and dealer agents, who are found in many cities and towns.

(C) Water

The Ghana Water Company Limited is responsible for the management (i.e. production and distribution) of pipe-borne water in most urban areas and towns. The Community Water & Sanitation Programme also assists in the management of potable water communities in smaller towns and villages in the districts.

To be connected to water, an investor must follow the following procedures:

- Investor needs to apply by completing the relevant application forms and paying the relevant fees;
- Through the District Offices of the GWCL, the area will be inspected, a drawing, size and pressure of the nearest pipe be determined;
- The applicant must pay the cost of connection in full before connection is effected.

For further information, contact:
The Managing Director
Ghana Water Company Limited
Post Office Box M. 194
Accra – Ghana
Tel: (+233-21) 666781-7
Fax: (+233-21) 663552

(D) Postal and Courier Services

The **Ghana Post Company Ltd,** operating as a public company, runs branches throughout the country and competes with private courier services.
There are seven (7) courier service providers in Ghana. The list of companies and their contacts are as follows:

Company	Telephone	Fax	Location/Email/Website
BKB Couriers (Ghana) Limited	(+233-21) 221817; 221801; 243498; 247380	(+233-21) 231625	324/4 Faanofa Street; Accra;Email: bkb@idngh.com http://www.bkbcouriers.co.uk/
DHL (Ghana) Ltd	(+233-21) 221552; 229722; 221647; 227035	(+233-21)	C.913/3 North Ridge, Crescent Road; Accra
EMS	(+233-21) 668137-8		Private Mail Bag, General Post Office; Accra
Federal Express (FEDEX)	(+233-21) 257921-2; 223852; 666659; 663725	(+233-21) 257928	No. 60 Mango Tree Ave.; Asylum Down; AccraEmail: iasghana@idngh.com iasghana@netplux.com Website: http://www.fedex.com/
TNT Express Worldwide	(+233-21) 773825; 775936		Trinity House, Ring Road; Accra
United Parcel Service (UPS)	(+233-21) 762509-10		Danquah Circle, Osu – Accra Email: Antrak@africaonline.com.gh Website:

			http://www.ups.com/
Universal Express	(+233-21) 774225; 765350		Kotoka International Airport; Accra

INVESTMENT INCENTIVES, BENEFITS AND GUARANTEES

The Ghana Investment Promotion Centre Act, 1994, provides for automatic incentives and benefits as follows:

CUSTOMS IMPORT DUTY EXEMPTIONS

	Tax Rate
There is custom duty exemption for agricultural, and industrial plant, machinery and equipment imported for investment purposes as contained in chapters 82, 84, 85, and 92 of the Customs Harmonized Commodity and Tariff Code. However, with the exception of goods imported specifically for the Educational, Health and Agricultural sectors, all import duty-exempted goods attract the relevant processing and/or other related fees or levies ranging between 0.5% and 1.0%.	**0**

The following attract concessionary duty as follows:

Heading No.	Tariff Description	Import Duty (%)	VAT (%)
82.08	Knives and Cutting Blades	5	0
84.71	Automatic Data Processing Machines and units thereof	0	12.5
85.01	Solar, Wind, & Thermal Energy Generating sets, Electric Generating sets of 375 KVA and above	5	0
98.07 98.08	Air-conditioners; Furnishing including Carpets, Bedding and Fixtures; Fans and Radio Sets; Refrigerators/Deep Freezers, Television Sets; Public Address Systems; and Crockery	10	0
44.07	Sawn, Chipped, Sliced or Peeled Wood	0	12.5
76.01	Aluminium Ingots	5	12.5
45.03	Floats for fishing nets (of natural corks)	0	12.5
58.08	Float cords for fishing nets	0	12.5
70.20	Floats for fishing nets (of glass)	0	12.5
78.06	Lead weights for fishing nets (of lead)	0	12.5
98.02.30 R00	Inputs for the manufacture of fishing nets & fishing ropes	0	12.5
98.10	Recording instruments for the music industry	0	12.5

1. Import duty is imposed on vehicles depending on the type of vehicle. All motor vehicleswith cylinder capacity not exceeding 1900 attract an import duty rate of 5%. Motor vehicles of cylinder capacity exceeding 1900 but not exceeding 3000 attract an import duty of 10%. Other vehicles of cylinder capacity exceeding 3000 and those designed for traveling on snow, golf cars and similar vehicles attract an import duty of 20%.
2. Commercial vehicles for the transport of goods such as trucks, tippers and lorries attract a duty of 5%.

3. Commercial buses with seating capacity of above 30 passengers, workshop vans, breakdown vehicles, mobile showrooms, ambulances, hearse and motor bikes are exempted from the payment of import duty.
4. All the type of vehicles referred to in **i, ii, iii** above attract a Value Added Tax (VAT) rate of 12.5%, except ambulances, which are VAT-exempt.
5. Exemptions **may** be granted from payment of customs import duty and other related charges for any special equipment that is not zero-rated upon application to the GIPC.

Source: Customs, Excise & Preventive Services

INCOME TAX INCENTIVES

(A) Corporate Tax

Listed Companies	**2005**	**2007**
Listed Companies	28%	25%
Newly Listed Companies	25% (for first 3 years)	
Income from Non-Traditional Exports		8%
Hotels		25%
The tax rate applicable to income derived by a financial institution from a loan granted to a farming enterprise for use by that enterprise in the production of its income		20%
The tax rate applicable to income derived by a financial institution from a loan granted to a leasing company for the use by that company for the funding of acquisition of assets for lease is		20%

Notes

"Non-Traditional Goods" means

- Horticultural productions.
- Processed and raw agricultural productions other than cocoa beans grown in Ghana.
- Wood products other than lumber and logs;
- Handcrafts;
- Locally manufactured goods.

(B) Exemptions

i. Tax Holiday (from start of operations)

a. **Real Estate**: The income of a company from a business of construction for sale or letting of residential premises is exempt for five (5) years from the date of commencement of operations.
b. **Rural Banks**: 10 years
c. **Agriculture and agro-industry**:

- Cocoa farmers and producers - income tax exempt
- Cattle ranching - 10 years
- Tree cropping (e.g. coffee, oil palm, shea butter, rubber and coconut) – 10 years

- Livestock excluding cattle and poultry - 5 years
- Fish farming, poultry and cash crops - 5 yearsAgro processing – the business of converting crops, fish or livestock produced in Ghana into edible canned or other packaged product other than in their raw state – 5 year

- Agro processing – the business of converting crops, fish or livestock produced in Ghana into edible canned or other packaged product other than in their raw state – 5 years

d. **Waste Processing** (including plastics and polythene) – 7 years
e. **Free Zones Enterprise/Development** - 10 years and 8% thereafter.

ii. Locational Incentives (Tax Rebates)

a) Manufacturing industries located in regional capitals other than

- Accra and Tema - 25 % rebate
- Elsewhere- 50% rebate

b) After the initial 5-year tax holiday period, agro-processing enterprises, which use local agricultural raw materials as their main inputs, shall have corporate tax rates fixed according to their location as follows:

- Accra-Tema – 20%
- Other Regional Capitals – 10%
- Outside Regional Capitals – 0%
- All over Northern, Upper East, Upper West Regions – 0%

(C) Capital Allowances
Capital allowances are granted to persons who own depreciable assets and use these assets in the production of income. Depreciable assets are grouped in Classes and the applicable capital allowance rates are as follows:

Class	Assets Included	Rate %
1	Computers and Data Handling Equipment	40%
2	i. Automobile, trailers, plant and machinery used in Manufacturing ii. Plantation Equipment	30%
	i. Mineral Petroleum exploration rights, locomotives, water transportation equipment in	80% of cost in year of purchase; 50% of residue annually thereafter; uplift of

3	respect of mineral and petroleum in year of operations. ii. Buildings, structures and works of permanent nature used in respect of mineral and petroleum exploration. iii. Plant and Machinery used in mining or petroleum operations.	5% on cost in the following year
4	Locomotives, water transportation equipment, aircraft equipment not included in other Class	20%
5	Buildings, structures and works of a permanent nature other than those mentioned in Class 3 above	10%
6	Intangible Assets, e.g. Goodwill	Useful Life

Note: Unutilised capital allowances are carried forward indefinitely.

CARRY FORWARD LOSSES

Tax losses are carried forward for five years and is lost if unutilised after the lapse of the fifth year. Only businesses involved in Manufacturing mainly for export, farming and mining have this right.

INVESTMENT GUARANTEES

i. Free Transferability of Capital, Profits and Dividends
The GIPC Act 478 provides guarantees to all enterprises, including free transferability through any authorized dealer bank in freely convertible currency of dividends or net profits attributable to the investment; payments in respect of loan servicing where a foreign loan has been obtained; remittance of proceeds (net of all taxes and other obligations) in the event of sale or liquidation of the enterprise or any interest attributable to the investment. Guarantees against expropriation of private investments provided under Act 478 are buttressed by the constitution.

ii. Insurance Against Non-Commercial Risks
Ghana is a signatory to the World Bank's **Multilateral Investment Guarantee Agency (MIGA) Convention**. This Convention guarantees coverage (insurance) against non-commercial risks such as transfer restrictions, breach of contract, expropriation, war and civil disobedience.

iii.Double Taxation Agreements
Ghana also uses Double Taxation Agreements (DTA) to rationalise tax obligations of investors who come from global tax sourced jurisdictions with a view to saving the investors the incidence of double taxation. Ghana has to date signed and ratified DTAs with **France** and the **United Kingdom**. Another DTA has been signed (but not ratified) with the **Republic of Germany**. It has also concluded (but yet to sign and ratify) same with **Belgium**, **Italy** and **Yugoslavia**.

iv. Investment Promotion and Protection Agreements
Ghana offers commitments at the bilateral level to protect investors and their investments. To date, Ghana has concluded 21 Investment Promotion and Protection Agreements (IPPAs). Some of these have been ratified while others are still awaiting ratification. Another 19 are pending for conclusion. The countries with whom the agreements have been signed and ratified are:

The United Kingdom
The People's Republic Of China

The Kingdom of The NetherlandsThe Kingdom of Denmark
The Republic of Germany The Swiss Confederation
The Republic of Malaysia.

The countries with whom agreements have been signed but awaiting ratification are:
The Republic of La Cote d'Ivoire
The Republic of Egypt
The United States of America
The Republic of France
The Republic of Zambia
The Republic of Cuba
The Republic of Yugoslavia
The Republic of Mauritania
The Republic of Guinea
The Republic of South Africa
The Republic of The Republic of Benin
The Republic of India
The Republic of Burkina Faso.

The countries with agreements pending are:
The Republic of South Korea
Canada
The Republic of Pakistan
The Republic of Ethiopia
The Republic of Israel
The Republic of Turkey
The Republic of Jamaica
The Republic of Nigeria
BelgiumThe Republic of Indonesia
The Republic of Philippines
The Republic of Mauritania
The Czech Republic
The Republic of Australia
The Republic Singapore
The Kingdom of Morocco
The Republic of Togo
The Republic of Finland
The Kingdom of Spain.

STRATEGIC AND LEGAL INFORMATION FOR CONDUCTING BUSINESS

THE WORLD BANK ASSISTANCE

HISTORY

Ghana is a country of firsts. In 1957, Ghana became the first country in Sub-Saharan Africa to emerge from colonialism. It experienced the highest GNP on the continent before an economic crisis in the late 1970s, and it experienced the trauma of military takeovers long before that became a trend in the region. It has also rebounded after launching one of the first and more stringent economic recovery programs in the region nearly a decade and a half ago. It is now pioneering the "Comprehensive Development Framework" (CDF) as a new way of managing the development process.

POLITICAL BACKGROUND AND CONTEXT

A new constitution was introduced in 1992, and Ghana's first multiparty elections were organized shortly thereafter. In 1996, Ghana enjoyed a smooth second-term election, conducted with full participation of all political parties and of the Ghanaian electorate, strengthening democratic institutions. Local assemblies were elected in all 110 Districts, and are assuming increasing responsibility for service delivery to the people of their Districts. Community elections were conducted successfully in June 1998, through non-partisan means, thus bringing representation down to the village and sub-District level.

The next presidential elections are planned for December 8, 2000. President Jerry John Rawlings, who has governed Ghana for most of the last two decades, will not be a candidate due to the term limits in the Constitution. He has thrown his support behind Vice President J.E.A Mills.

ECONOMIC BACKGROUND AND CONTEXT

Ghana's economy is mainly rural: cocoa, timber and pineapples are the main export crops; and mining (mainly gold) has become one of the biggest sources of foreign exchange. The emerging industrial sector's products include cassava, fruits and cocoa by-products

Ghana enjoyed the highest per capita income in the region at independence, but its economy went into a tailspin in the 1970s. By the early 1980s, per capita income had fallen by a third, and inflation was running at over 100 percent. In 1983, the Government launched an aggressive program of stabilization and economic liberalization. It sought to reduce budget deficits and create a market-friendly environment. In the decade that followed, growth averaged 5 percent and physical and social infrastructure was largely rehabilitated. The country still faces severe economic challenges. However, GDP growth for 1997-99 was over 4 percent, and there is strong evidence that poverty continues to fall, albeit slowly.

The Government of Ghana has been implementing a program of economic and structural reforms with the support of the IMF and the World Bank. The background to this program was issued in the Government's "Memorandum on Economic and Financial Policies," available at http://www.imf.org. A critical component of this is the Government's efforts to reform the key cocoa sector, for which they have published a clear policy statement, available at http://www.ghana.gov.gh. However, as Ghana enters the new millennium, it faces new challenges with the sharp decline in the international price of its two main exports of cocoa and gold.

Ghana's macroeconomic situation has deteriorated since mid-1999, reflecting a severe decline in its terms of trade and a shortfall in external assistance. The terms of trade fell by 10 percent in 1999 and by a further 16 percent in 2000, as the price of cocoa, the second main export earner, dropped by over 50 percent to a 20-year low, and imported oil prices tripled. This has led to a substantial run down in international reserves and a rapid slide in the Cedi. The nominal exchange rate has depreciated by about 125 percent since September 1999, and gross international reserves are currently below 1.5 months of imports. The Government has tightened fiscal and monetary policy to offset the adverse effects of the external shock. In line with the 2000 program agreed with the International Monetary Fund (IMF), Government increased the VAT rate from 10 to 12.5 percent, and raised petroleum taxes. The Government has set out a package of contingency expenditures equivalent to 1 percent of GDP to be deferred until the second half of the year. It has also launched an aggressive program to significantly raise divestiture receipts through the sale of Government shares in major public enterprises. The domestic primary surplus is targeted to increase to an unprecedented 4 percent of GDP (1.4 percent in 1999). Notably, tight monetary policy has limited the impact of the large devaluation and oil price hike on inflation, which was under 20 percent at end-June 2000.

DONOR COORDINATION

Donor coordination efforts are extensive. In addition to the Bank, key donors in Ghana include Canada, Denmark, France, Germany, Japan, Netherlands, U.K., and U.S.A. among the bilaterals. Multilateral donors include the African Development Band, EU, FAO/IFAD, UNDP, UNICEF and WHO. Following the 1997 Consultative Group (CG) meeting, the Government of Ghana and the Bank set up the "Mini CG," which meets quarterly under the co-chairmanship of the Minister of Finance and the Bank. This local entity follows up on CG decisions, reviews the country's economic situation, and addresses key issues in donor coordination. Partner groups perform similar functions for individual sectors, including health, education, roads, public finance management, community water supplies, governance, and decentralization. The recent development of sector programs in roads, basic education, and health has enhanced donor coordination considerably.

This approach to partnership made Ghana a natural candidate to be a leading pilot for the "Comprehensive Development Framework." A draft CDF for Ghana was presented at the Tenth Consultative Group meeting for Ghana, which was held for the first time in Accra on November 23-24, 1999.

WORLD BANK ROLE

The World Bank Group has played an active part in Ghana's economic recovery. The International Development Association (IDA), the Bank's interest-free lending arm for the poorest countries, currently finances about 25 active projects. Current disbursements have been running at about US$200 million per annum. Recent operations have included a second Economic Reform Support Operation and three "adaptable program loans" (the Bank's new instrument for providing extended support in challenging areas) for Community Water Supplies, Urban Development, and Agricultural Services.

The International Finance Corporation's (IFC) investments amount to US$60 million, and comprise of US$26 million in loans, US$7 million in equity US$14 million in quasi-equity and US$13 million in participation.

Ghana joined the Multilateral Investment Guarantee Agency (MIGA) in April 1988. So far, it has issued one guarantee of US$9 million for mining investment in 1993, which remained in place until the investor sold his interest in 1997. MIGA currently has 14 applications for guarantees for investments in mining, agribusiness, telecommunications, power and manufacturing.

The World Bank Institute (WBI) is also active in Ghana. In FY00, 260 participants from Ghana took part in WBI learning events, including 158 who participated in eight programs delivered locally. As in previous years, the most popular programs were World Links for Development (Education), strengthening parliament, training of journalists, and controlling corruption. The delivery of the GDLN center, hosted by the Ghana Institute of Management and Public Administration (GIMPA), is expected to significantly increase the number of participants in the coming years. It will also motivate WBI and GIMPA to work closely together in the context of WBI's Institutional Partnership Program, whereby GIMPA would help adapt WBI programs with a view to delivering them as part of its own curriculum.

CONTACTS

Mr. Peter Harrold
Country Director
World Bank Ghana Office
69, Dr. Isert Road, Accra, Ghana
Tel: 233-21-229681
Fax: 233-21-227887
Email: pharrold@worldbank.org

Ms. Theresa Jones
Country Program Coordinator
1818H Street NW, Washington DC 20433
Tel: (202) 473-5309
Email: tjones2@worldbank.org

US ASSISTANCE

Ghana is the principal ally of the United States in West Africa in promoting economic and political reform, and has repeatedly demonstrated - through both diplomacy and assistance provided by its armed forces - its commitment to helping resolve regional conflicts and promoting regional security. Ghana is a lead supporter of the Africa Crisis Response Initiative and has contributed troops to United Nations peacekeeping efforts around the world. Ghana is also in the forefront of African countries that have made significant progress in consolidating democracy and in restructuring their economies to be more efficient and internationally competitive.

Trade links between Ghana and the United States are expanding: U.S. exports to Ghana grew from $53 million in 1985 to $314 million in 1997, up $19 million from 1996, placing Ghana in third place (after Nigeria and South Africa) among African markets for U.S. exports. The interest in encouraging these positive trends is reflected in U.S. foreign policy objectives of increased economic prosperity and democratization, regional stability and improved quality of life in the developing world.

THE DEVELOPMENT CHALLENGE.

USAID's Strategy in Ghana

Ghana is the United States' third largest trading partner in sub-Saharan Africa. It plays a key role in promoting political and economic stability in the West African sub-region. Ghana has a strong tradition of supporting peacekeeping operations. In fact, Ghana is the fourth largest contributor to international peacekeeping. USAID/Ghana's program focuses on spreading participatory democracy; expanding trade opportunities; decreasing the spread of infectious diseases; and improving primary education.

ADVANCING GOOD GOVERNANCE

While Ghana is a democratic nation, its governance institutions remain weak. At the national level, Parliament lacks the capacity to serve as a check-and-balance to the executive branch. At the local level, District Assemblies rarely engage the communities they represent on development matters. USAID's democracy and governance program helps citizens interact with Parliament and local government. This exchange enhances responsiveness of Ghana's key governance institutions to citizens' requests. The program includes a focus on community involvement in development issues. For example, citizen groups in South Tongu in Ghana's Volta Region and their District Assembly have jointly embarked on a program to increase revenue collection. The groups are not only educating citizens about the need to pay their taxes, but are collecting the taxes at no cost to the Assembly. The result is more revenue to support improvements in the local education and health systems.

INCREASING PRIVATE SECTOR COMPETITIVENESS

Around 40 percent of Ghana's population lives on less than $1 per day and unemployment remains high. USAID's program helps farmers to get their produce to markets in the region, as well as Europe and the United States. USAID promotes policy and regulatory reforms in the financial, labor, land, energy, and telecommunication sectors to enable markets to work more efficiently. This includes providing assistance to small and medium-sized horticultural businesses to help meet regulatory and market-driven standards and attract foreign investment. Over the past seven years, Blue Skies, a fruit processing business, built a strong buyer-supplier relationship with small scale farmers of the Sugar Loaf pineapple. USAID helped the farmers that supply Blue Skies to obtain organic and food safety certification, enabling them to fetch premium prices in Europe for their processed fruit.

IMPROVING HEALTH

Despite major health gains over the last decade, infant and under-5 mortality rates have increased and HIV/AIDS still poses a threat. USAID's Health program focuses on individual and community health education; expanding access to health services; improving quality of health services; and strengthening institutional capacity to plan and manage health programs. HIV prevalence in Ghana has remained relatively stable, ranging between 2.2 and 3.1 percent of adults, and well below levels in neighboring countries. USAID's focus is on the most-at-risk groups to help slow the spread of the disease.

IMPROVING BASIC EDUCATION

Nationwide, primary school grade level competency in reading and math remains extremely low. USAID's program to improve primary education supports increasing girls' enrollment, improving reading skills, increasing community participation in schools, and preventing the spread of HIV/AIDS. To enhance reading comprehension, USAID encourages teaching Grade 1 children to read in their local language and then transitioning to English in Grade 2. To address teacher shortages in deprived communities of northern Ghana, USAID trains, places, and supports locally recruited teachers in understaffed schools. USAID has also established complementary education centers where school-age children who are unable to attend formal schools in northern Ghana receive classroom instruction after normal school hours.

ASSURING FOOD SECURITY

Thirteen percent of Ghanaians are undernourished. USAID provides commodities, primarily wheat, to address food security, particularly in the northern and central regions of Ghana. Eighty percent of the U.S. donation is monetized (sold to local millers). The proceeds are used to improve crop yields and storage, facilitate small and micro-credit programs, provide access to potable water and sanitation facilities, improve access to basic education, and enhance child health

OTHER DONORS.

The United States is the second largest bilateral donor in Ghana behind Japan. In 1998 the donor community at large pledged approximately $750 million. Donor assistance focuses on economic growth and poverty alleviation, human resource development, primary education, health services, family planning and decentralization of government. Other donors include: World Bank, European Union, Great Britain, Canada, Denmark, France, Germany, Netherlands, United Nations Development Program, and United Nation's Children's Fund.

ECONOMY & ECONOMIC DEVELOPMENT

Ghana achieved real economic growth of 4.6 percent in 1998 in spite of an energy crisis that slowed down economic activity in the first half of the year. The 1998 growth rate is a slight improvement over the 4.2 percent recorded in 1997. Agricultural growth was 5.3 percent, one percentage point above that of 1997. This performance is attributable to the cocoa, timber and logging sectors which grew by 11.0 and 22.1 percent respectively. The industrial sector was adversely affected by the energy crisis, recording a growth rate of 2.5 percent in 1998 as against 6.4 percent in 1997. The services sector grew at 6.0 percent, maintaining its lead as the fastest-growing sector of the economy.

The government remains under heavy pressure from international financial institutions and donors to adhere to a policy of fiscal discipline in order to set the stage for renewed growth. The year 1998 witnessed an adoption of far-reaching economic policy initiatives aimed at ensuring macro-economic stability. These measures injected considerable resilience into the economy. The Government of Ghana (GOG), in collaboration with the central bank (the Bank of Ghana), has been able to lower inflation to 9.4 per cent, the lowest since 1985, as well as effecting a fall in interest rates. Nevertheless, these efforts are threatened by the continued fall in the prices of gold and cocoa, emanating from the Asian financial crisis and sales of gold reserves by foreign banks.

2. PRINCIPAL GROWTH SECTORS

Gold mining remains the focus of growth in Ghana's industrial sector, although recent reductions in the price of gold may have a dampening effect on the economy for FY2000. Exploration work by most foreign mining firms has been put on hold, but current production in Ghana is continuing to expand. Cocoa production for the 1998/99 cocoa season is estimated by the U.S. Foreign Agricultural Service to be about 400,000 metric tons. This target could even be exceeded, since weather and rainfall conditions, which have been favorable, are the principal determinants of cocoa production. The liberalization of Ghana's telecommunications sector, including operation of a second network operator, should offer good opportunities for service and equipment providers. Several major hotel projects in Accra and elsewhere are indicators of increasing commercial interest in Ghana and a growing tourism sector.

3. GOVERNMENT ROLE IN THE ECONOMY

The GOG continues the process of divesting state-owned enterprises and disengaging from a direct role in the economy. The government has retained a minority stake in many divested enterprises but does not intend to play an active management role. The government does, however, play a major role in the air transport and cocoa sectors. Ghana Airways remains wholly owned by the GOG, which also retains a monopoly on the export of cocoa.

4. BALANCE OF PAYMENTS SITUATION

The government recorded a balance of payments surplus of USD 99 million for 1998 as against a surplus of USD 25 million in 1997. This is largely attributed to the improvement in the current accounts balance (including official transfers) from USD 590 million to USD 272 million. The trade deficit declined from USD 638 million in 1997 to USD 384 million in 1998, mainly due to an increase of about USD 350 million in export earnings. The trade deficit decline, coupled with a significant increase in net official transfers, resulted in the improved current accounts balance. Although the surplus on the capital account declined by about USD 121 million for the same period, it was enough to finance the current account deficit to generate a balance of payments surplus.

The government projects a balance of payments surplus of USD 60 million for 1999. This presumes an increase in exports of 9.7 percent, with cocoa and gold contributing about 30 and 38 percent respectively. The share of non-traditional exports is expected to move up to 14.6 percent of total exports as against 13.9 percent in 1998. Imports are forecast to grow by 2.4 percent.

The foreign exchange value of the cedi vis-a-vis the dollar declined by 4.1 percent in 1998 as against 22.7 percent in 1997. After adjustment for inflation, the cedi has appreciated in real terms since 1995. Although depreciating faster than in 1998, Ghana's local currency is expected to remain relatively stable in 1999. The Bank of Ghana (Ghana's central bank) maintains strict supervision of the local banks and foreign exchange bureaus in order to ensure compliance with the law.

5. INFRASTRUCTURE SITUATION

In the past, infrastructure shortcomings have created substantial impediments to domestic productivity and discouraged foreign direct investment. However, improvements continue to be made at most levels, especially in the telecommunications sector as a result of the privatization of Ghana Telecom and the granting of a second network operator license. The availability of wireless services is expanding and there has been much growth in voice traffic and data transmission systems.

The GOG has committed substantial resources to road building efforts, although the generally still poor quality of Ghanaian roads slows down the delivery of goods, especially during the rainy season.

The GOG has made significant efforts to address the Year 2000 problem by holding workshops, conferences and raising awareness through the media. A special Y2K Office has been established within the Ministry of Communications. Most banks and major financial institutions are now believed to be Y2K compliant. The Ghana Civil Aviation Authority has declared itself Y2K compliant, and compliance measures are presently underway in most GOG ministries and departments.

HISTORICAL BACKGROUND

GHANA'S ECONOMY HAS LEFT an indelible imprint on the country's social and political structures. Just as the presence of gold gave rise to the Asante confederacy and empire and attracted European traders and colonial rulers, so, too, were modern day politicians moved to try to protect the country's wealth by establishing the first socialist regime in twentieth-century Africa. As the ambitious plans initiated by Ghana's first president, Kwame Nkrumah, unraveled, however, military officers seized control of the country and promised to overturn what they perceived as a corrupt ruling class enriching itself from the nation's coffers. In the 1980s, military and civilian officials failed to revive the economy through stringent anti-corruption measures and embarked instead upon a restructuring of the economy.

The transformation of Ghana's economy undertaken in the 1980s was considered a test case for "structural adjustment" prescriptions advocated by international banking institutions. Faced with growing impoverishment in Africa as well as in much of the so-called developing world, the World Bank and the International Monetary Fund proposed radical programs to revive troubled economies and to restore their productivity. The government of Jerry John Rawlings turned to these agencies in 1983 and accepted their recommendations in exchange for assistance packages to ease Ghana's economic and social transformation. Foremost among the changes enacted in Ghana were the disengagement of the government from an active role in the economy and the encouragement of free-market forces to promote the efficient and productive development of local resources. The reformers cut government budgets, privatized state enterprises, devalued the currency, and rebuilt industrial infrastructure by means of assistance programs. As in other countries of Africa in the 1980s, government was identified as the problem, and free-market forces were seen as the solution.

By the 1990s, the effects of structural adjustment in Ghana were beginning to be assessed. According to the World Bank and other western financial institutions, the economy had become much more stable, and production was on a more solid footing than it had been a decade earlier. Exports were up, government deficits had been reduced, and inflation was down. Many Ghanaians, however, questioned whether the structural adjustment benefited all Ghanaians or just a few sectors of the economy. Critics of the World Bank charged, moreover, that it concentrated on infrastructure such as airports, roads, and other macro-economic projects that did little to improve the lives of the average Ghanaian.

Under the sway of free-market forces, production had increased in Ghana's traditionally strong sectors, cocoa and gold, thereby reverting to the pre-independence economic structure; still, a more broadly based economy had not developed. In addition, substantial loans had been incurred by the government to promote those sectors- -at the expense of recurrent budget expenditures such as health and education--without a compensatory increase in government revenues. Ironically, the tax breaks prescribed to encourage these sectors worked against increased government revenues, so that by 1992, tax revenues began to drop. In addition, jobs not only had been cut from the once bloated public sector but also had not expanded in the more successful export sectors. Although the government claimed its finances were much healthier in the 1990s than in the 1980s, the long-term economic and social impact of structural adjustment was uncertain.

Relying heavily on the exploitation of some non-renewable and even endangered resources, Ghana's economic recovery will have to expand to create a broader and better balanced economy. In addition to cocoa, Ghana's leading export commodities are gold, a nonrenewable resource, and timber, the harvesting of which has included more than eighteen endangered species of trees and has led to alarming deforestation. Furthermore, Ghana's ocean waters are seriously overfished, leading the government to ban the catching of shellfish.

According to the Ghanaian government, these resources could be used to develop local manufacturing, the goal Nkrumah tried to reach through direct state intervention thirty years ago. Local manufacturing could create jobs, cut the import bill, and provide a more diversified economic base. The question for Ghana is whether free-market forces will be more successful in promoting healthy economic expansion than the failed policies of direct state intervention.

Endowed with gold and oil palms and situated between the trans- Saharan trade routes and the African coastline visited by successive European traders, the area known today as Ghana has been involved in all phases of Africa's economic development during the last thousand years. As the economic fortunes of African societies have waxed and waned, so, too, have Ghana's, leaving that country in the early 1990s in a state of arrested development, unable to make the "leap" to Africa's next, as yet uncertain, phase of economic evolution.

As early as the thirteenth century, present-day Ghana was drawn into long-distance trade, in large part because of its gold reserves. The trans-Saharan trade, one of the most wide-ranging trading networks of pre-modern times, involved an exchange of European, North African, and Saharan commodities southward in exchange for the products of the African savannas and forests, including gold, kola nuts, and slaves. Present-day Ghana, named the Gold Coast by European traders, was an important source of the gold traded across the Sahara. Centralized states such as Asante controlled prices by regulating production and marketing of this precious commodity . As European navigational techniques improved in the fifteenth century, Portuguese and later Dutch and English traders tried to circumvent the Saharan trade by sailing directly to its southernmost source on the West African coast. In 1482 the Portuguese built a fortified trading post at Elmina and began purchasing gold, ivory, and pepper from African coastal merchants.

Although Africans for centuries had exported their raw materials--ivory, gold, kola nuts--in exchange for imports ranging from salt to foreign metals, the introduction of the Atlantic slave trade in the early sixteenth century changed the nature of African export production in fundamental ways. An increasing number of Ghanaians sought to enrich themselves by capturing fellow Africans in warfare and selling them to slave dealers from North America and South America. The slaves were transported to the coast and sold through African merchants using the same routes and connections through which gold and ivory had formerly flowed. In return, Africans often received guns as payment, which could be used to capture more slaves and, more importantly, to gain and preserve political power.

An estimated ten million Africans, at least half a million from the Gold Coast, left the continent in this manner. Some economists have argued that the slave trade increased African economic resources and therefore did not necessarily impede development, but others, notably historian Walter Rodney, have argued that by removing the continent's most valuable resource--humans--the slave trade robbed Africa of unknown invention, innovation, and production. Rodney further argues that the slave trade fueled a process of underdevelopment, whereby African societies came to rely on the export of resources crucial to their own economic growth, thereby precluding local development of those resources. Although some scholars maintain that the subsequent economic history of this region supports Rodney's interpretation, no consensus exists on this point. Indeed, in recent years, some historians not only have rejected Rodney's interpretation but also have advanced the notion that it is the Africans themselves rather than an array of external forces that are to blame for the continent's economic plight.

When the slave trade ended in the early years of the nineteenth century, the local economy became the focus of the so-called legitimate trade, which the emerging industrial powers of Europe encouraged as a source of materials and markets to aid their own production and sales. The British, in particular, gained increasing control over the region throughout the nineteenth century and promoted the production of palm oil and timber as well as the continuation of gold production. In return, Africans were inundated with imports of consumer goods that, unlike the luxuries or locally unavailable imports of the trans-Saharan trade, quickly displaced African products, especially textiles.

In 1878 cacao trees were introduced from the Americas. Cocoa quickly became the colony's major export; Ghana produced more than half the global yield by the 1920s. African farmers used kinship networks like business corporations to spread cocoa cultivation throughout large areas of southern Ghana. Legitimate trade restored the overall productivity of Ghana's economy; however, the influx of European goods began to displace indigenous industries, and farmers focused more on cash crops than on essential food crops for local consumption.

When Ghana gained its independence from Britain in 1957, the economy appeared stable and prosperous. Ghana was the world's leading producer of cocoa, boasted a well-developed infrastructure to service trade, and enjoyed a relatively advanced education system. At independence, President Kwame Nkrumah sought to use the apparent stability of the Ghanaian economy as a springboard for economic diversification and expansion. He began process of moving Ghana from a primarily agricultural economy to a mixed agricultural-industrial one. Using cocoa revenues as security, Nkrumah took out loans to establish industries that would produce import substitutes as well as process many of Ghana's exports. Nkrumah's plans were ambitious and grounded in the desire to reduce Ghana's vulnerability to world trade. Unfortunately, the price of cocoa collapsed in the mid-1960s, destroying the fundamental stability of the economy and making it nearly impossible for Nkrumah to continue his plans. Pervasive corruption exacerbated these problems. In 1966 a group of military officers overthrew Nkrumah and inherited a nearly bankrupt country.

Since then, Ghana has been caught in a cycle of debt, weak commodity demand, and currency overvaluation, which has resulted in the decay of productive capacities and a crippling foreign debt. Once the price of cocoa fell in the mid-1960s, Ghana obtained less of the foreign currency necessary to repay loans, the value of which jumped almost ten times between 1960 and 1966. Some economists recommended that Ghana devalue its currency--the cedi-- to make its cocoa price more attractive on the world market, but devaluation of the cedi would also have rendered loan repayment in United States dollars much more difficult. Moreover, such a devaluation would have increased the costs of imports, both for consumers and nascent industries.

Until the early 1980s, successive governments refused to devalue the currency (with the exception of the government of Kofi A. Busia, which devalued the cedi in 1971 and was promptly overthrown). Cocoa prices languished, discouraging cocoa production altogether and leading to smuggling of existing cocoa crops to neighboring countries, where francs rather than cedis could be obtained in payment. As production and official exports collapsed, revenue necessary for the survival of the economy was obtained through the procurement of further loans, thereby intensifying a self-destructive cycle driven by debt and reliance on vulnerable world commodity markets.

By the early 1980s, Ghana's economy was in an advanced state of collapse. Per capita gross domestic product (GDP--see Glossary) showed negative growth throughout the 1960s and fell by 3.2 percent per year from 1970 to 1981. Most important was the decline in cocoa production, which fell by half between the mid-1960s and the late 1970s, drastically reducing Ghana's share of the world market from about one-third in the early 1970s to only one-eighth in 1982-83. At the same time, mineral production fell by 32 percent; gold production declined by 47 percent, diamonds by 67 percent, manganese by 43 percent, and bauxite by 46 percent. Inflation averaged more than 50 percent a year between 1976 and 1981, hitting 116.5 percent in 1981. Real minimum wages dropped from an index of 75 in 1975 to one of 15.4 in 1981. Tax revenue fell from 17 percent of GDP in 1973 to only 5 percent in 1983, and actual imports by volume in 1982 were only 43 percent of average 1975-76 levels. Productivity, the standard of living, and the government's resources had plummeted dramatically.

In 1981 a military government under the leadership of Flight Lieutenant Jerry John Rawlings came to power. Calling itself the Provisional National Defence Council (PNDC), the Rawlings regime initially blamed the nation's economic problems on the corruption of previous governments. Rawlings soon discovered, however, that Ghana's problems were the result of forces more complicated than economic abuse. Following a severe drought in 1983, the government accepted stringent International Monetary Fund (IMF--see Glossary) and World Bank (see Glossary) loan conditions and instituted the Economic Recovery Program (ERP).

Signaling a dramatic shift in policies, the ERP fundamentally changed the government's social, political, and economic orientation. Aimed primarily at enabling Ghana to repay its foreign debts, the ERP exemplified the structural adjustment policies formulated by international banking and donor institutions in the 1980s. The program emphasized the promotion of the export sector and an enforced fiscal stringency, which together aimed to eradicate budget deficits. The PNDC followed the ERP faithfully and gained the support of the international financial community. The effects of the ERP on the domestic economy, however, led to a lowered standard of living for most Ghanaians.

STRUCTURE OF THE ECONOMY

Most government efforts to restore the productivity of the Ghanaian economy have been directed toward boosting the country's exports. These policies, however, have had numerous consequences. Following the initiation of the ERP in 1983 and the devastating drought of 1983, Ghana's GDP has registered steady growth, most of it attributable to the export sector, including cocoa and minerals and, to some extent, timber processing. The cost of this growth is apparent, however, in Ghana's growing external debts, which have financed rehabilitation of the export sector, and in the country's steady rate of inflation that has curbed consumer imports. The government has tried with limited success to avoid some of the country's historical pitfalls by broadening the range of both exports and trading partners. Nevertheless, prices for the goods that most Ghanaians purchase have been rising faster than the wages they receive for their work.

ROLE OF THE GOVERNMENT

In the 1990s, the government continued to play a decisive role in the direction and pace of economic development in Ghana. Under the Economic Recovery Program initiated in 1983, the Rawlings government tried to shift the burden of economic growth from government to the private sector through a dual strategy of cutting government spending and promoting private production. In particular, the government tried to boost export production through currency devaluations, tax incentives, and government-funded development projects. At the same time, budget deficits were almost entirely wiped out. These measures caused drastic cutbacks in recurrent government spending coupled with widespread privatization, while the government incurred further loans (and thereby debt) to balance the country's budget.

STATE ENTERPRISES

State-owned enterprises in Ghana date to the colonial period and especially to the post-World War II era. For example, the British organized a number of public utilities, such as water, electricity, postal and telegraph services, rail and road networks, and bus services. To foster exports of coffee, palm kernels, and cocoa, the Agricultural Produce Marketing Board was founded in 1949. In addition, the colonial government established the Industrial Development Corporation and the Agricultural Development Corporation to promote industries and agriculture. In the mid1970s , the National Redemption Council under I. K. Acheampong also emphasized state enterprises. The Acheampong government established a number of new enterprises and partly or wholly nationalized a number of foreign-owned companies, including the Ashanti Goldfields Corporation and Consolidated African Selection Trust. Intermittent efforts to improve performance and efficiency often led to the transferral of duties and functions to alternative state bodies but not to the wholesale privatization of ownership rights and assets.

By the 1980s, state enterprises were suffering along with most businesses in Ghana, but they were also held to blame for the economy's general condition. In particular, many were heavily subsidized and were draining much of the country's domestic loan capital. Under pressure from the World Bank and in accordance with the principles of the ERP, in 1984 the government began to sell state enterprises to private investors, and it initiated the StateOwned Enterprise Reform Program in 1988.

In 1984 there were 235 state enterprises in Ghana. The government announced that twenty-two sensitive enterprises would not be sold, including major utilities as well as transport, cocoa, and mining enterprises. In 1988 thirty-two were put up for sale, followed by a further forty-four in 1990 under what was termed the Divestiture Implementation Committee. By December 1990, thirty-four enterprises had been either partially or totally divested. Four were sold outright, a further eight were partially sold through share issues, and twenty-two were liquidated. Divestiture of fifteen additional enterprises was also underway, and by 1992 plans were afoot to privatize some of the nation's banks.

Joint ventures were set up for four enterprises, including two state mining companies, Prestea Goldfields and Ghana Consolidated Diamonds. In 1992 the Divestiture Implementation Committee considered resource-pooling programs to enable smaller domestic investors to buy up state enterprises. Such pooling would accelerate the program, but more importantly, it would enable the Provisional National Defence Council (PNDC) to deflect charges that it was auctioning off the nation's assets to foreigners.

The government also introduced a performance monitoring and evaluation system to improve state enterprise productivity and efficiency as well as to provide incentives for strong performers and disincentives for weak performers. By 1989 fifteen enterprises had responded positively, turning a combined pre-tax loss of ¢418 million from the previous year into pre-tax profits of ¢19 billion, following a 9 percent cut in costs and a 30 percent increase in sales. In early 1992, the chairman of the State Enterprises Commission announced that the government would pass legislation requiring state-owned enterprises to register as limited liability companies by 1993 to stimulate competition and to improve their performances.

BANKING AND CURRENCY

Control of money-supply growth and liquidity management have been among the ERP's most difficult tasks, and expansion has generally exceeded targets for most of the 1980s. The initial phase of monetary policy (1983-86) focused on reducing government borrowing from the domestic banking system and on using quantitative controls via credit ceilings. Although these succeeded in reducing domestic credit growth, larger than expected foreign earnings and the money market's inability to process them efficiently contributed to a rapid expansion in the broad money supply until the late 1980s.

The subsequent introduction of more dynamic monetary policies in 1989 involved a phase-in of indirect controls and market-based policy instruments. A further series of measures was introduced in 1990 to strengthen the responsiveness of interest rates to changes in liquidity conditions. There followed a phased increase in the Bank of Ghana's rediscount rate from 26 percent to 35 percent by mid-1991, the introduction of three- and five-year instruments later that year, and a widening of access to Bank of Ghana financial instruments in favor of the non-bank financial sector. The policies were quite effective. Money supply growth was brought convincingly under control in 1990 and 1991; however, a decline in interest rates and in monetary control, compounded by salary increases in the public sector, prompted monetary growth in 1992.

In January 1994, the Bank of Ghana relaxed its monetary policy. As a result, the government's 91-day treasury bill discount rate was lowered five percentage points to 27 percent. The interest rate equivalent of the discount rate fell from 34.78 percent to 28.95 percent. Savings deposit rates also fell in December 1993 from 17.5-22 percent to 15-22 percent. The wider range suggests competition for funds in the banking market. The range for longerterm money (two-year) declined from 22-32 percent to 25.2-28 percent.

LABOR FORCE

Despite the revival of the export sector, most Ghanaians continued to find employment with the government or to rely on informal employment for their livelihood. An increasing number of Ghanaians also turned to smuggling or to crime to earn a living. Reductions in the number of government workers had not been absorbed in the export sector by the early 1990s. At the same time, wages had not kept up with the cost of living. The government also sought to reform the education system, because increased education often led to better jobs and higher wages.

However, because students were expected to bear an increasing portion of the cost of their education, it was unlikely that the poorest Ghanaians would be able to take full advantage of the school system.

AGRICULTURE

Agriculture is Ghana's most important economic sector, employing more than half the population on a formal and informal basis and accounting for almost half of GDP and export earnings. The country produces a variety of crops in various climatic zones which range from dry savanna to wet forest and which run in eastwest bands across the country. Agricultural crops, including yams, grains, cocoa, oil palms, kola nuts, and timber, form the base of Ghana's economy.

Although Nkrumah attempted to use agricultural wealth as a springboard for the country's overall economic development, Ghanaian agricultural output has consistently fallen since the 1960s. Beginning with the drop in commodity prices in the late 1960s, farmers have been faced with fewer incentives to produce as well as with a general deterioration of necessary infrastructure and services. Farmers have also had to deal with increasingly expensive inputs, such as fertilizer, because of overvaluation of the cedi. Food production has fallen as well, with a decline in the food self-sufficiency ratio from 83 percent in 1961-66 to 71 percent in 1978-80, coupled with a four-fold increase in food imports in the decade prior to 1982. By 1983, when drought hit the region, food shortages were widespread, and export crop production reached an all-time low.

When the Rawlings government initiated the first phase of the ERP in 1984, agriculture was identified as the economic sector that could rescue Ghana from financial ruin. Accordingly, since that time, the government has invested significant funds in the rehabilitation of agriculture. Primarily through the use of loans and grants, the government has directed capital toward repairing and improving the transportation and distribution infrastructure serving export crops. In addition, specific projects aimed at increasing cocoa yields and at developing the timber industry have been initiated. Except for specific development programs, however, the government has tried to allow the free market to promote higher producer prices and to increase efficiency.

Although the government was criticized for focusing on exports rather than on food crops under the ERP, by the early 1990s the PNDC had begun to address the need to increase local production of food. In early 1991, the government announced that one goal of the Medium Term Agricultural Development Program 1991-2000 was to attain food self-sufficiency and security by the year 2000. To this end, the government sought to improve extension services for farmers and to improve crop-disease research. Despite the statements concerning the importance of food crops, however, the plan was still heavily oriented toward market production, improvement of Ghana's balance-of-payments position, and provision of materials for local industrial production. Furthermore, following World Bank guidelines, the government planned to rely more heavily on the private sector for needed services and to reduce the role of the public sector, a clear disadvantage for subsistence producers. In particular, industrial tree crops such as cocoa, coffee, and oil palm seedlings were singled out for assistance. Clearly, agricultural sectors that could not produce foreign exchange earnings were assigned a lower priority under the ERP.

The government attempted to reduce its role in marketing and assistance to farmers in several ways. In particular, the Cocoa Marketing Board steadily relinquished its powers over pricing and marketing. The government, furthermore, established a new farmers' organization, the Ghana National Association of Farmers and Fishermen, in early 1991 to replace the Ghana Federation of Agricultural Cooperatives. The new organization was to be funded by the farmers themselves to operate as a cooperative venture at the district, regional, and national levels. Although the government argued that it did not want to be accused of manipulating farmers, the lack of government financial support again put subsistence producers at a disadvantage.

COCOA

Cocoa production occurs in the forested areas of the country-- Ashanti Region, Brong-Ahafo Region, Central Region, Eastern Region, Western Region, and Volta Region--where rainfall is 1,000-1,500 millimeters per year. The crop year begins in October, when purchases of the main crop begin, while the smaller mid-crop cycle starts in July. All cocoa, except that which is smuggled out of the country, is sold at fixed prices to the Cocoa Marketing Board. Although most cocoa production is carried out by peasant farmers on plots of less than 3 hectares, a small number of farmers appear to dominate the trade. Indeed, some studies show that about one-fourth of all cocoa farmers receive just over half of total cocoa income.

In 1979 the government initiated reform of the cocoa sector, focusing on the government's role in controlling the industry through the Cocoa Marketing Board. The board was dissolved and reconstituted as the Ghana Cocoa Board (Cocobod). In 1984 it underwent further institutional reform aimed at subjecting the cocoa sector to market forces. Cocobod's role was reduced, and 40 percent of its staff, or at least 35,000 employees, were dismissed. Furthermore, the government shifted responsibility for crop transport to the private sector. Subsidies for production inputs (fertilizers, insecticides, fungicides, and equipment) were removed, and there was a measure of privatization of the processing sector through at least one joint venture. In addition, a new payment system known as the Akuafo Check System was introduced in 1982 at the point of purchase of dried beans. Formerly, producebuying clerks had often held back cash payments, abused funds, and paid farmer with false checks. Under the Akuafo system, a farmer was given a check signed by the produce clerk and the treasurer that he could cash at a bank of his choice. Plantation divestiture proceeded slowly, however, with only seven of fifty-two plantations sold by the end of 1990.

Although Ghana was the world's largest cocoa producer in the early 1960s, by the early 1980s Ghanaian production had dwindled almost to the point of insignificance. The drop from an average of more than 450,000 tons per year to a low of 159,000 tons in 1983-84 has been attributed to aging trees, widespread disease, bad weather, and low producer prices. In addition, bush fires in 1983 destroyed some 60,000 hectares of cocoa farms, so that the 1983-84 crop was barely 28 percent of the 557,000 tons recorded in 1964-65. Output then recovered to 228,000 tons in 1986-87. Revised figures show that production amounted to 301,000 tons in 1988-89, 293,000 tons in 1990-91, and 305,000 tons in 1992-93. After declining to 255,000 tons in 1993-94, the crop was projected to return to the 300,000 ton range in 1994-95.

In the early 1990s, Cocobod continued to liberalize and to privatize cocoa marketing. The board raised prices to producers and introduced a new system providing greater incentives for private traders. In particular, Cocobod agreed to pay traders a minimum producer price as well as an additional fee to cover the buyers' operating and transportation costs and to provide some profit. Cocobod still handled overseas shipment and export of cocoa to ensure quality control.

In addition to instituting marketing reforms, the government also attempted to restructure cocoa production. In 1983 farmers were provided with seedlings to replace trees lost in the drought and trees more than thirty years old (about one-fourth of the total number of trees in 1984). Until the early 1990s, an estimated 40 hectares continued to be added to the total area of 800,000 hectares under cocoa production each year. In addition, a major program to upgrade existing roads and to construct 3,000 kilometers of new feeder roads was launched to ease the transportation and sale of cocoa from some of the more neglected but very fertile growing areas on the border with Côte d'Ivoire. Furthermore, the government tried to increase Ghana's productivity from 300 kilograms per hectare to compete with Southeast Asian productivity of almost 1,000 kilograms per hectare. New emphasis was placed on extension services, drought and disease research, and the use of fertilizers and insecticides. The results of these measures were to be seem in rising cocoa production in the early 1990s.

OTHER COMMERCIAL CROPS

The main industrial crops are palm oil, cotton, rubber, sugar cane, tobacco, and kenaf, the latter used in the production of fiber bags. None is of strategic economic importance, and all, apart from oil palms, have suffered as a result of the country's economic difficulties. Despite claims that such crops could assist local industrialization efforts, the government has not focused the same attention on this sector as on export crops. For example, sugar cane output has diminished with the closure of the country's two sugar mills, which produced 237,000 tons per year in 1974-76, but only 110,000 tons in 1989.

The government has actually encouraged the export rather than the local processing of rubber, rehabilitating more than 3,000 hectares of plantations specifically for export production rather than revitalizing the local Bonsa Tire Company, which could produce only 400 tires per day in 1988 despite its installed capacity for 1,500 per day.

By the 1990s, the tobacco sector was expanding and moving toward higher export production. Ghana's dark-fired leaf probably grows too fast and requires too rich a soil to compete effectively with rival crops, but the potential for flue-cured and Burley varieties is good. Pricing difficulties had reduced tobacco production from 3,400 tons in the early 1970s to an estimated 1,433 tons in 1989. Output began to improve in 1990, however, reaching 2,080 tons.

The Leaf Development Company was established in 1988 to produce tobacco leaf for the local market and to lay the basis for a future export industry. In 1991, the company's first commercial crop amounted to 300 tons of flue-cured, 50 tons of Burley, and 50 tons of dark-fired tobacco (all green leaf weights), of which 250 tons were exported, earning US$380,000. In 1991 Rothmans, the British tobacco company, acquired a 49.5 percent stake in the company and took over management of the Meridian Tobacco Company in partnership with the state-owned Social Security and National Insurance Trust. Another firm, the Pioneer Tobacco Company, announced a 92 percent increase in post-tax profits of more than ¢1 billion for 1991. The company declared dividends worth ¢360 million, double the amount paid out in 1990.

Cotton production expanded rapidly in the early and mid-1970s, reaching 24,000 tons in 1977, but it fell back to one-third of this figure in 1989. Since the reorganization of the Ghana Cotton Development Board into the Ghana Cotton Company, cotton production has steadily increased from 4 percent of the country's national requirement to 50 percent in 1990. Between 1986 and 1989, Ghana saved US$6 million through local lint cotton production. The company expected that between 1991 and 1995, about 20,000 hectares of land would be put under cotton cultivation, enabling Ghana to produce 95 percent of the national requirement.

FORESTRY

Forests cover about one-third of Ghana's total area, with commercial forestry concentrated in the southern parts of the country. This sector accounted for 4.2 percent of GDP in 1990; timber was the country's third largest foreign exchange earner. Since 1983 forestry has benefited from more than US$120 million in aid and commercial credits and has undergone substantial changes, resulting in doubled earnings between 1985 and 1990. In 1993 timber and wood products earnings totalled US$140 million against a targeted level of US$130 million. Between January and November 1994, exports amounted to 919,000 tons and earned US$212 million.

Until the 1980s, forestry production suffered because of the overvalued cedi and deterioration of the transportation infrastructure. Log production declined by 66 percent during 1970- 81 and sawed timber by 47 percent. Exports fell from US$130 million in 1973 to US$15 million in 1983, and four nationalized firms went bankrupt during that period.

The forestry sector was given a large boost in 1986, mainly because of the World Bank's US$24 million timber rehabilitation credit, which financed imports of logging equipment. As a consequence, log production rose 65 percent in 1984-87, and export revenues rose 665 percent in 1983-88. Furthermore, the old Ghana Timber Marketing Board was disbanded and replaced by two bodies, the Timber Export Development Board--responsible for marketing and pricing, and the Forest Products Inspection Bureau--responsible for monitoring contracts, maintaining quality standards, grading products, and acting as a watchdog for illegal transactions. Some of the external financing underwrote these institutional changes, while much of the rest financed forestry management and research as well as equipment for logging, saw milling, and manufacturing.

The sector, however, faced several problems. The most important was severe deforestation. A century ago, Ghana's tropical hardwood forest extended from about the middle of the country southward to the sea. Moreover, nearly half the country was covered with forests, which included 680 species of trees and several varieties of mahoganies. Most of this wood has been cut. By the early 1990s, only about one-third of the country was still forested, and not all of this was of commercial value. This situation has forced the government to make difficult choices between desperately needed hard currency earnings and conservation. The Forest Resource Management Project, part of the ERP, was initiated in 1988, and in 1989 the government banned log exports of eighteen species. The government later extended the list and imposed high duties on other species, planning to phase out log and air-dried timber exports altogether by 1994.

Instead, the government hoped to increase sales of wood products to replace earnings from logs. Government figures showed that one cubic meter of lumber and plywood was worth more than twice as much as the same amount of logs; veneers earned five times as much; and other products, such as furniture and floorings, earned six times the price of an equivalent volume of logs. Improvements in the processing sector caused wood products (excluding lumber) to rise to about 20 percent of export earnings in 1991, accounting for 6.9 percent of volume exports. By comparison, wood products represented 11 percent of earnings and 5.5 percent of volume in 1985. The fall in the proportion of volume sales accounted for by logs was accompanied by a dramatic fall in their share in earnings, from 50-60 percent in the mid-1980s to 23 percent in 1990.

By the early 1990s, there were approximately 220 lumber processors in Ghana, but the industry operated under several constraints. Most overseas demand is for kiln-dried products, and Ghanaian manufacturers lack sufficient kilns to meet that demand.

The cheap air-dried processing method is not satisfactory because air-dried wood tends to destabilize over time. Foreign investment incentives are not so attractive in this sector as in others, for example, mining. Furthermore, infrastructure in the Western Region where lumber processing is located continues to be relatively neglected compared with mining and cocoa production regions.

Other difficulties include lack of expertise at technological and managerial levels. Scandals have been reported in Ghana's forestry industry since 1986, and they erupted again in early 1992. The most notable case involved African Timber and Plywood, once Ghana's largest exporter of round logs. In the mid-1980s, the government embarked on a US$36 million rehabilitation project to boost the company's production. In 1992 as much as US$2.3 million was alleged to have been siphoned off from the project through various malpractices, and a number of officials were arrested. Furthermore, the environmental group, Friends of the Earth, alleged that there had been additional thefts by numerous foreign companies totaling almost US$50 million in hard currency during the 1980s. In 1992 the government began investigating the activities of hundreds of companies, both foreign and local, that were alleged to have entered into a range of illegal dealings including smuggling, fraudulent invoicing, violation of local currency regulations, corruption, bribery, and nonpayment of royalties. The corruption is so wide spread, however, that it is unlikely that the Ghanaian authorities will stop timber-related crimes anytime soon.

FISHING

Fishing increased considerably in the late 1960s, from 105,100 tons of marine fish caught in 1967 to 230,100 tons in 1971. In 1982 the yield was 234,100 tons, composed of 199,100 tons of marine varieties and 35,000 tons of freshwater fish from Lake Volta. The industry was hit by fuel shortages, inadequate storage facilities, and the general economic difficulties of the 1970s and the 1980s. Nevertheless, by 1988 the fish catch was 302,900 tons; by 1991 it amounted to 289,675 tons, down from more than 319,000 tons in 1990.

Large-scale poaching by foreign vessels has severely depleted fish stocks in Ghana's 200-nautical-mile maritime Exclusive Economic Zone, causing major government concern. The most affected stocks are sea bottom-feeding fish. Tuna stocks reportedly remain unaffected. A 1992 Ministry of Food and Agriculture report recommended that the government accelerate mobilization of surveillance and enforcement units and step up regulation of trawler fleets. That same year, the government passed a fisheries law to curb overfishing and to help protect the marine environment. Fishermen were banned from catching specified shellfish, and all fishing vessel operators were required to obtain licenses. The law provided for a regulatory body--the Fisheries Monitoring, Control, Surveillance, and Enforcement Unit--as well as a fisheries advisory council. These organizations, however, both of which are underfunded and undermanned, are unlikely to stop illegal fishing activities anytime soon.

MINING AND PETROLEUM INDUSTRIES

Ghana's mineral sector had started to recover by the early 1990s after its severe decline throughout the 1970s. One indicator of the scale of decline was that by 1987, only four gold mines were operating in Ghana, compared with eighty in 1938. Throughout the 1970s, the output of gold, as well as bauxite, manganese, and diamonds, fell steadily. Foreign exchange shortages inhibited mine maintenance, new exploration, and development investment. The overvalued cedi and spiraling inflation exacerbated mining companies' problems, as did smuggling and the deteriorating infrastructure. Energy supplies failed to meet the industry's growing needs; foreign exchange shortages constrained oil imports, and domestically generated hydroelectricity was unable to make up the shortfall.

After 1983, however, the government implemented a series of measures to enhance the sector's appeal. In 1986 new mining legislation for the gold and diamond sectors replaced the previous complex and obsolete regulations, and a generous incentives system was established that allowed for external foreign exchange retention accounts, capital allowances, and a flexible royalties payment system. Since then the sector has benefited from a wave of fresh investment totaling US$540 million since 1986, and by the early 1990s mining was the country's second highest foreign exchange earner.

Under legislation passed after 1983, the government liberalized and regularized the mining industry. For the first time, the government made small claim-holding feasible, with the result that individual miners sold increasing amounts of gold and diamonds to the state-operated Precious Minerals Marketing Company. In 1990 the company bought 490,000 carats of diamonds and 20,000 ounces of gold and earned a total of US$20.4 million through sales, 70 percent of it from diamond sales and 30 percent from gold bought from smallscale operators. Diamond output totaled 688,000 carats in 1991 and 694,000 carats in 1992, while gold production amounted to 843,000 fine ounces in 1991 and 1,004,000 fine ounces in 1992. Furthermore, the government succeeded in attracting significant foreign investment into the sector and, by early 1991, had signed over sixty mining licenses granting prospecting rights to international companies. To forestall domestic criticism of large-scale foreign control of the sector, the government announced in mid-1991 the establishment of a state-controlled holding company to buy shares in mines on behalf of private, that is, foreign, investors.

GOLD

Ghana has produced and exported gold for centuries. In precolonial times, present-day Ghana was one source of the gold that reached Europe via trans-Saharan trade routes. In the fifteenth century, Portuguese sailors tried to locate and to control gold mining from the coast but soon turned to more easily obtained slaves for the Atlantic slave trade. Most gold mining before the mid-nineteenth century was alluvial, miners recovering the gold from streams. Modern gold mining that plumbs the rich ore deposits below the earth's surface began about 1860, when European concessionaires imported heavy machinery and began working in the western areas of present-day Ghana. The richest deposit, the Obuasi mine, was discovered by a group of Europeans who sold their rights to E.A. Cade, the founder of Ashanti Goldfields Corporation (AGC). Since the beginning of the twentieth century, modern mining in the Gold Coast has been pursued as a large-scale venture, necessitating significant capital investment from European investors.

Under British colonial rule, the government controlled gold mining to protect the profits of European companies. The colonial government also restricted possession of gold as well as of mercury, essential in recovering gold from the ore in which it is embedded. Following independence, foreign control of the sector was tempered by increasing government involvement under the Nkrumah regime; however, production began to decline in the late 1960s and did not recover for almost twenty years. In the mid-1960s, many mines began to hit poorer gold reefs. Despite the floating of the international gold price in the late 1960s, few investors were willing to invest, and the government failed to provide the capital necessary to expand production into new reefs. Of the two major gold mining enterprises, neither the State Gold Mining Corporation nor AGC (40 percent controlled by the government) expanded or even maintained production.

Under the ERP, the mining sector was targeted as a potential source of foreign exchange, and since 1984, the government has successfully encouraged the rejuvenation of gold mining. To offer incentives to the mining industry, the Minerals and Mining Law was passed in 1986. Among its provisions were generous capital allowances and reduced income taxes. The corporate tax rate was set at 45 percent, and mining companies could write off 75 percent of capital investment against taxes in the first year and 50 percent of the remainder thereafter. The government permitted companies to use offshore bank accounts for service of loans, dividend payments, and expatriate staff remuneration.

Companies are permitted to retain a minimum of 25 percent of gross foreign exchange earnings from minerals sales in the accounts, a level that can be negotiated up to 45 percent. Reconnaissance licenses are issued for one-year renewable periods, prospecting licenses are valid for three years, and mining licenses are in force for up to thirty years. The government has the right to 10 percent participation in all prospecting and to extend its share if commercial quantities of a mineral are discovered. In response, between 1985 and 1990 eleven companies became active with foreign participation, representing investments totaling US$541 million. Since 1986 there has been a gradual recovery in overall production.

More than 90 percent of gold production in the early 1990s came from underground mines in western Ashanti Region, with the remainder coming from river beds in Ashanti Region and Central Region. AGC, the country's largest producer, mined 62,100 fine ounces in January 1992, the highest monthly production ever recorded since the company began operation in 1897. The company also lowered its costs in relation to production during the last quarter of 1991 from 0.26

percent in October to 0.24 percent in December. Production during the company's fiscal year of October 1990 to September 1991 was 569,475 fine ounces, 42 percent more than the previous year's figure of 400,757 fine ounces and the largest amount ever produced by the mine. The second largest amount produced was 533,000 fine ounces, produced in 1972.

AGC planned major expansions in the early 1990s funded by World Bank loans. In early 1991, the corporation announced the discovery of new reserves estimated at more than 8 million ounces, in addition to its known reserves of 22.3 million ounces. The new reserves include lower-grade and remnant ores that the corporation had been unwilling to mine because of high costs. AGC planned to lower costs through capital-intensive operations and a sharp reduction of labor costs. It also planned then to raise output from a projected 670,000 fine ounces for 1992 to more than 1 million fine ounces a year in 1995. The expansion was to be funded by an International Finance Corporation loan package totaling US$140 million. AGC was to put up the balance, estimated to exceed US$200 million.

AGC was not the only company to benefit from an upsurge in production. Despite its increased production, the company's overall share of the domestic gold market declined from 80 percent to 60 percent in the same period that other operators entered the industry. Provisional figures for 1991 showed that two new mines, Teberebie and Billiton Bogoso, produced 100,000 fine ounces each, while other companies, including State Gold Mining Corporation, Southern Cross Mining Company, Goldenrae, Bonte, and Okumpreko, were stepping up production.

Several other enterprises were on the drawing board or were about to open by mid-1992. The British company Cluff Resources had raised US$10.2 million to finance a new mine at Ayanfuri. The company had been involved in exploration since 1987 and planned to produce as much as 50,000 ounces of gold annually. A CanadianGhanaian joint-venture gold mine and associated processing facilities was commissioned in mid-1991 in Bogoso, western Ghana. Finally, in May 1992, a joint-venture company was created to prospect for gold in the Aowin Suamang district in Western Region. Shareholders in the new company included the Chinese government (32.68 percent), private investors in Hong Kong (32 percent), the Ghanaian government (10 percent) and private Ghanaian interests.

In 1992, Ghana's gold production surpassed 1 million fine ounces, up from 327,000 fine ounces in 1987. In March 1994, the Ghanaian government announced that it would sell half of its 55 percent stake in AGC for an estimated US$250 million, which would then be spent on development projects. The authorities also plan to use some of the capital from the stock sale to promote local business and to boost national reserves. The minister of mines and energy dispelled fears that the stock sale would result in foreign ownership of the country's gold mines by saying that the government would have final say in all major stock acquisitions.

DIAMONDS

The government also is trying to expand Ghana's diamond mining industry, which has produced primarily industrial grade gems from alluvial gravels since the 1920s. More than 11 million carats of proven and probable reserves are located about seventy miles northwest of Accra. The main producer is the state-owned Ghana Consolidated Diamonds (GCD), which operates in the Birim River Basin. In the 1960s, the company mined 2 million carats of diamonds a year, but annual production in 1991 amounted to only 146,000 carats. This downturn resulted from technical problems and GCD's weak financial position. Production from all mines came to 688,000 carats in 1991 and to 694,000 carats in 1992.

In the early 1990s, the government announced plans to privatize its diamond-mining operations and to expand production. At Accra's invitation, De Beers of South Africa agreed to undertake an eighteen-month feasibility study to determine the extent of the Birim River Basin diamond reserves. The survey was to cost US$1 million. A De Beers subsidiary will be the operator and manager of GCD, while Lazare Kaplan International, a New York-based diamond polishing and trading company, will produce and market the diamonds.

In 1989 the government established the Precious Minerals Marketing Corporation (PMMC) to purchase minerals from small producers in an effort to stem diamond smuggling. Estimates suggested that as much as 70 percent of Ghana's diamonds were being smuggled out of the country in the mid-1980s. In its first sixteen months of operation, the PMMC bought 382,423 carats of diamonds and 20,365 ounces of gold and sold 230,000 carats of diamonds worth US$8 million. The corporation also earned ¢130 million in 1991 on its jewelry operations, up 48 percent from the previous year, and it planned to establish joint marketing ventures with foreign firms to boost sales abroad. Nevertheless, because of new complaints over raw gem sales, the government in March 1992 ordered an investigation into the operations of the state agency and suspended its managing director.

MANGANESE

Ghana is one of the world's leading exporters of manganese; however, only 279,000 tons were produced in 1992, compared with the all-time high of 638,000 tons in 1974-75. Ghana has reserves exceeding 60 million tons, and considerable rehabilitation of the sector took place in the 1980s. Ghana National Manganese Corporation's mine and the surrounding infrastructure were repaired, helping to raise production from a low of 159,000 tons in 1983 to 284,000 tons in 1989 and 247,000 tons in 1990. The corporation earned US$20 million from its exports in 1991, up from US$11.6 million in 1989 and US$14.2 million in 1990. Approximately US$85 million was also invested by private investors at the newly explored Kwesikrom deposit.

PETROLEUM EXPLORATION

Although commercial quantities of offshore oil reserves were discovered in the 1970s, by 1990 production was still negligible. In 1983 the government established the Ghana National Petroleum Corporation (GNPC) to promote exploration and production, and the company reached agreements with a number of foreign firms. The most important of these permitted US-based Amoco to prospect in ten offshore blocks between Ada and the western border with Togo. Petro Canada International has prospected in the Tano River Basin, and Diamond Shamrock in the Keta Basin. In 1989 three companies, two American and one Dutch, spent US$30 million drilling wells in the Tano basin. On June 21, 1992, an offshore Tano basin well produced about 6,900 barrels of oil daily.

In the early 1990s, GNPC reviewed all earlier oil and gas discoveries to determine whether a predominantly local operation might make exploitation more commercially viable. GNPC wanted to set up a floating system for production, storage, off-loading, processing, and gas-turbine electricity generation, hoping to produce 22 billion cubic feet per day, from which 135 megawatts of power could be generated and fed into the national and regional grid. GNPC also won a contract in 1992 with Angola's state oil company, Sonangol, that provides for drilling and, ultimately, production at two of Sonangol's offshore oilfields. GNPC will be paid with a share of the oil.

The country's refinery at Tema underwent the first phase of a major rehabilitation in 1989. The second phase began in April 1990 at an estimated cost of US$36 million. Once rehabilitation is completed, distribution of liquified petroleum gas will be improved, and the quantity supplied will rise from 28,000 to 34,000 barrels a day. Construction on the new Tema/Akosombo oil products pipeline, designed to improve the distribution system further, began in January 1992. The pipeline will carry refined products from Tema to Akosombo Port, where they will be transported across Lake Volta to northern regions. Distribution continues to be uneven, however. Other measures to improve the situation include a US$28 million project to set up a national network of storage depots in all regions.

The Tema Lube Oil Company commissioned its new oil blending plant, designed to produce 25,000 tons of oil per year, in 1992. The plant will satisfy all of Ghana's requirements for motor and gear lubricants and 60 percent of the country's need for industrial lubricants, or, in all, 90 percent of Ghana's demand for lubricant products. Shareholders include Mobil, Shell, and British Petroleum (together accounting for 48 percent of equity), Ghana National Petroleum Corporation, and the Social Security and National Insurance Trust.

MANUFACTURING AND TOURISM

MANUFACTURING

At independence in 1957, the Nkrumah government launched an industrialization drive that increased manufacturing's share of GDP from 10 percent in 1960 to 14 percent in 1970. This expansion resulted in the creation of a relatively wide range of industrial enterprises, the largest including the Volta Aluminum Company (Valco) smelter, saw mills and timber processing plants, cocoa processing plants, breweries, cement manufacturing, oil refining, textile manufacturing operations, and vehicle assembly plants. Many of these enterprises, however, survived only through protection. The overvalued cedi, shortages of hard-currency for raw materials and spare parts, and poor management in the state sector led to stagnation from 1970 to 1977 and then to a decline from 1977 to 1982.

Thereafter, the manufacturing sector never fully recovered, and performance remained weak into the 1990s. Underutilization of industrial capacity, which had been endemic since the 1960s, increased alarmingly in the 1970s, with average capacity utilization in large- and medium-scale factories falling to 21 percent in 1982. Once the ERP began, the supply of foreign exchange for imported machinery and fuel substantially improved, and capacity utilization climbed steadily to about 40 percent in 1989. Nevertheless, by 1987 production from the manufacturing sector was 35 percent lower than in 1975 and 26 percent lower than in 1980.

Ghana's record with industrialization projects since independence is exemplified by its experience with aluminum, the country's most conspicuous effort to promote capital-intensive industry. This venture began in the mid-1960s with the construction of a 1,186-megawatt hydroelectric dam on the lower Volta River at Akosombo. Built with assistance from Britain, the United States, and the World Bank, the Akosombo Dam was the centerpiece of the Volta River Project (VRP), which the Nkrumah government envisioned as the key to developing an integrated aluminum industry based on the exploitation of Ghana's sizable bauxite reserves and its hydroelectric potential. Foreign capital for the construction of an aluminum smelter in Tema was obtained from US-based Kaiser Aluminum, which acquired a 90 percent share in Valco, and from USbased Reynolds Aluminum, which held a 10 percent share. Valco became the principal consumer of VRP hydroelectricity, using 60 percent of VRP-generated power and producing up to 200,000 tons of aluminum annually during the 1970s.

Changing global economic conditions and severe drought dramatically affected the Ghanaian aluminum industry during the 1980s. The discovery of vast bauxite reserves in Australia and Brazil created a global oversupply of the mineral and induced a prolonged recession in the aluminum trade. Under these conditions, Valco found it far more economical to import semi-processed alumina from Jamaica and South Korea than to rely on local supplies, despite the discovery in the early 1970s of sizable new deposits at Kibi. Valco's refusal to build an aluminum production facility brought Kaiser and Reynolds into bitter conflict with the government.

Severe drought compounded the effects of unfavorable market conditions by reducing the electricity generating capacity of the Akosombo Dam and by forcing a temporary shutdown of the smelter from 1983 to 1985. Aluminum production was slow to recover in the wake of the shutdown. In the early 1990s, aluminum production and exports continued to be negligible.

Drastic currency devaluation after 1983 made it exceptionally expensive to purchase inputs and difficult to obtain bank credit, which hurt businessmen in the manufacturing sector. Furthermore, the ERP's tight monetary policies created liquidity crises for manufacturers, while liberalization of trade meant that some enterprises could not compete with cheaper imports. These policies hurt industries beset by long recession, hyperinflation, outmoded equipment, weak demand, and requirements that they pay 100 percent advances for their own inputs. Local press reports have estimated the closure of at least 120 factories since 1988, mainly because of competitive imports. The garment, leather, electrical, electronics, and pharmaceuticals sectors have been particularly hard hit. In 1990, even the New Match Company, the only safety match company in the country, closed.

ERP strategies made it difficult for the government to assist local enterprises. Committed to privatization and the rule of freemarket forces, the government was constrained from offering direct assistance or even from moderating some policies that had an obviously detrimental impact on local manufacturers. Nevertheless, the Rawlings government initiated programs to promote local manufacturing.

In 1986 the government established the Ghana Investment Center to assist in creating new enterprises. Between 1986 and 1990, the vast majority of projects approved--444 of 621--were in the manufacturing sector. Projected investment for the approved ventures was estimated at US$138 million in 1989 and at US$136 million in 1990. In the initial phase, timber was the leading sector, giving way in 1990 to chemicals. In 1991 the government established an office to deal with industrial distress in response to complaints that "unrestrained imports" of foreign products were undermining local enterprises. The 1992 budget included assistance for local industrialists; ¢2 billion was set aside as financial support for "deserving enterprises."

The dominant trends in manufacturing, nonetheless, were the involvement of foreign capital and the initiation of joint ventures. Significant new enterprises included a US$8 million Taiwanese-owned factory, capable of turning out ten tons of iron and steel products per hour, which began trials at Tema in 1989. Although approximately 500 projects had been approved since the investment code came into force in 1985, almost half had still not been launched by the end of 1989. Between 90 and 95 percent of the approved projects were joint ventures between foreign and local partners, 80 percent of which were in the wood industry. Restructuring of the sector was proceeding through divestiture, import liberalization, and promotion of small-scale industries.

TOURISM

Under Ghana's 1985 investment code, tourism is a priority sector with incentives and benefits for investors. The government hopes to triple its foreign exchange earnings from tourism under a five-year tourism plan, based on a projection that between 1991 and 1995, the number of tourists visiting Ghana every year will double from the 1991 base of 145,000. Jobs in the tourism industry are projected to reach 270,000, with more created in other sectors that derive business from the tourist trade. There are also incentives for star-rated hotels, approved tourist villages and beaches, and holiday recreational resorts. Investors are involved in the development of other tourist attractions, such as waterfalls, beaches, forts, castles, and historical sites, and even in specialized restaurants, tourist coaches, and buses. Incentives in this sector include tax and rate exemptions on building properties for three years in addition to investment and depreciation allowances.

FOREIGN INVESTMENTS AND ASSISTANCE

Despite efforts to increase private capital participation in the Ghanaian economy, in the early 1990s foreign investments continued to be sparse, and the economy relied heavily on aid and loans. By 1991 the external debt exceeded US$4 billion, and it was nearly US$4.3 billion in 1992, an amount equal to the level of assistance provided by donors over the previous decade. The country continued to experience trade and service deficits despite increased exports.

INVESTMENT

Despite efforts to induce foreign investment in the economy, interest has been restricted primarily to the mining sector. Although at least eleven mining companies enjoyed some foreign participation by 1990, the government had succeeded in creating only two joint ventures in former state enterprises outside the mining industry.

In 1985 the government adopted an investment code to encourage foreign investment. It excluded the petroleum and mining sectors for which the government introduced a separate code in 1986, it offered special conditions for agriculture, manufacturing (for export, using local raw materials, and for the production of agricultural equipment, spare parts, and machine tools), construction, and tourism. Agricultural projects were given a 45 percent corporate income tax allowance, a 100 percent allowance on plant and equipment, and a 10 percent investment allowance. In manufacturing and construction, the investment allowance was 7.5 percent, with depreciation and capital allowances of 40 percent and 50 percent, respectively, the latter two halved in subsequent years. Finally, in tourism, the investment allowance was 7.5 percent, and the depreciation allowances were 50 percent for plant and 20 percent for buildings, which also were halved in subsequent years. In all cases, imports required for the projects were exempted from duties. Additional tax reductions were granted to projects located in Kumasi and Sekondi-Takoradi, while other areas (excluding Accra-Tema) were given even larger reductions.

Some activities (retail and wholesale trade, except where employed capital was over US$500,000; land transport; travel; advertising; estate agencies) were reserved for Ghanaian-owned firms. Foreign investors were required to supply a minimum of US$60,000 in the case of partnerships with Ghanaians, or US$100,000 in the case of fully owned enterprises. Only net foreign exchange earning ventures were allowed to be fully owned by foreigners. The code guaranteed investments against nationalization, and where disputes needed arbitration, they were to be settled through existing international forums. Transfers abroad were allowed for dividend payments, debt servicing, charges for technology transfers, or liquidation of enterprises. Implementation of the code and processing of applications by potential investors were made the responsibilities of the Ghana Investment Center.

In mid-1993 Minister of Finance Kwesi Botchwey announced that a new investment code had been presented to Ghana's parliament. Under the new code, minimum foreign capital requirements for joint ventures will be dropped from US$60,000 to US$10,000, and the minimum for fully owned foreign enterprises will be reduced to US$50,000. Companies established solely for export will be exempt from the minimum capital requirement. The new code outlaws government expropriations and provides a five-year tax holiday for the agricultural and real estate sectors.

PRACTICAL AND LEGAL INFORMATION FOR CONDUCTING BUSINESS

INVESTMENT AND LEGAL CLIMATE

The Ghana Investment Promotion Centre Act, 1994, provides for automatic incentives and benefits as follows: (See GIPC Incentive brochure for full details)

CUSTOMS IMPORT DUTY EXEMPTIONS

There is duty exemption for plant, machinery, equipment and parts imported for investment purposes as contained in chapters 82, 84, 85 and 98 of the Customs Harmonized Commodity and Tariff Code.	Tax Rate 0

1. The following however attract concessionary duty.

Heading No	Tariff Description
82.08	Knives and Cutting Blades
84.71	Automatic Data Processing Machines and units thereof
85.01	Electric Motors and Generators (Excluding Generating Sets)
85.02	Electric Generating Sets and Rotary Converters (less than 375 kVA)
98.07 and 98.08	Air-conditioners; Furnishing including Carpets, Bedding and Fixtures; Fans and Radio Sets; Refrigerators/Deep Freezers; Television Sets; Public Address Systems; and, Crockery

2. Exemptions may be granted from customs import duty and other related charges for any special equipment that is not zero-rated upon application to the GIPC.

INCOME TAX INCENTIVES

A. **Corporate Tax Rate - 32.5% in all sectors except:**
   i. income from non-traditional export - 8%
   ii Hotels - 25%

B. **Exemptions**
   i. **Tax Holiday (from start of operations)**
      a. Real Estate: rental income from residential and commercial premises - first 5 years after construction.
      b. Rural Banks: 10 years
      c. Agriculture and agro-industry:
         - cocoa farmers and producers - income tax exempted
         - cattle ranching - 10 years exemption

- tree cropping (e.g. coffee, oil palm, sheabutter, rubber and coconut) 10 years exemption
- livestock excluding cattle and poultry - 5 years exemption
- fish farming, poultry and cash crops - 5 years exemption
- manufacturing company, using predominantly local raw materials processing crops, fish or livestock - 3 years exemption

d. Manufacturing enterprises which add substantial value to local raw materials - first 3 years exemption.
e. Air and Sea transport (non-resident) - income tax exempted.
f. Free Zones Enterprise/Development - 10 years exemption and 8% corporate tax thereafter.

ii. **Locational Incentives (Tax Rebates)**
Manufacturing companies pay the following corporate tax rate if located in:-

- Accra/Tema - 32.5%
- Regional capitals (25% Rebate) - 24.375%
- Elsewhere (50% Rebate) - 16.25%

CAPITAL ALLOWANCES

The rates of capital allowances remain unchanged as follows:

iii. **Companies in Banking, Finance, Insurance, Commerce**

	Depreciation Allowance	**Annual Allowance**
Buildings	10%	3%
Plant & Equipment		
Electrical	20%	12.5%
Non-electrical	20%	7.5%
Vehicles	20%	20%
Cars	20%	15%
Computers	20%	15%

iv. Notes:

- Depreciation allowance is computed on cost in the year of purchase and is granted once in the lifetime of the asset and is taken into account in calculating residual balance.
- Annual allowance is granted on residual balance.

v. **All other companies**

Depreciation allowances

Type of expenditure	Rate	No of years
Qualifying plant expenditure	50% on cost	2 years
Qualifying building	20% on cost	5 years

Unutilised capital allowances are carried forward indefinitely.

CARRY FORWARD LOSSES

- All companies except mining and insurance companies can carry forward losses for five years.
- Insurance companies carry forward losses indefinitely.
- For mining companies, losses are carried forward indefinitely but restricted to the capital allowance granted for the year.

This is explained by the example below:

	S1 **¢'bn**	**S2** **¢'bn**
Net loss as per financial statement	(3)	(3)
Add back - net non allowable expenses e.g. depreciation	1	1
Adjusted loss before capital allowance	(2)	(4)
Capital allowance	2	2

Notes:

- Under S1 both adjusted loss of 2 billion cedis and capital allowance of 2 billion are carried forward.
- Under S2 adjusted loss will be restricted to the capital allowance figure of 2 billion cedis. Therefore the loss to be carried forward is 2 billion cedis and the capital allowance of 2 billion cedis.

INVESTMENT GUARANTEES

Act 478 provides guarantees to all enterprises, including free transferability through any authorized dealer bank in freely convertible currency of dividends or net profits attributable to the investment; payments in respect of loan servicing where a foreign loan has been obtained; remittance of proceeds (net of all taxes and other obligations) in the event of sale or liquidation of the enterprise or any interest attributable to the investment. Guarantees against expropriation of private investments provided under Act 478 are buttressed by the constitution.

All prospective investors are most welcome to take advantage of the generous incentives under the liberalized environment offered by the new investment regime - GIPC Act, 1994 (Act 478).

TAX INCENTIVES

Provided under the Income Tax Decree 1975 (SMCD 5) administered by the Internal Revenue Service (IRS)

TARIFF EXEMPTIONS - Items listed in this section are allowed in duty free or under concessionary duty rates. These Customs Import Duty Exemptions are administered by Customs Excise and Preventive Service (CEPS).

TOOLS AND IMPLEMENTS

Heading No.	H.S. Code	Tariff Description	
82.02		Hand Saws; blades for saws of all kinds (including slitting, slotting or toothless saw blades).	
	8202.20 R00	-	Band saw blades
		-	Circular saw blades (including slitting or slotting saw blades).
	8202.31 H00	-	With working, part of steel
	8202.32 X00	-	With working part of materials
		-	Other saw blades
	8202.91 K00	-	Straight saw blades, for working metal
	8202.99 H00	-	Other
82.07		Interchangeable tools for hand tools, whether or not power-operated, or for machine-tools (for example, for pressing, stamping, punching, tapping, threading, drilling, boring, broaching, milling, turning or screw driving), including dies for drawing or extruding metal, and rock drilling or earth boring tools.	
		-	Rock drilling or earth boring tools
	8207.11 X00	-	With working part of sintered metal carbide or cermets
	8207.12 K00	-	With working part of other material

	8207.20 K00	-	Dies for drawing or extruding metal
	8207.30 B00	-	Tools for pressing, stamping or punching
	8207.20 N00	-	Tools for tapping or threading
	8207.50 F00	-	Tools for drilling, other than for rock drilling
	8207.60 B00	-	Tools for boring or broaching
	8207.70 K00	-	Tools for milling
	8207.80 B00	-	Tools for turning
	8207.90 N00	-	Other interchangeable tools
82.08		Knives and cutting blades, for machines or for mechanical appliances	
	8208.10 X00	-	For metal working
	8208.20 B00	-	For wood working
	8208.30 W00	-	For kitchen appliances or for machines used by the food industry
	8208.40 R00	-	For agricultural, horticultu al or forestry machines
	8208.90 R00	-	Other
82.09	8209.00 H00	Plates, sticks, tips and the like for tools, unmounted, of sintered metal carbides or cermets	

NUCLEAR REACTORS, BOILERS, MACHINERY AND MECHANICAL APPLIANCES; PARTS THEREOF

Heading No.	H.S. Code	Tariff Description	
84.01		Nuclear reactors; fuel elements (cartridges), non- irradiated, for nuclear reactors, machinery and apparatus for isotopic separation .	
	8401.10 N00	-	Nuclear reactors
	8401.20 F00	-	Machinery and apparatus for isotopic separation, and parts thereof.

	8401.30 H00	-	Fuel elements (cartridges), nonirradiated
	8401.40 K00	-	Parts of nuclear reactors
84.02			Steam or other vapour generating boilers (other than central heating hot water boilers capable also of producing low pressure steam); super- heated water boilers.
		-	Steam or other vapour generating boilers
	8402.11 F00	-	Watertube boilers with a steam production exceeding 45t per hour
	8402.12 L00	-	Watertube boilers with a steam production not exceeding 45t per hour
	8402.19 N00	-	Other vapour generating boilers, including hybrid boilers
	8402.20 L00	-	Super-heated water boilers
	8402.90 B00	-	Parts
84.03			Central heating boilers other than those of heading No. 84.82.
	8403.10 F00	-	Boilers
	8403.90 B00	-	Parts
84.04			Auxiliary plant for use with boilers of heading No. 84.02 or 84.03 (for example, economisers, super-heaters, soot removers, gas recoverers); condensers for steam or other vapour power units.
	8404.10 L00	-	Auxiliary plant for use with boilers of heading No. 84.82 or 84.03
	8404.20 X00	-	Condensers for steam orother vapour power units

	8404.90 W00	-	Parts
84.05		Producer gas or water gas generators, with or without their purifiers; acetylene gas generators and similar water process gas generators, with or without their purifiers.	
	8405.10 H00	-	Producer gas or water gas generators, with or without their purifiers, acetylene gas generators and similar water process gas generators, with or without their purifiers
	8405.90 N00	-	Parts
84.06		Steam turbines and other vapour turbines.	
		-	Turbines:
	8406.11 K00	-	For marine propulsion
	8406.19 H00	-	Other
	8406.90 R00	-	Parts
84.07		Spark-ignition reciprocating or rotary internal combustion piston engines.	
	8407.10 X00	-	Aircraft engines
		-	Marine propulsion engines:
	8407.21 W00	-	Outboard motors
	8407.29 B00	-	Others
		-	Reciprocating piston engines of a kind used for the

			propulsion of vehicles of Chapter 87:

ELECTRICAL MACHINERY AND EQUIPMENT AND PARTS THEREOF, SOUND RECORDERS AND REPRODUCERS, TELEVISION IMAGE AND SOUND RECORDERS AND REPRODUCERS, AND PARTS AND ACCESSORIES OF SUCH ARTICLES

Heading No.	H.S. Code		Tariff Description
85.01			Electric motors and generators (excluding generating sets)
	8501.10 R00	-	Motors of an output not exceeding 37.5 W
	8501.20 L00	-	Universal AC/DC motors of an output exceeding 37.5 W
		-	Other DC motors; DC generators:
	8501.31 KOO	-	Of an output not exceeding 750 W
	8501.32 B00	-	Of an output exceeding 750 W but not exceeding 75 KW
	8501.33 B00	-	Of an output exceeding 75 KW but not exceeding 375 KW
	8501.34 W00	-	Of an output exceeding 375 KW
	8501.40 W00	-	Other AC motors single-phase
		-	Other AC motors, multi-phase
	8501.51 N00	-	Of an output not exceeding 750 W
	8501.52 R00	-	Of an output exceeding 750 W but not exceeding 75 KW
	8501.53 F00	-	Of an output exceeding 75 KW
		-	AC generators (alternators):

	8501.61 F00	-	Of an output not exceeding 75 KVA
	8501.62 L00	-	Of an output exceeding 75 KVA but not exceeding 375 KVA
	8501.63 H00	-	Of an output exceeding 375 KVA but not exceeding 750 KVA
	8501.64 X00	-	Of an output exceeding 750 KVA
85.02		Electric generating sets and rotary converters.	
		-	Generating sets with compression ignition, internal combustion piston engines (diesel or semi-diesel engines):
	8502.11 L00	-	Of an output not exceeding 75 KVA
	8502.12 H00	-	Of an output exceeding 75 KVA but not exceeding 375 KVA
	8502.13 K00	-	Of an output exceeding 375 KVA
	8502.20 H00	-	Generating sets with spark-ignition, internal combustion piston engines
	8502.30 K00	-	Other generating sets
	8502.40 B00	-	Electric rotary converters
85.03	8503.00 R00	Parts suitable for use solely or principal with the machines of heading No.85.01 or 85.02.	
85.04		Electrical transformers, static converters (for example, rectifiers) and inductors.	
		-	Liquid dielectric transformers:

	8504.21 B00	-	Having a power handling capacity not exceeding 650 KVA
	8504.22 B00	-	Having a power handling capacity exceeding 650 KVA but not exceeding 10,000 KVA
	8504.23 W00	-	Having a power handling capacity exceeding 10,000 KVA
		-	Other transformers
	8504.31 W00	-	Having a power handling capacity not exceeding 1 KVA
	8504.32 N00	-	Having a power handling capacity exceeding 1 KVA but not exceeding 16 KVA
	8504.33 R00	-	Having a power handling capacity exceeding 16 KVA but not exceeding 500 KVA
	8504.34 N00	-	Having a power handling capacity exceeding 500 KVA
	8504.40 B00	-	Static converters
	8504.50 F00	-	Other inductors
	8504.90 N00	-	Parts

GOODS ADMISSIBLE AT CONCESSIONARY DUTY RATES WHEN IMPORTED BY ENTERPRISES UNDER THE GHANA INVESTMENT PROMOTION CENTRE ACT

Heading No.	H.S. Code	Enterprise	Tariff Description	Rate of Duty
98.07	9807	Hotels	The following materials in the appropriate quantities: i) Refrigerators/Deep freezers ii) Television Sets iii) Airconditioners iv) public Address System v) Furnishing including carpets, bedding and fixtures vi) Fans vii) Radio Sets viii) Crockery	0
98.08	9808	Restaurants, including fast food,	The following materials, in the appropriate quantities:	0

		chairs with a seating capacity of thirty or more.	i) Airconditioners ii) Crockery iii) Referigerators/Deep freezers iv) Furnishing including carpets	
98.09	9809	Local film production and electronic media duly approved by the appropriate authority	The following equipments in the appropriate quantities: i) Transmission apparatus for radio telephones, radio telegraphs, radio or television broadcasting whether or not incorporating reception apparatus. ii) Sound recording apparatus iii) Reproducing apparatus iv) Televisioin cameras and accessories.	0

Note: The expression "in the appropriate quantities" shall relate to size, number of rooms, seating capacity etc.

All items listed in Chapters 82, 84, 85 and 98b of the Customs Harmonised Commodity and Tariff Code were zero-rated under Customs and Excise (Duties and other Taxes) Act 1996, Act 512.

However, Act 545 – the Customs and Excise (Duties and other Taxes) Amendment Act 1998 – amended the principal enactment by the substitution of the following rates of duties and taxes as they relate to the GIPC Act, 1994 (Act 478).

Heading No.	Tariff Description	Import Duty (%)	Sales Tax (%)
82.08	Knives and Cutting Blades	5	0
84.71	Automatic Data Processing Machines and units thereof	0	15
85.01	Electric Motors And Generators (Excluding Generating Sets)	5	0
85.02	Electric Generating Sets and Rotary Converters (less than 375 kVA)	5	0
98.07 and 98.08	Air-conditioners; Furnishing including Carpets, Bedding and Fixtures; Fans and Radio Sets; Refrigerators/Deep Freezers; Television Sets; Public Address Systems; and, Crockery	10	0

INVESTMENT INCENTIVES UNDER THE INCOME TAX DECREE (GHANA) 1975 (SMCD5)

Income Tax Incentives provided under the Income Tax Decree, 1975 (SMCD5) as amended, include:

TAX HOLIDAY (FROM START OF OPERATIONS):

a. **Real Estate:**
Rental income from residential and commercial premises - the first 5 years after construction. Income accruing to a company engaged in the construction, sale or letting of residential premises - during the first 5 years of start-up of operations.

b. **Rural Banks:**
10 years

c. **Agriculture & Agro - Industry:**

- Cocoa farmers & producers: Income Exempted
- Cattle ranching: 10 years
- Tree crops (eg. coffee, oil palm, sheabutter, rubber & coconut): 10 years
- Poultry, Fishing & Cash Crops: 5 years

d. **Air and Sea Transport (non-resident):** Income Exempted

- The President may exempt any persons or class of persons from all or any provision of the Decree subject to the approval of Parliament.

CAPITAL ALLOWANCES:

e. Depreciation (accelerated) allowance applicable to all sectors except banking, finance, commerce, insurance, mining and petroleum.

- Qualifying Plant Expenditure: Depreciation rate of 50% per annum for 2 years.
- Qualifying Building Expenditure: Depreciation rate of 20% per annum for five (5) years.

NB: * Sectors which enjoy accelerated depreciation allowance do not enjoy annual allowances.

f. Depreciation (normal) allowance applicable to banking, finance, commerce, insurance, mining and petroleum and to be enjoyed **only once** in the year of assessment for which the asset is **first used by owner of asset:**

- Qualifying Plant Expenditure: 20% Depreciation allowance of
- Qualifying Building Expenditure: Depreciation allowance of 10%.
- Qualifying Mining Expenditure: Depreciation allowance of 25%.

(NB *Depreciation allowance for Plantation is 10%)

g. Annual allowance applicable to banking, finance, commerce, insurance **after** the enjoyment of the depreciation allowance referred to in (b) above:

- Machinery: Annual allowance at the rate of 10%.
- Plant: Annual allowance at the rate of 7 1/2%
- Furniture, Fixtures and Fittings: Annual allowance at the rate of 7 1/2%
- Buildings (excluding residential property): Annual allowance at the rate of 5% for mining and timber and 3% for other sectors.

- Ships, trawlers, Ferry Boats, Lighters and tug boats, Barges, Dredges and Pontoons: Annual allowance at the rate of 5%.
- Aeroplanes and Helicopters: Annual allowance at the rate of 10 %% for aeroplanes and 71/2 for helicopters.
- Qualifying mining and timber expenditure: Annual allowance at the rate of 15%.

2. Rates of Annual allowance on Plant, Machinery etc. applicable to specific items at discretionary rates are as provided below:

Amplifiers (Cinema)	7 1/2%
Bicycle	20%
Brickmaking machines	5%
Motor Cars & Trailers	15 %
Carts	5%
Cash Register	7 1/2%
Cinema Projectors	10%
Electric Dynamos, Motors and General Plant	12 1/2%
Engine boilers and shafting (Sawmills and Printing)	7 1/2%
Engines - Diesel	10%
Engines - Internal Combustion (stationery)	10%
Fixtures (General)	7 1/2%
Lorries	20%
Machinery (General)	10%
Oil Storage Tanks - Bolted	7 1/2%
Oil Pipelines & Fitting	7 1/2%
Rivoted & Welded	7 1/2%
Petrol Pumps (fixed, portable or underground)	12 1/2%
Photo-finish (Racing)	10%
Printing and Binding machines	7 1/2%
Printing Type	12 1/2%

Railway Wagons	10%
Refrigeration Plan	12 1/2%
Seating (Cinema)	7 1/2%
Soap Manufacture: Filling Machines	12 1/2%
Soap Manufacture: Pressing Machines	7 1/2%
Soap Manufacture: Stills	7 1/2%
Textile Design Rollers	10%
Turnstiles (Cinema)	10%
Typewriting and Calculating Machine	15%
Diesel Locomotives	12 1/2%
Motor Van	20%

Notes:

(A) Tools and Implements: No Capital Allowance, but are allowed on replacement basis.
(B) Where an item is not mentioned in (d) the rates under (a), (b) and (c) will apply.

LOCATION INCENTIVES (TAX REBATE)

- Manufacturing industries located in regional capitals other than Accra and Tema - 25% rebate.
- All other manufacturing industries located outside regional capitals - 50% rebate.

CORPORATE TAX RATES

35% in all Sectors except:

- Income from non-traditional exports - 8%
- Hotels - 25%

EXEMPTION FROM INCOME TAX PAYABLE

On the provision of accommodation for employees on farms and building, timber, mining and construction sites.

LOSS - CARRY - OVER

- All sectors - 5 years
- Except insurance business - unlimited.

EXEMPT FROM THE MINIMUM CHARGEABLE INCOME TAX

- Exemption from minimum chargeable income of 5% turnover during the first five years.

A CAPITAL EXPENDITURE FOR RESEARCH AND DEVELOPMENT

by manufacturing company in Ghana is (approved by the Minister of Trade and Industry) fully deductible.

WITHHOLDING TAX

- The withholding tax rate on dividends is 10%.
- The withholding tax on royalties, management and technology transfer fees is 15%.
- The withholding tax rate on interest has been reduced from 30% to 10%

TRADE REGULATIONS AND STANDARDS

TRADE BARRIERS, INCLUDING TARIFFS, NON-TARIFF BARRIERS AND IMPORT TAXES

COMMERCIAL BARRIERS

Traditional barriers to U.S. exports and investment include: (1) limited Ghanaian purchasing power; (2) complex land tenure system; (3) lack of U.S. interest due to the relatively small market size; (4) limited and costly financing resources for U.S. exporters and Ghanaian buyers; (5) stronger attraction of other overseas markets; (6) more favorable credit terms by European suppliers to local importers; (7) limited information; (8) inadequate credit facilities for local importers; (9) perceived British domination of the market due to traditional ties with Britain; (10) high inflation rate; (11) inadequate business infrastructure, particularly in the telecommunications and road sectors; and (12) bureaucratic hurdles for some documentation.

TARIFFS AND IMPORT TAXES

Ghana is currently using the Harmonized System (HS) Customs Code in classifying goods. Taxes assessed on the basis of weight, value or volume are subject to change annually. Goods arriving in country may be subject to import duty, value-added tax (VAT), special tax, and import excise duty. Duties are imposed on certain categories of exports as well.

Generally, the import rates imposed on various goods for the current year are as follows: agricultural and industrial machinery, educational materials, and solar cells and panels - zero duty; interchangeable tools of Chapters 82, 84, and 85 – 5 percent ad valorem; raw materials, computer software, and unrecorded media for sound recording - 10 percent ad valorem; and all other goods - 20 percent ad valorem, which is the standard rate of duty. Aside from a few items that are exempt from the payment of customs duty, all imports are subject to import duty plus VAT. The VAT is currently 12.5 percent and is calculated on the duty-inclusive value of the goods at rates contained in the HS manual. The GOG reduced the additional 20 percent special tax on some selected "non-essential" imported goods to 10 percent and for some products it has been removed. These include cosmetics and toiletries, used clothing, poultry products, edible oil, and grapes and apples. There is a 0.5 percent ECOWAS levy on all imports from non-ECOWAS countries and 0.5 percent EDIF levy on all imports. For further information please check the

CEPS website, www.cepsghana.org.

Imports into Ghana come under two main categories: (1) import on collection, whereby any person may import into Ghana before paying for the goods (prior approval from the Bank of is required); and, (2) conventional importation, in which the importer needs to go through the banking system to establish a Letter of Credit (L.C.) or make provision for foreign exchange.

CUSTOMS VALUATION

In general, all imports are subject to customs duties. Law provides exemptions for government, privileged persons, organizations and institutions.

In April 2000, Ghana changed the valuation of imports for the purpose of assessing ad valorem tax from the Brussels Definition of Value (BDV) assessment method to the Customs Valuation Code (CVC) value assessment method of the World Trade Organization (WTO). Pre-Shipment Inspection (PSI) has been abolished and replaced by a Destination Inspection Scheme (DIS). This implies that under the DIS, imports will only be inspected at the port of clearance in Ghana as against inspection prior to export to Ghana under the PSI.

Under the CVC several methods are being used to assess the value of imports. The use of these methods is expected to be more transparent than the BDV and also facilitate the clearing of goods of ports. For more information on the methods applied please visit www.cepsghana.org.

Gateway Services limited and G.S.B.V. Company Limited are responsible for the inspection of all goods imported into Ghana.

Regulatory Agencies

Governmental agencies responsible for regulating business activities include:

Taxation: Internal Revenue Service
P.O. Box 2202
Accra
Tel: 233-21-664961
Fax: 233-21-664938

VAT Service
P.O. Box 17177
Accra
Tel: 233-21-228725
Fax: 233-21-230286

Monetary Bank of Ghana
Transactions: P.O. Box 2674
Accra
Tel: 233-21-666902/666361
Fax: 233-21-662996

Labor Issues: Ministry of Manpower Development &
Employment
P.O. Box M.84
Accra
Tel: 233-21-665421
Fax: 233-21-667251

Copyrights: Copyrights Office
Private Mail Bag
Ministries Post Office
Accra
Tel: 233-21-229190
Fax: 233-21-224282

Standards/ Ghana Standards Board
Labels: P.O. Box M245
Accra
Tel: 233-21-500065 or 500066
Fax: 233-21-776092

Food and Drugs Board
P.O. Box C2783
Cantonments, Accra
Tel: 233-21-228864
Fax: 233-21-228864

Company Registrar-General's Department
Registration: P.O. Box 118
Trademarks/Patents: Accra
Tel: 233-21-664691-3
Fax: 233-21-662043

IMPORT LICENSES

The import license system was abolished in 1989. However, for some items a permit or certificate is still required. These include drugs, all communications equipment, mercury, gambling machines, handcuffs, arms and ammunition, and live plants and animals.

Ghana has no quotas for imported items.

Agencies to which one must apply for permits/certificates to import certain items are as follows:

Gold Coins, Uncut Ministry of Finance &
Diamonds, Goods Economic Planning
Bearing Designs in P.O. Box M.40, Accra
Imitation of Money, Tel: 233-21-665421/665441
Handcuffs, Machines Fax: 233-21-667069
For Duplicating Keys:

Arms and Ammunition; Ministry of Interior
Gambling Machines: P.O. Box M.42
Accra
Tel: 233-21-665421/665198
Fax: 233-21-667450

Communications National Frequency &
Equipment: Registration Board
P.O. Box 1627
Castle Annex, Accra

Tel: 233-21-666932
Fax: 233-21-665347

Drugs: Ministry of Health
P.O. Box M.44
Accra
Tel: 233-21-665421/665323
Fax: 233-21-663810

EXPORT CONTROLS

With a few exceptions, there are no controls on exports. The main categories of restricted exports include military hardware and antiques and collector's items more than 50 years old, including works of art. These items require special permits and certificates as a prerequisite for their exportation. Other items that require permits are game and wildlife, timber products, precious minerals and live plants. Allowing private participation has broken the government-owned Cocoa Marketing Board's (COCOBOD) monopoly over the export of cocoa beans. Prohibited exports include items specified by law, narcotics, parrots, and Ghanaian currency in excess of 5,000 cedis (approximately $0.70). Agencies to which one must apply for permits and certificates to export various items are:

Antiques: Ghana Museums & Monuments Board
Head Office, Barnes Road
C/O P.O. Box M.40
Accra
Tel: 233-21-221633/221635/222401

Precious Minerals: Precious Minerals Marketing Corp.
(PMMC)
P.O. Box 108
Accra
Tel: 233-21-664931/4 or 773368
Fax: 233-21-662586

Wildlife: Department of Game & Wildlife
P.O. Box M.239
Accra
Tel: 233-21-664654/666129
Fax: 233-21-666476

Live Plants: Ministry of Agriculture
Plant/Animal Quarantine Dept.
Box M.37
Accra
Tel: 233-21-665421
Fax: 233-21-665363

Dangerous Weapons: Ministry of Interior
P.O. Box M.42
Accra
Tel: 233-21-665421/665198
Fax: 233-21-667450

IMPORT DOCUMENTATION

An Import Declaration Form (IDF) must cover most classes of goods imported into the country. An importer completes an IDF, which is obtained locally, and presents it to a one of the two Destination Inspection Scheme (DIS) companies depending on whether the goods are coming by sea or air. The IDF is presented to Gateway Services Limited if goods will come by sea or to GSBV Company Limited if goods will be received by air. In order to clear the goods through customs, the importer must complete a designated Customs Entry form and present a bill of lading from the foreign exporter, a commercial invoice, an IDF, and Final Customs Valuation Report (FCVR) issued by a DSI company. Other documents required are income tax certificate, Ghana Shipper's Notification Form and a packing list.

TEMPORARY ENTRY

The laws of Ghana provide for the entry of certain goods conditionally relieved from payment of import duties and taxes. Such goods must be imported for a specific purpose and must be intended for re-export within three months, in the original condition of entry, or after having undergone further processing or repair. If goods brought into Ghana under temporary entry permit are to be sold, the Customs Excise and Preventive Service (CEPS) must be notified and appropriate taxes settled in full before the sale. For trade show materials, CEPS insists that goods and samples be re-exported within three months of their entry.

LABELING, MARKING REQUIREMENTS

The GOG continues to enforce a product-labeling law of general applicability, which took effect in 1992. By law, imports and locally produced goods in virtually all categories (notable exceptions include petroleum and fish) must clearly identify the goods shipped (in English), the ingredients or components, the point of origin, and establish a date of expiration for perishables. Improperly identified food and drugs are held for testing by the Ghana Standards Board (GSB) where approved goods are released upon payment of a fine and unapproved goods are confiscated for disposal.

PROHIBITED IMPORTS

Import prohibitions include: narcotics, mercuric medicated soap, toxic waste, contaminated goods, foreign cigarettes without a warning notice, foreign soil, counterfeit notes and coins of any country, and any goods prohibited by local law.

STANDARDS

The Ghana Standards Board (GSB) is the authority responsible for developing and promulgating standards as well as ensuring the quality of goods imported into Ghana. The GSB has promulgated approximately 160 Ghanaian standards and adopted over 300 foreign standards for certification purposes. These standards cover a wide range of products. Both manufacturers and importers are required to register with the GSB.

The GSB has not yet adopted the ISO 9000 for Ghana. The GSB actively encourages local businesses to adopt the ISO 9000 standards in order to make them more competitive. There is a special emphasis on inputs for non-traditional exports. Some multi-national private sector companies have already adopted the ISO 9000 series.

The Food and Drug Board (FDB) also regulates and certifies food, drugs, cosmetics, and other products which have health implications for the consuming public. This situation has led to some duplication of activities by GSB and FDB. The Ministry of Trade and Industry is in the process of resolving this problem.

Ghana uses 220V, 50 cycles for electricity and the metric system of measurement. Operating standards usually follow the British or European norm.

FREE TRADE ZONES/WAREHOUSES

A Free Trade Zone was established in May 1996. The free zone consists of a parcel of land near Tema Steelworks, Ltd. In the Greater Accra Region and two other sites located at Mpintsin and Ashiem, near Takoradi. The seaports of Tema and Takoradi, as well as the Kotoka International Airport, and all the lands related to these areas are a part of the free zone. The law also permits the establishment of single factory zones outside or within the areas mentioned above. Under the law, a company qualifies to be a free zone company if it exports more than 70 percent of its products. Among the incentives for free zone companies are a ten-year corporate tax holiday and zero duty on its imports.

To make it easy for a potential free zone developer to acquire the various licenses and permits to operate, the Ghana Free Zones Board provides a "one-stop approval service" to assist in the completion of all formalities. A lack of resources has limited the effectiveness of the Board, however. To further facilitate operations in the zones, nationals of OECD countries, Canada, East Asian countries and the Republic of South Africa can, in principle and with sufficient advance notice, obtain entry visas at the airport, although this process does not always work smoothly. All foreign employees of businesses established under the program will require work and residence permits.

Contact address for the Secretariat is as follows:

Ghana Free Zones Board
Ministry of Trade & Industry Annex
P.O. Box M.47
Accra
Tel: 233-21-670534/670532
Fax: 233-21-670536
E-mail: freezone@africaonline.com.gh
Contact: Mr. Kojo Ntim Atuahene – Executive Director

Most large Ghanaian banks as well as a number of private sector companies and individuals own bonded warehouses.

MEMBERSHIP IN FREE TRADE ARRANGEMENTS

Ghana is a member of the World Trade Organization (WTO) and is a signatory to the ACP-EU Partnership Agreement, which replaced the Lomé Convention, a trade and aid agreement between the European Union and 46 of Europe's former colonies and dependencies in Africa, the Caribbean and the Pacific (the ACP group). The ACP-EU arrangements guarantee duty free entry into EU member states for a number of commodities and products produced in ACP countries. Ghana is also one of the beneficiaries of the U.S. African Growth and Opportunity Act (AGOA) quota and duty free status. Ghana is a member of ECOWAS, the Economic Community of West African States. ECOWAS, which groups both Anglophone and Francophone states of the region, has as its goal a customs union, which is to lead eventually to a full common market and the free movement of labor. Original ECOWAS arrangements called for full tariff exemptions for companies that are at least 25 percent owned by citizens of member states, and exemptions for goods which are at least 40 percent manufactured within ECOWAS. In March 2000, the

ECOWAS governments introduced a 0.5 percent levy on all products that are imported from non-member ECOWAS countries.

Implementation of ECOWAS initiatives has been slow. In order to complement its relatively small market size, the GOG is seeking to make Ghana the "Gateway" to the West African market through a project sponsored by the World Bank. The project seeks to make Ghana a trade hub for penetration into the 250 million people West African regional market.

MARKETING PRODUCTS AND SERVICES

DISTRIBUTION AND SALES CHANNELS

The channels of distribution available to U.S. suppliers of goods and services in Ghana are wholesalers, retail outlets, and agents or distributors. Some suppliers sell directly to the government while others sell to indigenous associations. The most important trading center for U.S. products and the most populous area of the country is the Accra/Tema Metropolitan area (pop. approx. 3.5 million). Other large cities, in order of size and importance for marketing U.S. products, are Kumasi (pop. approx. 1.5 million), Sekondi/Takoradi (pop. approx. 400,000), Tamale (pop. approx. 400,000), Sunyani (pop. approx. 200,000) and Cape Coast (pop. approx.150, 000.) Exporters are advised to consider the requirements of the product and the potential market before choosing a distribution channel.

USE OF AGENTS/DISTRIBUTORS; FINDING A PARTNER

While there are no laws requiring the retention of a local agent or distributor for a foreign company exporting to Ghana, American companies wishing to enter the Ghanaian market are strongly advised to retain a business person or persons resident in Ghana to market their products. An agent or distributor should possess a thorough understanding of the economy. If the exported product requires servicing, qualified personnel and a reasonable inventory of spare parts must be considered. Exporters should be aware that agents and distributors commonly represent several product lines.

While in the past Ghanaians had a preference for made-in-Britain and Asian goods, there has been increased interest of late in American products because of their perceived superior quality. While European competitors market their geographic proximity as a competitive advantage, Ghanaian businessmen and women have expressed their willingness to pay a sometimes higher price (because of transportation costs) for an American product since American companies enjoy the reputation in Ghana for providing excellent after-sales service. It should be noted that transportation costs from the U.S. are also dropping because of new direct air connections between Accra and New York and Baltimore, as well as shipping from Baltimore directly to the port of Tema in Ghana.

The CS can help locate agents and distributors through the International Partner Search (IPS) program. Information regarding this program is available through the Commercial Service district offices located in all 50 states and Washington, DC. The cost of a report is USD 250.

Exporters may also wish to use the International Company Profile (ICP), a service for checking the reputation, reliability and financial status of a prospective trading partner. The information is in the form of a confidential report, along with a recommendation from commercial officers at the U.S. Embassy as to the suitability of the company as a trading partner. A fee of USD 100 per company is charged.

Prior to committing to a long-term relationship, exporters are advised to visit Ghana to gain firsthand knowledge of the country. The Commercial Service offers a unique facility for U.S.

business people - the Gold Key Service, a custom-tailored service for U.S. firms planning to visit a country. It provides the following:

- Up to four scheduled appointments per day with a potential agent/distributor or contact
- Services of a Commercial Specialist on all calls
- Use of our offices in Accra's business center
- Unlimited uses of our phone and fax for local calls (use our international lines at cost)
- Basic secretarial and receptionist service
- In-depth business, economic and political briefing by an American officer

Your one-time low cost:
--USD150 is required for the first day of the service and USD120 for each subsequent day.
--An additional USD100 per day for a business escort to your meetings, if requested.

Please inform the Commercial Service Accra at the address below at least three weeks before your departure to Ghana in order to facilitate this process.

The Commercial Service
United States Embassy Accra
Department of State
Washington, DC 20521-2020

or

P. O. Box 194
Accra,
Tel: (233-21) 235096, 229179
Fax: (233-21) 235096/776008
Email: comserv@ghana.com

FRANCHISING

There is a growing interest in franchising in Ghana, an area that has potential for development, especially by smaller U.S. businesses. Under-capitalization of many companies discourages greater use of this approach to business.

DIRECT MARKETING

Wholesale establishments and many retail outlets are concentrated in Accra. These include company headquarters, branch banking, supermarkets and specialty shops. Several companies have opened branches in Kumasi and Takoradi. Both within and outside of Accra, most of the small-scale retail outlets are individual proprietorship operations that lack specialization. U.S. companies will require some presence in Ghana either through an agent, a distributor or a small business.

JOINT VENTURES/LICENSING

The Ghanaian Investment Code provides legislative encouragement for joint venture activities. However, joint venture arrangements with Ghanaian firms should carefully spell out areas of responsibility. Some local entrepreneurs operate under the impression that all costs will be borne by the foreign investor while expertise in selling to the local market is all that is required of them. Many potential local joint venture partners have little equity to offer and merely seek to capitalize on their knowledge of the local business environment.

ESTABLISHING AN OFFICE; THE GHANA INVESTMENT PROMOTION CENTER (GIPC)

All investors intending to invest in Ghana should first contact the Ghana Investment Promotion Center (GIPC). The GIPC is a government agency with two primary objectives: (1) the encouragement and promotion of investment in the Ghanaian economy, and (2) the coordination and monitoring of all investment activities.

One of the goals of the GIPC is to guide an entrepreneur through the local business registration process including handling the formalities to register, incorporate, modify or dissolve a local company. The GIPC was established under the Ghana Investment Promotion Center Act of 1994 as a one-stop shop for economic, commercial and investment information for entrepreneurs interested in starting a business or investing in Ghana. The GIPC utilizes databases, documentation, formal presentations, investment missions, country-specific investment fora and basic counseling services to carry out its activities. Under the GIPC Act of 1994, investment projects in all sectors of the economy, other than the mining and petroleum sectors, are free to establish without prior approval of the GIPC. Mining and petroleum sector projects have to be approved or licensed by the Minerals Commission and the Ghana National Petroleum Corporation.

The first step in the incorporation of a company is normally to ascertain from the Registrar of Companies whether the desired name is available. When this is cleared, a copy of the proposed regulations of the company must be delivered to the Registrar for registration. The regulations must contain the following: (1) the name of the company, (2) the nature of the business or the objects for which the business is being established, (3) the names of the first directors, and (4) the limits of the powers of the directors with regard to the provisions of the Code. The Registrar has five working days to complete the registration formalities if application documents are received in good order. Upon registration of the regulations, the Registrar certifies under his/her seal that the company is incorporated by awarding a Certificate of Incorporation, which makes the company a body corporate with legal identity. After registration of the business entity, business enterprises are free to implement their projects, import equipment and clear it through Customs, Excise and Preventive Services (CEPS).

The principal forms of business organizations do not differ too much from U.S.-based companies. Apart from state-owned enterprises, there are (1) companies, including branches of foreign firms, (2) partnerships and joint ventures, and (3) sole proprietorships. Under the Companies Code, a company can take any of the following forms: (1) limited liability company or a company having the liability of its members limited to the amount, if any, unpaid on the shares respectively held by it, (2) company limited by guarantee or a company having the liability of its members limited to such amount as the members may respectively undertake to contribute to the assets of the companies in the event of its being liquidated; and (3) an unlimited company or a company not having any limit on the liability of its members.

A company may be registered as a public or a private company. Every company with limited liability must include the word "Limited" as the last part of its name. All companies incorporated in Ghana must have at least one shareholder and two directors. The Act also requires all companies to file annual returns with the Registrar of Companies.

Prior to establishing a business entity in Ghana, it is advisable to consult a local attorney. The cost for the service and registering the business should not exceed USD 200. The Commercial Service maintains an up-dated list of attorneys in Ghana, several of whom have worked and/or studied in the United States.

7. Selling Factors/Techniques

Ghana maintains strong historical, cultural and economic links with Britain. Other major foreign investments are from Germany, China and India. However, there is an increasing demand for U.S.-made goods and a liking for things "American" in general. It is nonetheless important that U.S. companies establish and maintain a high level of personal contact within Ghana; it is generally not possible to mount a successful enterprise via telephone, email or fax contact alone.

Ghanaian values are very traditional, and this tendency extends to business dealings as well. People are extremely polite; it is customary to greet everyone you meet. Even a long-term partner or business contact is usually greeted with an exchange of pleasantries, followed by a handshake and inquiries about one's health, family and relatives. Never walk into a person's office or begin a telephone conversation without a greeting. The few newcomers who have made the mistake of beginning a conversation without the necessary greeting report being told by their host(s), "But you have not greeted me (us)." Ghanaians are often referred to as "the friendliest people on the continent." They are warm and receptive to outsiders, are very accommodating and will go the extra mile to be helpful. Ghanaians like regular, face-to-face contact and personal visits are warmly welcomed. While paying personal visits may not always be the most efficient or inexpensive method, it is generally regarded as the most effective method of handling new trade initiatives.

Although many Ghanaian businesspeople are well traveled and understand the Western saying "time is money," it is advisable for the business visitor to Ghana to adapt to a pace of business and life that is slower than in the U.S.

The Lebanese and Asian (primarily Indian) communities play an important role in business in Ghana. Many Lebanese businesspeople are third and fourth generation Ghanaian citizens, and while they may educate their children in Lebanon (and Britain) and travel there for business and recreation, they consider Ghana their home in a real sense.

ADVERTISING AND TRADE PROMOTION

There are more than a dozen advertising agencies in Accra. A few of the larger companies offer the full range of publicity and sales promotion services in the main population areas. Three of them, Lintas, Design & Display Publicity, and Media Majique are affiliates of American companies. While many of the smaller companies advertise themselves as "advertising" companies, they are engaged primarily in designing and printing. The Commercial Service can be of assistance in identifying suitable companies for brand representation and the identification of leading publications with general or specialized readership. There are also several companies that offer market research.

MAJOR NEWSPAPERS AND BUSINESS JOURNALS:

Daily Graphic Ghanaian Chronicle
Ghanaian Times The Financial Post
Business and Financial Times
High Street Journal

The first two publications, Daily Graphic and Ghanaian Times, are state-owned dailies and have the largest reach, while the others are privately owned and circulate in the metropolitan areas. Ghanaians own more than 2 million television sets and over 13 million radios, and are accustomed to consumer-oriented commercials and advertising, as well as public service announcements. With three free-on-air television networks currently being broadcast in the capital (G.T.V., TV3 and Metro TV), and over 20 pay-per-view networks rebroadcast by satellite, advertising through the media has taken a quantum leap. There are now over 49 FM radio stations throughout the country (up from only one in 1994), and these all feature regular advertisements. Suppliers of imported products are expected to provide advertising and promotional support, particularly if it is a new product or brand. As well as radio and television spots there are also posters, point of sale displays and billboards. Trade shows are an increasingly popular means of reaching the Ghanaian buyer. (See Chapter 12, Trade Events in Ghana.)

Packaging is important to the Ghanaian consumer. Eye-catching, colorful designs appeal to the consumer. Extended shelf life in a warm and humid environment is an important factor.

PRICING PRODUCT

Ghanaians tend to be very price conscious with respect to most purchases. Increasing sophistication is leading some buyers away from the low cost alternatives that result eventually in higher replacement costs. Costs should be computed on a CIF (Cost, Insurance and Freight) basis.

Local sources of commercial credit are extremely limited. Real interest rates on deposits are sometimes negative, giving individuals little incentive to hold savings in bank accounts. People prefer to hold cash, so that the amount of currency in circulation is large when compared with bank deposits. Domestic bank lending to the private sector is constrained by high interest rates. U.S. exporters are advised to utilize an irrevocable, confirmed letter of credit, especially if they are non-resident and new to the Ghanaian market.

The Commercial Service can help exporters formulate sound credit policies applicable to local markets and credit information on individual Ghanaian firms through the International Company Profile (ICP) program (see Chapter IV, 2 for details). Information about ICPs is also available through the Commercial Service district offices located in all 50 states and Washington, DC. Similar information can be obtained from private agencies.

SALES SERVICE/CUSTOMER SUPPORT

Goods sold in Ghana are frequently subjected to heavy use and are often not maintained in accordance with the manufacturer's recommendations. Service contracts, product recalls, and work performed under warranty are not widely familiar, but are becoming more and more commonplace.

There is a genuine interest in Ghana in trading with the U.S. Businessmen and women cite after-sales support and the high quality of American goods as reasons for the interest. High-tech or heavy industrial equipment such as computer hardware and software, telecommunications equipment, photocopiers, automobiles, air conditioning/refrigeration units, heavy mining and earth-moving equipment have all enjoyed reasonable success in the Ghanaian economy of late. Readable service manuals, frequent personnel training and an adequate inventory of spare parts are important for success in the Ghanaian market.

SELLING TO THE GOVERNMENT

Currently, there are varying procedures for selling to government. A unified code is, however, under preparation. Government is estimated to account for 50-70 percent of imports into Ghana. While the Ghana Supply Company (GSC) has historically acted as the principal purchasing agent of government, this authority has gradually been eroded as heads of departments are allowed to directly undertake purchases of supplies and equipment. The Ministry of Finance intervenes actively in the process of procurement of goods and works through the Central, Regional, and

District Tender Boards. For GSC purchases, a 45-day tendering period on procurement contracts being let is provided. The point of contact for GSC is

The Chief Executive
Ghana Supply Company
P.O. Box M 35
Accra
Tel: 233-21-228131
Fax: 233-21-668452

Special project implementation or management units are usually set up to implement projects funded with foreign aid, bilateral and multilateral funds. Purchases of goods and works are made in line with the funding agency's guidelines and those of the World Bank. Notice for tenders are usually put up in the major national dailies and some foreign newspapers. There is usually a nominal charge to purchase the bid documents.

The Ghana National Procurement Agency (GNPA), a state-owned entity, sometimes makes purchases on behalf of the government for items such as rice, sugar and edible oil. The point of contact for GNPA is

The Chief Executive
P.O. Box 15331
Accra-North
Tel: 233-21-228321; 228829; 228387
Fax: 233-21-221049

PROTECTING PRODUCT FROM INTELLECTUAL PROPERTY RIGHTS (IPR) INFRINGEMENT

The protection of intellectual property is an evolving area of law in Ghana but strides have been made in recent years to afford protection to a variety of intellectual property under both local and international law. Ghana is a member of the World Intellectual Property Organization (WIPO) and the English-speaking African Regional Industrial Property Organization (ESARIPO).

NEED FOR A LOCAL ATTORNEY

It is advisable to consult a local attorney to ensure that the company is following all the appropriate laws and procedures with regard to employment and other matters. There are a number of labor laws that regulate employer-employee relations in Ghana.

LEADING SECTORS FOR U.S. EXPORTS AND INVESTMENT

BEST PROSPECTS FOR NON-AGRICULTURAL GOODS AND SERVICES

1 - Telecommunications Equipment
2 - Computers and Peripherals
3 - Automobiles/Light Trucks/Vans
4 - Electrical Power Systems
5 - Construction and Earth Moving Equipment
6 - Mining Industry Equipment
7 - Food Processing and Packaging Equipment
8 - Hotel/Restaurant Equipment
9 - Travel and Tourism Services

The data below are estimates based on Ghana Statistical Service figures. Estimates for 2000 and 2001 take into consideration the direction of government policies, economic and political conditions and the views of market participants. All data are in millions of U.S. dollars.

TELECOMMUNICATIONS EQUIPMENT (TEL)

As a result of the GOG's liberalization of its telecommunications sector, annual growth has been significant. Imports are mainly for landline projects, private mobile telephone services, and broadband data transfer services. Major imports include switching and transmission equipment, telephone, and fax machines, radio and television equipment, and cellular radiotelephones.

The national network operators have programs underway to meet their performance targets under their licenses. The key competing countries are Japan, Malaysia, France, and the U.K. Demand is expected to rise in 2001 as result of a substantial credit received by Ghana Telecom for its expansion program.

	1999E	2000E	2001E
$M $M $M			
a. Total Market Size 97	54	68	
b. Total Local Production	0	0	0
c. Total Exports	0	0	0
d. Total Imports	97	54	68
e. Imports from the U.S.	10	12	15

COMPUTERS AND PERIPHERALS (CPT)

The market for computers continues to expand as government and businesses try to facilitate work and improve productivity. The main imports are desktop personal computers, floppy diskettes, printers, and monitors. The U.S. remains a major supplier in the computer equipment market in Ghana. Other suppliers are Japan, U.K., East Asian countries and, lately, South Africa.

A growing number of firms serve the Ghanaian hardware and software markets. Local assembling is growing as a way of becoming more price competitive. Improved local servicing capacity coupled with growth of offshoot activities including shareware, software design, computer graphics, and systems consulting spurs demand. There is a rising demand for used Pentium computers.

	1999E	2000E	2001E
	$M	$M	$M
a. Total Market Size	25	28	35
b. Total Local Production	0	0	0
c. Total Exports	3	3	4
d. Total Imports	28	31	39
e. Imports from the U.S.	10	12	15

The above statistics are unofficial estimates.

AUTOMOBILES/LIGHT TRUCKS/VANS (AUT)

Ghana has no significant domestic assembly of motor vehicles and thus relies exclusively on imports of these products. Used vehicles (5-10 years old) constitute about 70 percent of vehicles imported into Ghana. Effective June 1998, the GOG banned the importation of motor cars and commercial vehicles that are more than 10 years old, abolishing the penalty on older vehicles. There is a bill before Parliament to revise the age upward to 15 years.

Low-income levels make older cars more attractive. The general trend is toward vehicles with smaller engine (1200-1800cc) capacity and those that can run on liquefied gas. Under the new tax rates, they attract import duty of 5 percent plus a 12.5 percent VAT.

In the new vehicles market, U.S. cars are becoming very popular, as it is increasingly easier to obtain replacement parts. Right-hand steering motor vehicles are forbidden in Ghana.

	1999E	2000E	2001E
	$M	$M	$M
a. Total Market Size	437	299	300
b. Total Local Production	0	0	0
c. Total Exports	3	3	3
d. Total Imports	440	302	303
e. Imports from the U.S.	33	36	32

The above statistics are unofficial estimates.

ELECTRICAL POWER SYSTEMS (ELP)

The 1998 energy crisis brought in its wake the need to prepare to meet present and future energy demands. Present demand deficit is about 600MW. The GOG plans to increase generating capacity to 2600MW, primarily through gas-fired plants financed by independent power producers. Capital investment by the utilities is expected to help stimulate the market for generation, transmission, and distribution equipment.

Demand for electric generators is expected to decline owing to the improvement in the reliability of power supply from the electric utility. However, generators still form part of many households' as well as industry contingency plans.

	1999E	2000E	2001E
	$M	$M	$M
a. Total Market Size	45	42	40
b. Total Local Production	0	0	0
c. Total Exports	8	5	4

d. Total Imports	53	47	44
e. Imports from the U.S.	15	12	10

CONSTRUCTION AND EARTHMOVING EQUIPMENT (CON)

Earthmoving equipment is in demand for use in road construction, mining operations and in commercial and residential property development. Price and financing terms are key considerations for buyers where sales are not linked to external assistance programs. Reconditioned equipment has very good prospects, especially that which has easily obtainable replacement parts. Non-U.S. producers of construction and earthmoving equipment have been somewhat slow to enter the Ghanaian market, but there are indications that they are becoming more aggressive.

	1999E $M	2000E $M	2001E $M
a. Total Market Size	313	241	220
b. Total Local Production	0	0	0
c. Total Exports	0	0	0
d. Total Imports	313	100	108
e. Imports from the U.S.	50	30	28

The above statistics are unofficial estimates.

MINING INDUSTRY EQUIPMENT (MIN)

Although the mining sector continues to enjoy strong growth in Ghana, the slump in the world price of gold may lead to delayed purchases of some equipment. Gold extraction is the focus of most activity, but bauxite, manganese, salt, and diamonds are also being mined in Ghana. Ghana now produces over one million ounces of gold annually and is the second-largest producer in Africa. The industry leader, Ashanti Goldfields Corporation, was partially privatized in 1994. American, Australian and South African firms are also active in the Ghanaian gold mining industry.

U.S. suppliers face strong competition from Japanese, European, Australian, and South African manufacturers. U.S. products have, however, earned a reputation for high quality, reliability and good value.

	1999E $M	2000E $M	2001E $M
a. Total Market Size	50	35	32
b. Total Local Production	0	0	0
c. Total Exports	0	0	0
d. Total Imports	50	35	32
e. Imports from the U.S.	16	12	10

The above statistics are unofficial estimates.

FOOD PROCESSING AND PACKAGING EQUIPMENT (FPP)

New supermarkets and other food stores in the Accra/Tema and Kumasi areas have increased the available outlets for processed foods and thus increased demand for these items. There are numerous opportunities for the supply of equipment to canners and bottlers of beer, soft drinks, fruit juices and locally-produced fresh produce, particularly tomatoes and pineapples. Companies are eager to produce more attractive packaging for many consumer food products. The ability of local food processors to produce quality packaging is very limited and there is much room for improvement.

Major imports include fruit, cocoa, vegetable, and beverage processing equipment. Due to the relatively small market, small output capacity equipment is preferable. Local engineering firms can be good outlets for the sale of assembly components.

	1999E	2000E	2001E
	$M	$M	$M
a. Total Market Size	38	25	23
b. Total Local Production	0.3	0.4	0.5
b. Total Exports	0	0	0
d. Total Imports	37.3	24.6	22.5
e. Imports from the U.S.	8	6	6

The above statistics are unofficial estimates.

HOTEL/RESTAURANT EQUIPMENT (HTL)/HOUSEHOLD CONSUMER GOODS (HCG)/CONSUMER ELECTRONICS (CEL)

Construction of new hotels and restaurants to cater for the growing number of tourists and businesspeople coming to Ghana is the main factor driving demand. Currently, several major hotels are under construction and will supply an additional 2000 rooms when complete. This is expected to spur the demand for commercial refrigerators, ovens, dishwashers and display cabinets.

	1999E	2000E	2001E
	$M	$M	$M
a. Total Market Size	53	56	55
b. Total Local Production	5	4	3
c. Total Exports	2	3	3
d. Total Imports	50	55	55
e. Imports from the U.S.	10	8	8

The above statistics are unofficial estimates.

TRAVEL AND TOURISM SERVICES (TRA)

International travel and tourism is gradually emerging as a key services sector in the Ghanaian economy. Foreign exchange earnings from tourism increased from USD 81 million in 1990 to over USD 386 million in 2000. The number of tourists arriving in 2000 was about 400,000, and this is projected to rise. The GOG's program to market Ghana as the gateway to West Africa, and the use of Accra as host to major international conferences is expected to spur demand for airline and lodging services. To respond to the growing traffic of business travelers and holidaymakers to Ghana, there is a growing need for more travel and tourism-related businesses, such as tour and travel operators and management services, as well as investments in tourism infrastructure.

	1999E	2000E	2001E
	$M	$M	$M
a. Total Market Size	304	386	425

BEST PROSPECTS FOR AGRICULTURAL PRODUCTS

WHEAT

There is no cultivation of wheat in Ghana. All the wheat consumed in Ghana is imported, with about 95% of the imports coming from the U.S. and the rest from Canada and the EU. Almost every household in Ghana eats wheat (flour) in one form or another. It is eaten primarily as bread, which has recently become more of a staple food for Ghanaians. With population increases and a rising demand also for wheat bran for livestock and poultry, demand for the importation of wheat will be sustained. Total wheat milling capacity in Ghana is about 400,000 MT.

	1999E	2000E	2001E
MT MT MT ('000)			
a. Total Consumption	250	210	N/A
b. Total Local Production	0	0	0
c. Total Exports	0	0	0
d. Total Imports	250	270	N/A
e. Imports from the U.S.	220	250	N/A

MT ('000) = Thousand Metric Tons

RICE

Rice is cultivated in all the agricultural regions in Ghana. It is grown mainly in the valley bottoms, employing traditional farming practices. Modern scientific methods of rice cultivation through mechanization and irrigation are increasing gradually, particularly in the northern savanna zones and the Accra Plains of the Greater Accra Region. Nevertheless, local rice cultivation does not meet local demand. Rice is therefore imported to augment local production from Pakistan, Korea, India, Thailand, Japan and the USA, with imports from the USA accounting for about 65% of total imports. Ghanaian banks are usually reluctant to issue Letters of Credit to importers; hence, it is difficult to operate the USDA/CCC GSM-102 program for the importation of rice and other U.S. agricultural products from the U.S.

	1999E	2000E	2001E
MT MT MT (Millions)			
a. Total Consumption	300	350	N/A
b. Total Local Production	120	130	N/A
c. Total Exports	0	0	0
d. Total Imports	180	220	N/A
e. Imports from the U.S.	80	100	N/A

MT ('000) = Thousand Metric Tons

The above statistics are unofficial estimates.

FROZEN BEEF/CHICKEN/TURKEY

The cattle industry in Ghana is based mainly on extensive pastoral or free-range systems among subsistence farmers. The northern savanna zone accounts for the bulk of cattle production. Ineffective control of cattle diseases and the unavailability of veterinary drugs are the two major problems facing the cattle industry in Ghana. Poultry production in about 65 percent of the total market is mainly "backyard/Free Range", with a high chick mortality rate. Large quantities of meat, meat products and poultry parts are therefore imported into Ghana to satisfy local consumption.

Available figures from the Ministry of Food and Agriculture (MOFA) indicate that beef and dairy products account for about 68 percent of meat and animal products imported into Ghana. Chicken forms about 13 percent of the imports. The U.S. accounts for about 9 percent of beef imports, and 11 percent of dairy product imports, after France (22 percent), Holland (21 percent) and Poland (12 percent.) This is mainly due to higher shipping costs from the U.S.

	1999E	2000E	2001E
	MT	MT	MT (Millions)
a. Total Consumption	91	100	N/A
b. Total Local Production	55	65	N/A
c. Total Exports	0	0	0
d. Total Imports	36	35	N/A
e. Imports from the U.S.	3	15	N/A

Note: MT ('000) = Thousand Metric Tons

The above statistics are unofficial estimates.

SIGNIFICANT INVESTMENT OPPORTUNITIES

The GOG has divested itself of more than two-thirds of the more than 300 enterprises previously owned by the state. Some potentially attractive sectors hitherto considered to be strategic enterprises have not yet been privatized, but the Government has announced its intentions to do so. They include the oil refinery, power and water utilities, ports and railways, and banks. Government's monopoly on the export of cocoa was also removed in 1999 by allowing the private sector to participate in cocoa export.

Although some of the remaining companies have suffered from inadequate investment and their assets are obsolete, there are attractive opportunities in some sectors for American firms interested in entering the Ghanaian market. Poultry farms, fishing operations, mining companies, hotels and timber companies are included among the enterprises still to be sold. The Divestiture Implementation Committee (DIC) was established by the government to implement the divestiture policy.

The gold mining industry attracts significant foreign investment to Ghana. American, Canadian, Australian and South African companies are represented. The Minerals Commission is responsible for overseeing foreign investment in the mining sector. The GOG is directing attention on the domestic refining of gold and its use for jewelry.

Telecommunications and power generation are two additional sectors that may be of particular interest to potential investors. The liberalization of Ghana's telecommunications industry has created opportunities for providers of a variety of communications services. Ghana's growing electricity demand and the government's willingness to consider private sector solutions to this problem offers opportunity to independent power producers. Several major American companies are already active in this sector. Horticultural products, a wide range of agricultural products, electronics, value-added wood products, seafood and cosmetics could also offer significant investment opportunities to the American business community. Ghana's selection as one of the beneficiaries of the U.S. African Growth and Opportunity Act (AGOA) quota and duty free status opens the door to some investment opportunities, especially in the textile and apparel sector.

The Government of the United States acknowledges the contribution that outward foreign direct investment makes to the U.S. economy. U.S. foreign direct investment is increasingly viewed as a complement or even a necessary component of trade. American firms that have operations abroad sell roughly 60 percent of U.S. exports. Recognizing the benefits that U.S. outward investment brings to the U.S. economy, the United States undertakes initiatives such as Overseas Private Investment Corporation (OPIC) programs, investment treaty negotiations and business facilitation programs that support U.S. investors.

TRADE AND PROJECT FINANCING

THE BANKING SYSTEM

Ghana's formal banking sector comprises the central bank - the Bank of Ghana - nine (9) commercial banks, three (3) development banks, five (5) merchant banks and over one hundred rural unit banks. Until recently the sector was dominated by state-owned institutions and showed few signs of competition. Within the last three years, however, two state-owned banks have been privatized under the government's Divestiture Implementation Program, and others were recently advertised for divestiture. Non-banking financial institutions (NBFIs) comprise a Stock Exchange, 17 insurance companies, the Social Security and National Insurance Trust (SSNIT), three (3) discount houses, the Home Finance Company, numerous building societies, two venture capital company, a unit trust and 6 leasing companies. The Bank of Ghana is responsible for the overall regulation and supervision of the banking and financial services market.

COMMERCIAL BANKS

Ghana Commercial Bank Limited
Standard Chartered Bank Limited
Barclays Bank Limited
The Trust Bank Limited
SSB Bank Limited
International Commercial Bank Limited
Metropolitan and Allied Bank (Ghana) Limited
Stanbic Bank (Ghana) Limited
UniBank (Ghana) Limited

Commercial banks offer services such as current and savings accounts, telegraphic transfers, safe custody deposits, sale of traveler's checks and foreign transactions including the establishment of letters of credit.

DEVELOPMENT BANKS

Agricultural Development Bank Limited
National Investment Bank Limited
Prudential Bank Limited

MERCHANT BANKS

Merchant Bank (Ghana) Limited
Ecobank (Ghana) Limited
CAL Merchant Bank Limited
First Atlantic Merchant Bank Limited
Amalgamated Bank Ltd.

Merchant banks offer services such as acceptances, new issues, private placing and public offers of shares for sale, underwriting of new issues and offers of shares for sale, corporate finance and consulting services, registrar's services for public and private companies, stockbroking services, management of investment portfolios and leasing and hire purchase services.

FOREIGN EXCHANGE BUREAUS (FOREX)

Foreign exchange bureaus (known as Forex bureaus) are in operation throughout Ghana. The cedi can be exchanged for foreign currency at any Forex location.

HOW TO FINANCE EXPORTS/METHODS OF PAYMENT

The formal banking institutions have been unable to provide the needed intermediation between savers and investors. Demand deposits are the main source of funds for banks, and loans and advances account for a relatively small portion of their assets. High reserve requirements have prevented banks from building up their loan portfolios, and most banks have preferred the attractive and relatively risk-free returns from holding government securities.

The non-bank financial institutions (NBFIs) have yet to emerge as significant players in the financial system. That could change in the medium term with the introduction of new legislation for the sector. The contractual savings institutions have also undertaken a "safe" posture by investing in short-term government securities. Other than real estate, NBFIs have provided little medium- and long-term finance to the economy.

4. TYPES OF EXPORT FINANCING AND INSURANCE AVAILABLE

Traditional trade finance instruments such as letters of credit, collections, and funds transfer are available to the exporter. If a letter of credit is chosen, the exporter should require an irrevocable, confirmed letter of credit to ensure prompt, reliable payment.

The Export-Import Bank of the U.S. (EX-IM Bank) supports short- and medium-term programs for U.S. exports to Ghana. EX-IM Bank programs support the exports of products and services from the private sector that create American jobs. For a more detailed description on the mission of the agency, access the EX-IM Bank website at www.exim.gov.

The USDA's GSM-102 and GSM-103 Credit Guarantee Programs and Facility Credit Guarantee Program provide access to financing for imports of wheat, rice, feed grains, vegetable oil, protein meal, dairy products, as well as agricultural equipment. The payment guarantee to the U.S. exporter is for a minimum of 90 days and a maximum of one year.

Participating banks in the program are:

Agricultural Development Bank Limited
Barclays Bank Limited
CAL Merchant Bank Limited
Ecobank (Ghana) Limited
First Atlantic Merchant Bank
Ghana Commercial Bank Limited
Merchant Bank (Ghana) Limited
Standard Chartered Bank Limited
SSB Bank Limited

The limit for the West Africa region is USD 50 million. The GSM-102 and GSM-103 programs are generally available only to high quality importers with a good credit history and substantial assets with the guarantor bank. To date, support for the program on the part of Ghanaian banks has been lukewarm at best.

TYPES OF PROJECT FINANCING AVAILABLE

Several organizations offer project financing and insurance for exporters to Ghana. For example, the World Bank's International Finance Corporation (IFC) and the U.S. Overseas Private

Investment Corporation (OPIC) offer financing and insurance products to exporters. For a more detailed description on the mission of the agency, access the OPIC website at www.opic.gov.

The U.S. Trade and Development Agency (TDA) provides loans to U.S. businesses bidding for the GOG-sponsored procurement as well as funds for feasibility studies. For more information on the programs of the TDA, access their website at www.tda.gov. Also see chapter VIII 4 for U.S. EXIM financing.

GHANAIAN BANKS AND THEIR CORRESPONDENT U.S. BANKS

A few of the Ghanaian merchant and commercial banks have correspondent U.S. banks. Those banks include the following:

GHANAIAN BANK CORRESPONDENT U.S. BANK

Barclays Bank (Ghana) Limited Barclays Bank P.L.C., NY

Ecobank (Ghana) Limited Citibank, NY
Bankers Trust, NY

Standard Chartered Bank Limited Standard Chartered Bank of America

Ghana Commercial Bank Limited Morgan Guaranty Trust, NY
Citibank, NY
Chemical Bank, NY

SSB Bank Limited Citibank, NY
Chemical Bank, NY

Agricultural Development Bank Limited Citibank, NY
ABN-AMRO Bank, NY
Bankers Trust, NY

CAL Merchant Bank Limited Chemical Bank, NY
First Union National Bank, NJ

Merchant Bank (Ghana) Limited Citibank, NY
Union Bank of Switzerland, NY
Swiss Bank Corporation, NY

National Investment Bank Limited Chemical Bank, NY
Citibank, NY

Stanbic Bank Limited

UniBank (Ghana) Limited

SELECTED LAWS AND REGUALTIONS AFFECTING BUSINESS

INVESTMENT LAW

ESTABLISHMENT OF GHANA INVESTMENT PROMOTION CENTRE AND RELATED PROVISIONS

PART I - ESTABLISHMENT OF GHANA INVESTMENT PROMOTION

CENTRE AND RELATED PROVISIONS

Establishment of Centre

1. (1) There is established by this Act a body corporate to be known as the Ghana Investment Promotion Centre, referred to in this Act as the "Centre".

(2) The Centre shall have perpetual succession and a common seal and may sue and be sued in its corporate name.

1. The Centre shall have power for the discharge of any of its functions, to acquire and to hold movable and immovable property, to dispose of property and to enter into any contract or other transaction.

Object of Centre

2. (1) The object of the Centre is to encourage and promote investment in the Ghanaian economy.

(2) The Centre shall be the agency of government to co-ordinate and monitor all investment activities to which this Act applies.

Function of the Centre

3. For the purpose of section 2, the Centre shall have the following functions -

(a) initiate and support measures that will enhance the investment climate in the country for both Ghanaian and non-Ghanaian companies;

(b) promote investments in and outside Ghana through effective promotional means;

(c) collect, collate, analyse and disseminate information about investment opportunities and sources of investment capital, and advise upon request on the availability, choice or suitability of partners in joint-venture projects;

(d) register and keep records of all enterprises to which this Act is applicable;

(e) identify specific projects and invite interested investors for participation in those projects;

(f) initiate, organize and participate in promotional activities such as exhibitions, conferences and seminars for the stimulation of investments;

(g) maintain liaison between investors and Ministries, Government departments and agencies, institutional lenders and other authorities concerned with investments;

(h) provide and disseminate up-to-date information on incentives available to investors;

(i) assist incoming and existing investors by providing support services including assistance to procure authorities and permits required for the establishment and operation of enterprises;

(j) evaluate the impact of the Centre on investments in the country and recommend appropriate changes where necessary;

(k) register and keep records of all technology transfer agreements relating to investments under this Act; and

(l) perform such other functions as are incidental to the attainment of the object of this Act.

The Board of the Centre

4. (1) The governing body of the Centre shall be a Board which shall be responsible for the discharge of the functions of the Centre.

(2) The Board shall consist of -

(a) a Chairman;

(b) a Vice-Chairman;

(c) the Chief Executive of the Centre; and

(d) five other members at least three of whom shall be persons selected from outside the public services.

(3) The members of the Board shall be appointed by the President in consultation with the Council of State.

(4) The President shall in making the appointments under this section have regard to the expertise, knowledge and experience of the persons in matters relating to investments in Ghana.

(5) The Vice-Chairman shall be elected by the members from among their number; and where the Chairman is a person appointed from the public services, the Vice-Chairman shall be elected from the members appointed from outside the public services.

(6) A member of the Board other than the Chief Executive shall hold office for a term of four years and is eligible for re-appointment.

(7) A member of the Board may at any time resign his office in writing addressed to the President or may be removed from office by the President in consultation with the Council of State for stated reasons.

(8) Members of the Board shall be paid such allowances as the Minister responsible for Finance shall determine.

Meetings of the Board

5. (1) The Chairman shall preside at all meetings of the Board and in his absence the Vice-Chairman shall preside and in the absence of both the Chairman and Vice-Chairman, the members present shall elect one of their number to preside.

(2) The quorum for a meeting of the Board shall be four including the Chief Executive.

(3) The Board may co-opt any person to act as adviser at a meeting of the Board, except that a person co-opted does not have the right to vote on any matter before the Board for decision.

(4) The validity of the proceedings of the Board shall not be affected by a vacancy among its members or by a defect in the appointment or qualification of a member.

(5) Except as otherwise expressly provided for under this Act, the Board shall determine the procedure for its meetings.

Committee of the Board

6. The Board may for the discharge of the functions of the Centre appoint committees of the Board comprising members of the Board or non-members or both and may assign to them such function as the Board may determine except that a committee composed entirely of non-members may only advise the Board.

Chief Executive of the Centre

7. (1) The Centre shall have a Chief Executive who shall be appointed by the President acting in accordance with the advice of the Board given in consultation with the Public Services Commission.

(2) The Chief Executive shall hold office on such terms and conditions as the President may on the advice of the Board determine.

(3) Subject to such general directions as the Board may give, the Chief Executive shall be responsible for the day-to-day administration of the Centre and the implementation of the decisions of the Board.

The Secretary and other staff of Centre

8. (1) The Board shall have an officer to be designated the Secretary who shall perform the functions of keeping accurate records of proceedings and decisions of the Board and such other functions as the Chief Executive may direct.

(2) The President may acting in accordance with the advice of the Board given in consultation with the Public Service Commission, appoint for the Centre the Secretary and such other officers and employees as it may require for the effective implementation of its functions.

(3) The President may in writing delegate to the Board the power of appointment vested in him under subsection (2) of this section.

(4) The Board may engage such consultants and advisers as it may require for the proper and efficient discharge of the functions of the Centre.

Departments of the Centre

9. The Board may, on the recommendations of the Chief Executive, create such departments in the Centre as it may consider necessary for the efficient discharge of the functions of the Centre.

Responsibility for the Centre

10. The Centre shall be responsible to the President.

Expenses and Funds of Centre

11. (1) The Government shall provide to the Centre out of monies approved by Parliament such sums as may be necessary for the efficient discharge of the functions under this Act.

(2) The Centre may levy such fees and charges for its services as may be determined by the Board.

(3) All sums of money received on account of the Centre shall be paid into such bank accounts as may be determined by the Board.

(4) The Centre may with the approval of the Board invest as it considers fit any monies not required for immediate use.

Accounts and Audit of the Centre

12. (1) The Centre shall keep proper books of accounts and proper records in relations to the accounts and shall prepare at the end of each financial year within a period of six months after the end of the financial year, a statement of its accounts in such form as the Auditor-General may direct.

(2) The books of accounts of the Centre shall each year be audited by the Auditor-General or an auditor approved by him and a report on the audit shall be submitted to the Board.

Financial year of Centre

13. The financial year of the Centre shall be the same as the financial year of the Government.

Annual Report

14. (1) The Board shall submit to the President within two months after the receipt of the auditor's report, a report on the activities and operations of the Centre during the preceding year.

(2) The annual report of the Centre shall include -

(a) a copy of the audited accounts of the Centre together with the Auditor-General's report on it; and

(b) such other information as the President may request.

(3) The President shall through a Minister designated by him present to Parliament a report on the activities and operations of the Centre.

Relationship with other public authorities

15. All government departments, government agencies and other public authorities shall co-operate fully with the Centre in the performance of its functions under this Act.

Stationing of public officers at the Centre

16. Notwithstanding section 15 of this Act, the President may on the advice of the Board in writing request the Registrar-General, the Director of Immigration and the head of any government Department to station at the offices of the Centre such public officers as may be specified therein and the request shall be complied with.

PART II - PROVISIONS RELATING TO INVESTMENT

Application of Act

17. This Act does not apply to mining and petroleum enterprises.

Enterprises reserved for Ghanaians

18. The enterprises specified in the Schedule to this Act are reserved for Ghanaians and may not be undertaken by a non-Ghanaian.

Enterprises eligible for foreign participation and minimum foreign capital requirement.

19. (1) Except as provided in sections 17 and 18 and subject to this Act and any other law, a non-Ghanaian may invest and participate in the operation of any enterprise in Ghana.

(2) An enterprise in which foreign participation is permitted under subsection (1) of this section shall not be established or operated by a non-Ghanaian unless

(a) in the case of a joint enterprise with a Ghanaian partner, there is investment by the non-Ghanaian of foreign capital of not less than US$10,000.00 or its equivalent worth in capital goods by way of equity participation; or

(b) where the enterprise is wholly owned by a non-Ghanaian there is an investment of foreign capital of not less than US$50,000.00 or its equivalent worth in capital goods by way of equity capital.

(3) Notwithstanding subsection (1) of this section, in the case of a trading enterprise involving only the purchasing and selling of goods which is either wholly or partly owned by a non-Ghanaian, there shall be an investment of foreign capital or its equivalent in goods worth at least US$300,000.00 by way of equity capital and the enterprise shall employ at least 10 Ghanaians.

Export trading enterprises exempted

20. (1) The minimum capital requirement specified in section 19 shall not apply to -

(a) portfolio investments; or

(b) an enterprise set up solely for export trading.

(2) For the purpose of this section, "export trading" includes export of goods or produce that originate from Ghana.

Establishment of enterprises

21. (1) Subject to this Act, a person who intends to establish an enterprise to which this Act applies shall incorporate or register the enterprise in accordance with the Companies Code, 1963 (Act 179) or such other laws as are relevant to the establishment of the enterprise.

(2) On the submission of an application for the incorporation of an enterprise under subsection (1) of this section, the officers responsible for the incorporation and registration shall, where the documents of the applicant are in order, complete the processing of the application and issue the requisite certificate to the applicant within a period not exceeding five working days from the date of the submission of the application.

Registration of enterprises with the Centre

22. (1) An enterprise in which foreign participation is permitted under section 19 of this Act shall after its incorporation or registration be registered with the Centre.

(2) The Centre, shall, within five working days from the date of receipt of completed registration forms of the Centre register the enterprise where it is satisfied that -

(a) all relevant documents for registration are in order; and

(b) the minimum foreign equity capital requirement has been complied with.

Benefits and incentives

23. An enterprise shall be entitled to such benefits and incentive as are applicable to such enterprise under the Income Tax Decree 1975 (S.M.C.D. 5) and under Chapters 82, 84, 85 and 98 of the Customs Harmonised Commodity and Tariff Code scheduled to the Customs, Excise and Preventive Service Law, 1993 (P.N.D.C.L. 330) and any other law for the time being in force.

Exemption of non-zero

24. Any enterprise which desires to avail itself of the incentives provided under section 23 of this Act but whose plant, machinery, equipment or parts thereof are not zero-rated under the Customs Harmonised Commodity and Tariff Code scheduled to the Customs Excise and Preventive Service Law, 1993 (P.N.D.C.L 330) may submit an application for exemption of import duties, sales tax or excise duties on the plant, machinery, equipment or parts thereof to the Centre.

Incentives for special investment

25. For the purpose of promoting identified strategic or major investments, the Board may in consultation with such appropriate state agencies as the Board may determine and with the approval of the President, negotiate specific incentive packages in addition to the incentive provided under section 23 of this Act for such period as the Board may specify.

Priority areas

26. (1) The Board may, with the approval of the President, by legislative instrument, specify priority areas of investment and prescribe applicable incentives and benefits.

(2) Instruments issued under subsection (1) shall be signified under the hand of the Chairman of the Board or in his absence the Vice-Chairman.

Investment guarantees, transfer of capital, profits and dividends

27. Subject to this section an enterprise to which this Act applies shall be guaranteed unconditional transferability through any authorised dealer bank in freely convertible currency of -

(a) dividends or net profits attributable to the investment;

(b) payments in respect of loan servicing where foreign loan has been obtained;

(c) fees and charges in respect of any technology transfer agreement registered under this Act; and

(d) the remittance of proceeds (net of all taxes and other obligations in the event of sale or liquidation of the enterprise or any interest attributable to the investment.

Guarantee against expropriation

28. (1) Subject to subsections (2) and (3) of this section

(a) no enterprise shall be nationalized or expropriated by Government ; and

(b) no person who owns, whether wholly or in part, the capital of any enterprise shall be compelled by law to cede his interest in the capital to any other person.

(2) There shall not be any acquisition of an enterprise to which this Act applies by the State unless the acquisition is in the national interest for a public purpose and under a law which makes provision for -

(a) payment of fair and adequate compensation; and

(b) a right of access to the High Court for the determination of the investor's interest or right and the amount of compensation to which he is entitled.

(3) Any compensation payable under this section shall be paid without undue delay and authorization for its repatriation in convertible currency, where applicable, shall be issued.

Dispute settlement procedures

29. (1) Where a dispute arises between an investor and Government in respect of an enterprise, all efforts shall be made through mutual discussion to reach an amicable settlement.

(2) Any dispute between an investor and Government in respect of an enterprise to which this Act applies which is not amicably settled through mutual discussions may be submitted at the option of the aggrieved party to arbitration as follows: -

(a) in accordance with the rules of procedure for arbitration of the United Nation Commission of International Trade Law; or

(b) in the case of a foreign investor, within the framework of any bilateral or multilateral agreement on investment protection to which the Government and the country of which the investor is a national are parties; or

(c) in accordance with any other national or international machinery for the settlement of investment dispute agreed to by the parties.

(3) Where in respect of any dispute, there is disagreement between the investor and the Government as to the method of dispute settlement to be adopted, the choice of the investor shall prevail.

Immigration quota

30. (1) Every enterprise with a paid-up capital of
US$ 10,000.00 but less than US. $100,000 or its equivalent in cedis, shall be entitled to an initial automatic maximum immigrant quota of one person.

(2) Every enterprise with a paid-up capital of
US $100,000 but less that US $500,000.00 or its equivalent in cedis shall be entitled to an initial automatic maximum immigrant quota of two persons.

(3) Every enterprise with a paid-up capital of
US $500,000.00 or more or its equivalent in cedis shall be entitled to an initial automatic maximum immigrant quota of four persons.

(4) Except as provided in subsections (1), (2), and (3) of this section, all applications for immigrant quota with respect to an investment in Ghana shall be submitted to the Centre.

(5) An application submitted under this section shall be dealt with by the Immigration Service in consultation with the Centre.

Assistance to enterprise

31. The Centre shall provide to an enterprise such assistance and guidance as the enterprise may require and shall act as liaison between the enterprise and the relevant government departments, agencies and other public authorities.

Personal remittances

32. There shall be provided to expatriate personnel employed or engaged in an enterprise to which this Act is applicable, banking facilities through authorised dealer banks for making remittances abroad except that such remittances shall not exceed the total official wage of the expatriate personnel.

Technology transfer agreement

33. (1) A person who establishes an enterprise may enter into such technology transfer agreement as he considers appropriate for his enterprise.

(2) All technology transfer agreements entered into under subsection (1) shall be registered with the Centre.

(3) All technology transfer agreements shall be governed by any regulations for the time being in force relating to such agreements.

PART III - GENERAL PROVISIONS

Official secrecy and duty of public officers

34. (1) A person who in the course of his official duties in the administration of this Act has possession of or control over any document or information obtained under this Act and who communicates such document or information or any part of it to any other person to whom he is not authorised to communicate it by any enactment or by the Board commits an offence and is liable on summary conviction to a fine not exceeding ¢500,000 or to imprisonment for a term not exceeding one year or to both.

(2) A public officer who has a duty to perform under this Act and fails to perform that duty or performs the duty recklessly shall be liable to such disciplinary action as the Board or the appropriate disciplinary authority may determine.

Offences and penalty

35. (1) Every enterprise to which this Act applies shall permit an officer or a designated agent of the Centre to enter its premises at any reasonable time in pursuit of the monitoring function of the Centre.

(2) A person who without lawful excuse refuses to admit an officer or designated agent of the Centre on to the business premises of the enterprise or otherwise obstructs an officer or a designated agent of the Centre acting under subsection (1) of this section commits an offence and is liable on summary conviction to a fine not exceeding ¢2 million.

Repeal and Savings

36. The following enactments are repealed or revoked as the case may be -

Investment Code, 1985 (P.N.D.C.L. 116);

Investment Code (Amendment) Law, 1992 (P.N.D.C.L. 292);

Investment Code (Area of Special Priority) Instrument,1991 (L.I. 1519);

Investment Code (Immigrant Quota) Regulations, 1992 (L.I. 1543);

Selective Alien Employment Tax Decree. 1973 (N.R.C.D. 201);

Selective Alien Employment Tax (Amendment) Decree, 1974 (N.R.C.D. 248);

Selective Alien Employment Tax (Amendment) (No. 2) Decree, 1974 (N.R.C.D. 268);

Selective Alien Employment Tax (Amendment) Law, 1988 (P.N.D.C.L. 196);

The Import and Export Trade and Industry (Specification of minimum foreign capital investment by non-Ghanaian citizens) Act, 1980 (Act 402)

Transtitional Provisions

37. (1) Notwithstanding the repeal of the Investment Code, 1985 (P.N.D.C.L. 116) any agreement executed under it and in force immediately before the commencement of this Act shall continue in force as if made under this Act.

(2) Any application pending before the Ghana Investments Centre established under the Investment Code, 1985 (P.N.D.C.L. 116) shall confer benefits previously enjoyed under the agreement before the commencement of this Act be deemed to be pending before the Centre established under this Act.

(3) Any agreement continued in force by virtue of subsection (1) of this section shall confer benefits previously enjoyed under the agreement before the commencement of this Act and also such other benefits as may be applicable to the enterprise under this Act.

(4) Where an enterprise in existence immediately before the commencement of this Act has duly complied with the Investment Code, 1985 (P.N.D.C.L. 116) in relation to any, minimum equity requirement or employed capital specified in that Code, the enterprise shall be deemed lawful notwithstanding any provision of this Act to the contrary.

(5) All immigrant quota in existence immediately before the coming into force of this Act in respect of an enterprise to which this Act is applicable shall continue in force until expiration or unless renewed under this Act.

(6) All technology transfer agreements registered with the Ghana Investment Centre shall be deemed to be registered with the Centre established under this Act.

Transfer of assets, liabilities and staff

38. (1) All assets, rights, obligations and liabilities of the Ghana Investments Centre established under the Investment Code, 1985 (P.N.D.C.L. 116) and in force immediately before the coming into force of this Act, are transferred to the Ghana Investment Promotion Centre established under this Act.

(2) All persons employed by the Ghana Investments Centre immediately before the coming into force of this Act shall, on the coming into force of this Act be deemed to have been duly appointed under this Act.

Regulations

39. (1) The Board may by legislative instrument make regulations -

(a) providing for anything that is to be prescribed under this Act;

(b) relating to technology transfer;

(c) generally for carrying out the principles and object of this Act;

(2) Any instrument issued under subsection (1) shall be under the signature of the Chairman of the Board or in his absence that of the ViceChairman.

Interpretion

40. In this Act unless the context otherwise requires -

"benefits" includes facilities, entitlements and exemptions conferred on an enterprise to which this Act applies;

"capital" means all cash contributions, plant, machinery, equipment, buildings, spare parts, raw materials and other business assets other than goodwill;

"direct investment" means investment made to acquire a lasting interest in an enterprise operating in the economy of Ghana and intended to give the investor an effective control in the management of the enterprise;

"enterprise" means an industry, project, undertaking or business to

which this Act applies or an expansion of that industry, undertaking, project or business or any part of that industry, undertaking, project or business and where there is foreign participation means such an enterprise duly registered with the Centre;

"foreign capital" means convertible currency, plant, machine, equipment, spare parts, raw materials and other business assets other than goodwill that enter Ghana with no initial disbursement of Ghana's foreign exchange and are intended for the production of goods and services related to an enterprise to which this Act is applicable;

"foreign loan" means loan obtained from outside Ghana and denominated in any currency other than the currency of Ghana;

"Ghanaian" means any citizen of Ghana or any company, partnership or association or body (whether corporate or unincorporate) the majority capital or financial interest in which is owned by citizens of Ghana and includes the State and a statutory corporation;

"indirect investment" means any act or contract whereby an investor makes a contribution, whether tangible or intangible, to an enterprise in Ghana without obtaining an equity interest in the enterprise but is entitled to returns based on profits generated by the enterprise;

"investment" includes direct and indirect investments and portfolio investments;

"Government" means the Government of the Republic of Ghana;

"market" means a public or open place established by local custom or by the appropriate local government council for the purpose of buying and selling and any other public place used substantially for that purpose;

"mining" includes any operation for exploration, prospecting, winning or obtaining of minerals, precious metals or precious stones;

"own" in relation to an enterprise, includes the holding of any proprietary interest in the enterprise;

"Petroleum" means crude oil or natural gas or a combination of both;

"Portfolio investment" means an investment in shares or bonds which are mandatorily convertible into share or other securities traded on the Ghana Stock Exchange.

"Technology transfer agreement" means an agreement relating to an enterprise to which this Act applies that involves:

(i) the assignment, sale or use of foreign patents, trademarks or other industrial property rights.

(ii) the supply of foreign technical know-how or technological knowledge;

(iii) foreign technical assistance, design and engineering, consultancy or other technical services in whatever form they may be supplied.

(iv) foreign managerial, marketing or other services.

except that an agreement shall not be regarded as a technology transfer agreement for the purposes of this Act if its duration does not exceed a period of eighteen months.

TRAVEL TO GHANA

IMPORTANT INFORMATION FOR TRAVEL

LOCATION:
Ghana is located on the West Coast of Africa, along the Gulf of Guinea, and is boarded by Cote d'ivoire, Togo and Burkina Faso. The Country covers an area of 238,305km2.

CAPITAL:
The Capital is on the Greenwich Meridian (zero line of longitude) with a population of 3 million.

CLIMATE:
Northern Ghana has a rainy season from about April to October. The rest of the year is hot and dry with temperatures up to 38oC. In southern Ghana the rains last from April to June and again from September to October. Generally temperatures are between 21o and 32oC.

AIRPORT:
Kotoka International Airport is situated 12km from Accra city centre. Domestic Airports are located at Kumasi,(Ashanti Region), Sunyani, (Brong Ahafo Region) Tamale, (Northern Region). Hotel shuttle buses and taxis are available.

TRAVEL DOCUMENTS AND VISAS:
A valid passport is required by all visitors and visa except for citizens of ECOWAS states. These can be obtained from the nearest Ghanaian diplomatic missions and consulate. Group visas for tourist may be issued at entry to Ghana if prior arrangements were concluded between the Tour Operator, the **Ghana Tourist Board (GTB)** and the Ghana Immigration Service.

For further details, contact:
The Director,
Ghana Immigration Service,
Box M. 53,
Ministries Post Office,
Accra-Ghana.
Tel: 224445 Fax: 777401.

HEALTH:
Visitors must be in possession of a current medical certificates showing vaccination against Yellow Fever.

CUSTOMS:
Tourist can bring in personal items duty free, but for details of trade goods and specialist equipment please contact the

Customs, Excise and Preventative Service:
Box 68, Accra, Ghana.
Tel: 666845/668274
or the nearest Ghanaian diplomatic mission.

CURRENCY:
Ghana's currency is the cedi (¢) which is equal to 100 pesewas. It comes in ¢500, ¢1000 and ¢5000 bills. Coins come in the denominations of ¢10,¢20, ¢50, ¢100, ¢200, ¢500.

Rates of exchange are posted daily by banks and forex bureaux. There are no restrictions on the amount of foreign currency that can be brought into Ghana. This must however, be stated on the currency form.

BANKING:
Banks and forex bureaux are available at the airport and in all main towns.

BANKING HOURS:
Monday-Thursday - 0830-1400
Friday - 0830-1500

COMMERCIAL HOURS:
Monday-Friday - 12.30 - 1330-1700

PHOTOGRAPHY:
Ghana is a photographers paradise with so many spectacular sights. However, as an expression of courtesy always seek people's consent before taking pictures of them. Photographic equipments should be declared to customs on arrival.

PEOPLE AND LANGUAGE:
The official language of Ghana is English, although many other languages like Twi, Fante, Ga, Ewe, Hausa and Dagbani are spoken.

RELIGION:
The main religious groups in Ghana are Christian, Muslim, and those who follow traditional faiths. Places of worship are found all over the Country.

MEDICAL FACILITIES:
Good medical facilities are found in all the cities and major towns.

ELECTRICITY:
Electrical supply is normally 200-220 volts.120 volts appliances will require an adaptor.

COMMUNICATIONS:
The IDD code for Ghana is +233. Telephone fax and telex services are available in all main towns, and hotels.

TRANSPORT:
Good roads reach most parts of Ghana, and long distance buses, tro-tros (local minibuses) and taxis are widely available.

There is a rail service between Accra, Kumasi and Takoradi. The Volta Lake Transport Company has a lake transport service from Akosombo in the south to Buipe Port in the north.

There are two international seaports at Tema and Takoradi.

SHOPPING:
Ghana is a great place to shop. Local Ghanaian fashion is world-renowned and Ghana is the home of authentic Kente cloth. Shops in the main towns are filled with jewellery, leather goods and basketware.

The markets are places to buy excellent handicrafts and drums, and souvenirs of every description. A great opportunity to practice your bargaining skills.

EXPORTATION OF HANDICRAFTS:
Anybody wishing to export antiques must obtain a certificate from the Museums and Monuments Board.

However the underlisted items can be exported without permit:- textiles (print, Kente, accessories), wooden objects (wood carvings of contemporary products), Basketry/other woven articles, pottery and ceramics items of contemporary products metal works of contemporary design and manufacture; art object art work of contemporary design and production.

For enquiries, contact :
The Director,
National Museums and Monuments Board,
P. O. Box 7343,
Accra.

DRIVING:
Ghana drives on the right, a current international driving licence is required.

PUBLIC HOLIDAYS:

New Year's Day	January 1
Independence Day	March 6
Good Friday	March/April
Easter Monday	March/April
Eid il Fitr	February
Eid il Adza	April
May Day	May 1
Republic Day	July 1
Farmers Day	1st Friday in Dec.
Christmas Day	December 25
Boxing Day	December 26

WHAT TO WEAR:
Light cotton clothing is preferable. A jacket and tie may be required for business meetings.

TRADITIONAL COURTESIES:
Ghanaians are a conservative people and respect traditional courtesies.A handshake, using the right hand is the acceptable greetings.

Visitors to remote villages or shrines should visit the local elder, taking a small gift such as a bottle of local schnapps.

1. SUNSHINE IN PLENTY
Ghana has a tropical climate with moderate temperatures, constant breeze and clear, continuous sunshine most of the year. Temperatures range is 21-32oC in the South and 22-36oC in the North.

2. BEAUTIFUL, UNSPOILT
SANDY BEACHES Along the length of its Atlantic Coast are miles of palmfringed historic forts and castles built in the 15th and 18th centuries by Europeans trading in gold and slaves.

Beach resorts are being put up to cater for the growing market for beach tourism in Ghana.

3. A RICH AND UNIQUE CULTURE
Ghana offers the best of sights and sounds in the form of tropical forests, savannah, wildlife parks, festivals, cocoa farms, local dishes, costume and music. Our colourful kente cloth and traditional African wear are an added attraction.

4. HISTORICAL FORTS, CASTLE AND MONUMENTS
Ghana's golden coastline along the Gulf of Guinea is unique in Africa for the number of ancient forts and castles built by the various European nations - initially by the Portuguese and later by the Swedes, Dutch, Danish, British and Prussians.

Two of these are a "must see". The Elmina Castle built by the Portuguese in 1482 and the Cape Coast Castle built by the Swedes in 1653 which houses the West African Historical Museum.

5. FASCINATING WILDLIFE AND VEGETATION
Ghana has a varied plant and wildlife system ranging from the dense tropical rain forest in the Southwest through deciduous forest in the middle belt to dry savannah country in Northern Ghana, where the Mole National Park provides sanctuary to Antelopes, monkeys, elephants, lions, kobs, leopards and many more wildlife.

The Kakum National Park near Cape Coast is a tropical rain forest with a canopy walkway enabling one to have a better view of the flora and fauna in there.

6. HOSPITALITY
The Ghanaian traditional Hospitality is proverbial. As a country that has enjoyed political stability for a long time, its citizens the are most friendly in Africa.

Ghana is indeed safer than most if not all other African countries you've been to or heard of.

GHANA ATTRACTIONS

HISTORICAL GHANA

Formerly Gold Coast, Ghana became independent from Britain on March 6, 1957, the first black African colony to achieve independence. Ghana occupies the pinnacle spot in Pan-African history having lit the torch for African Emancipation and became home to famous Pan-Africanists such as W.E.B. Du Bois and George Padmore. Dr. Kwame Nkrumah whose mausoleum adds to Accra's landscape was Ghana's first President.

European power struggles between the 15th and 19th centuries started with the Portuguese who built Elmina Castle in 1482 followed by the Dutch, Swedes, Danes, Prussians and the British looking for fortunes in gold and ivory.

This intense commercial rivalry ended with the growth of the tragic trade in slavery - all 42 European castles and fortifications being used as dungeons for the millions who lost their lives or whose descendants compose the African diaspora today. Cape Coast Castle, one of the best preserved, is becoming an official museum of the Slave Trade.

- Over 30 forts and castles including Elmina and Cape Coast Castles are recognized by UNESCO as World Heritage Monuments.
- Sites of wars between the British and the indigenous population especially the Ashanti peoples.
- The Mausoleums of great Pan-Africanists like Dr. Kwame Nkrumah and Dr. W. E. B. Du Bois; memorials to George Padmore and others.

THE CASTLES OF GHANA

The forts and castles along the coast of Ghana date back to the 15th Century and were built and occupied at different times by European traders and adventurers from Portugal, Spain, Denmark, Sweden, Holland, Germany and Britain to safeguard trading posts.

Several of them changed hands on numerous occasions in bloody battles or by treaty, and all have a fascinating history.

Today, some have been restored and have a variety of uses while some are in ruins. Most are open to the public.

1. ANKOBRA - Fort Eliza Cathargo - Built by the Dutch in 1702; only traces of ruins are now visible.
2. AXIM - Fort S. Antonio - Portuguese trading post, 1502. Destroyed by the townspeople in 1514. Second fort built by the Portuguese on present site in 1515.
3. BEYIN - Fort Appolonia - Dutch lodge 1660. British Fort built between 1750 and 1770. Reconstructed between 1962 and 1968.
4. PRINCESS TOWN - Groot-Friedrichsburg or Fort Hollandia - Danish lodge 1658, fort built in 1683.
5. TAKRAMA - Fort Sophie Louise Lodge built by Brandenburgers in 1690, English fort 1691. Present day: Only the foundations are visible.
6. AKWIDA - Fort Dorothea - Built by Brandenburgers, 1685. Present day: ruins.
7. DIXCOVE - Fort Metal Cross. The fort on the bay (Dick's or Dickies Cove). Work commenced in 1683. Restored 1954-66.
8. BUTRI - Fort Batensteyn - Swedish post 1650-2. Dutch fort built, 1656.

9. SEKONDI - Fort Orange. Built by the Dutch probably in 1640.

10. Shama - Fort St. Sebastian. Built as a Dutch lodge in 1526. Portuguese Fort built in 1590. Restored 1954-7.

11. KOMENDA - Fort Vredenburg - English trading post 1663.

12. ELMINA - Fort St. Jorge. Portuguese reached Elmina (Del Mina) in 1471. Built by Portuguese, 1482. First European fort on the Gold Coast, improved before 1500.

13. ELMINA - For St. Jago (Conraadsburg). Chapel built between 1555 and 1558 by the Portuguese. Turned into a lodge and watch tower. Restored 1956-60.

14. ELMINA - Watchtower. Presumably Dutch but of unknown date, restored in 1956.

15. CAPE COAST -Cape Coast Castle. Built as a lodge by the Dutch in 1630 on an abandoned lodge built earlier by the Portuguese. Extensively rebuilt before 1757-80. Present day: Cape Coast Castle Museum.

16. CAPE COAST- Fort Victoria- Built by the English in 1702.

17. CAPE COAST- Fort William - Built by the British 1819-20.

18. CAPE COAST- Fort MacCarthy - Built by the British 1822.

19. MOURIE (Near Cape Coast)-Fort Nassau. Dutch post, 1598. Dutch fort built 1612.

20. ANOMABU - Fort William. Built by the Dutch 1640. Restored 1954.

21. KORMANTSE - Fort Amsterdam. Dutch trading post 1598. Dutch Lodge built 1631, fort rebuilt by the English in 1645.

22. AMOKU (near Ankaful, Saltpond). French post built 1786.

23. TANTUM - English post intermittently occupied from 1662. English fort built in 1724

24. APAM - Fort Leydsaemheyt (Fort Patience). Built by the Dutch, 1696-1702.

25. SENYA BERAKU - Fort Geodehoop (Good Hope) Dutch Fort established, 1667.

26. ACCRA - Fort James. It is likely that there was a Portuguese lodge in the middle of the 16th century (probably by 1576).

27. ACCRA - Fort Crevecoer (Ussher Fort). Dutch post built in 1642.

ACCRA- Christianborg Castle. A Portuguese fortified house,1500. Swedish lodge built in 1652. Rebuilt and used as a residence of the British Governor of Gold Coast, 1877-1957. Residence of Prime Minister of Ghana and renamed Government House, Osu, 1957. Became the official residence of Dr. Nkrumah (President), 1960 and has since remained the seat of government. Frequently rebuilt with additions in recent years. Not open to the public.

29. TESHIE - Fort Augustaborg. Dutch post built in 1730-40.

30. PRAMPRAM - Fort Vernon British post in 1740.

31. ADA - Fort Kongenstein. Portuguese trading place, 16th century.

32. KETA - Fort Prinsenstein. Danish post established c.1714

GREATER ACCRA REGION

- **The National Museum**

Located on Barnes Road, this fine museum houses a fascinating collection of Ghana's historical treasures.

- **Independence Square**

The venue for many national celebrations, dominated by the Independence Arch and the memorial to the Unknown Soldier.

- **Accra International Conference Centre**

Its 1600-seater plenary hall is the most important meeting venue in Ghana, and often plays host to important international gatherings.

- **The National Theatre**

The distinctive architecture of this modern building encompasses an important national centre for the performing arts.

- **The Du Bois Memorial Centre for Pan-African Culture**

A source of inspiration to many, this Centre now houses a research library and gallery of manuscripts, as well as the grave of this famous African-American scholar and his wife.

- **The George Padmore Research Library of African Affairs**

A famous research and educational centre for African-American studies.

- **Kwame Nkrumah Mausoleum**

This is the last resting place of the first President of Ghana, and a famous pan-Africanist.

- **Osu Castle**

Formally known as Christianborg Castle and built in 1659, by the Danes it has been the seat of Government since the early 1920s. It is the official residence of the Government of Ghana and not open to the public.

- **Accra Zoo**

A small, but fascinating, collection of many birds and animals indigenous to Africa, now part of an ongoing conservation programme.

- **Centre for National Culture**

The Centre's arts and crafts bazaar and traditional textile market is the best place in Accra to find traditional handicrafts from all over Ghana.

- **University of Ghana - Legon**

Ghana's premier centre of higher education, it was founded in 1948. Set in beautiful gardens, including a striking botanical garden, it also houses the School of Performing Arts and the Balme Library.

- **Kokrobite Beach Resort**

25km west of Accra, Kokrobite is also home to the Academy of African Music and Arts.

- **The Markets of Accra**

Amongst the most famous markets of Accra are Makola market located on Kojo Thompson Road, and the Osu Night Market, where market stalls are illuminated by hundreds of lanterns and candles.

- **Shai Resource Reserve**

The conservation area in the Shai Hills is part of Ghana's commitment to the preservation of its natural heritage and wildlife.

- **Ada Popular Resort**

Ada Popular resort area is a favourite base for watersports and game fishing.

ATTRACTIONS & EXCURSIONS IN THE ASHANTI REGION

Kumasi and the Asante heritage Kumasi is the capital of the Asante kingdom and the local highlights are:

- **The Crafts of the Asante**

The craft villages surrounding Kumasi include:

- Bonwire - 18km NE of Kumasi - Kente Weaving
- Pankronu - 3km N of Kumasi - pottery
- Ahwiaa - 6km N of Kumasi - wood carvings
- Ntonsu 10km from Kumasi -Adinkra cloth making

- Asuofia/Asamang-Barakese Road - beadmaking
- Ampabame Krofrom - 10km from Ahodwo-brass smiths Goldsmiths and Silversmiths can be seen in Kumasi
-

The Natural Attractions of Ashanti

The Ashanti Region is great for its unexplored unspoilt natural attractions. For birds and butterflies the forests are the place to go, while wildlife can be spotted around the lakes and in the nature reserves.

The following locations are great for trekking, or just rewarding forest walks:

- Lake Bosomtwe - 35km S of Kumasi
- Bobiri Forest Reserve - 35km SE of Kumasi
- Owabi Bird Sanctuary -23km NW of Kumasi
- Bomfobiri Wildlife Sanctuary - 50km from Kumasi
- Digya National Park - From Kumawu to Atebubu
- Atwia Rock Formations - 40km from Kumasi
- Mframabuom Caves-Kwamang, 55km from Kumasi
- Obuasi Gold Mines

For details of visits to the Ashanti Gold Mine - available on Tuesdays and Thursdays - contact the P.R. Manager on (233-0582-494).

The Cultural Attractions of the Asante

The traditional culture of the people is one of the attractions of the Ashanti Region. Important illustrations can be discovered at:

- Asantemanso Village
- Kumanwu Town
- Kentinkronu Shrine
- Adarko Jachie Shrine
- Ejisu Besease Shrine
- Statues of Kumasi
- Patakro Shrine

ATTRACTIONS & EXCURSIONS IN THE VOLTA REGION

Lake Volta Estuary

The estuary is an area of great scenic beauty, with river and ocean beaches, and picnic spots shaded by palm trees. The sand bars are the nesting grounds for sea birds, and endangered species of turtle are still found here.

The Keta-Angaw Lagoon Basin

Important wetlands and breeding grounds for migratory birds. Tafi Monkey Village The sacred monkey sanctuaries around Tafi Atome, some 5km away from the Avatime Hills.

The Waterfalls of the Volta Region

Although some may be seasonal, all are set in attractive wooded or mountain settings.

- **Wli Falls** - 20km from Hohoe, in the Wli Nature Reserve
- **Tagbo Falls** - Liate Wote
- **Tsatsadu Falls** - 10km from Hohoe
- **Aflambo Falls** - Leklebi
- **Amedzofe-Gbadzeme Falls**

Kalakpa Game Production Reserve

At Abutia Kloe, 15km from Ho, the reserve has increasing species of migratory and indigenous birdlife, buck, buffalo and monkeys.

Kyabobo National Park

A newly designated national park in the foothills of Mt. Djebobo, on the border with Togo.

Grottos and Caves

In the limestone hills, the grottos and caves are dramatic. Not to be missed are:

- The ancestral caves of Likpe - 14km from Hohoe
- The grottos of Kpando - Agbehoe and Aziavi
- The caves of Nyagbo and Logba
- Caves and iron mining - Akpafu

HISTORICAL SITES

Fort Prinzenstein, Keta

- Cape St. Paul Lighthouse, Woe

German historical sites at Kpando, Ho, Amedzofe, Kpedze

ATTRACTIONS & EXCURSIONS IN THE WESTERN REGION

- **The Castles of the Western Region**

The Western Region is another region with a rich heritage demonstrated by the number of castles still open to visitors.

The best examples in the region are:

- Fort St. Appolonia at Beyin
- Fort Metal Cross at Dixcove (1693)

- Fort Batensteyn (1656) at Butri
- Fort Groot Friederichsburg at Princess Town
- Fort S. Antonio at Axim (1515)
- Fort Dorothea (ruins) at Akwida
- Fort Sebastian at Shama

- **The Village on Stilts of Nzulezu**

An amazing village where life goes on in the centre of Lake Tadane, just 90km west of Takoradi. The houses are built on stilts, and traditional village life adapts to the watery conditions.

The excursion from Beyin involves a walk through the reeds at the lake's edge, and a trip in a dugout canoe to the village. The village welcomes visitors every day except Thursday, which is a sacred day.

- **Akatekyi Crocodile Pond**

Akatekyi Crocodile Pond 30km West of Takoradi, the local fetish priest entices the crocodiles from the water with a live chicken. Bring a bottle of schnapps for the libation. Visitors are welcome every day except Wednesdays, a sacred day.

- **The Beaches of the Western Region**

The Western Region is famous for some of the best beaches in Ghana. Just the right spot to relax after a tour.

Some of the most popular are:

- Busua Pleasure Beach - only 5km from Fort Metal Cross
- Sports Club Beach - behind the Atlantic Hotel in Takoradi
- Ajua Beach-just 200 metres from Dadowa Lagoon
- Princess Town Beach - off the Takoradi/Elubo highway
- Miamia Beach - a secluded beach with rocky coves, perfect for picnics

---

- **The Mines of Western Region**

The Western Region has several mines that may be visited, by prior arrangement.

The main sites are:

- Tarkwa Goldmines - founded in the 1800s just 92km north-west of Takoradi
- Nsuta Manganese Mine-20km south-east of Tarkwa and

Prestea Goldmines - 40km north of Tarkwa

MAJOR FESTIVALS IN GHANA

FESTIVAL	PLACE	PERIOD

Akwasidae	Manhyia, Kumasi	Every six weeks
DipoKrobo	Odumase	February
Gologo	Talensi, Tong-Zuf	March
Aboakyer	Winneba	1st Sat. in May
Asafotufiam	Ada	July/August
Damba	Tamale, Wa	July/August
Bakatue	Elmina	1st Tues. in July
Fetu Afahye	Cape Coast	1st Sat in September
Kobine	Lawra	September
Homowo	Accra	August/September
Kundum	Axim, Takoradi	August/September
Odwira	Akropong	September
Apoo	Wenchi/Techiman	October
Hogbetsotso	Anloga	1st Sat in November
Mmoaninko	Ofinso	November
Fiok	Centime	December
Fao	Navrongo	January

MAJOR INTERNATIONAL EVENTS IN GHANA

No.	Event	Date (1998-2000)	Venue	Remarks
1	Black History Month	Feb. '98	Accra, Ghana	-
2	6th Ghana international trade fair	Feb. 27-March 9 1998	Accra, Ghana	A general fair on all sectors.
3	Grand Sales '98	July/August 1998	Accra, Ghana	A generalised fair to boost internal trade.
4	Ghana Transport Fair	September 1998	Accra, Ghana	A specialised fair on transport
5	2nd Ghana International Book Fair	November 1998	Accra, Ghana	A specialised fair on books, printing and related machinery

6	Masqueraders Festival	Jan 1999	Cape Coast, Ghana	-
7	2nd ECOWAS FAIR	Feb - March 1999	Accra, Ghana	A generalised fair for the sub-region
8	Grand Sales '99	July/August 1999	Accra, Ghana	A good generalised fair to boost internal trade
9	Computech '99	September 1999	Accra, Ghana	A specialised fair on information and technology
10	7th Ghana International Trade Fair	Feb/March 2000	Accra, Ghana	A generalised fair on all sectors
11	Grand Sales '2000	July/August 2000	Accra, Ghana	A generalised fair to boost internal trade.
12	3rd Ghana International Book Fair	November 2000	Accra, Ghana	A specialised fair on books printing and related machinery.

SUPPLEMENTS

GHANA AND U.S. CONTACTS

KEY COUNTRY CONTACTS IN GHANA

MINISTRIES AND OTHER GOVERNMENT OF GHANA ENTITIES

Ministry of Trade and Industry
P.O. Box M47
Ministries,Accra
Hon. Dr. John Abu, Minister
Tel: 233-21-665421/663327
Fax: 233-21-668263

Ministry of Finance & Economic Planning
P.O. Box M.40
Ministries, Accra
Hon. Kwame Peprah, Minister
Tel: 233-21-665421/665441
Fax: 233-21-667069

Ministry of Foreign Affairs
P.O. Box M.53
Ministries, Accra
Hon. James Victor Gbeho, Minister
Tel: 233-21-664008
Fax: 233-21-664008

Ministry of Tourism
P.O. Box 3106
Ministries, Accra
Hon. Mike Gizo, Minister
Tel: 233-21-666049/666314/666426
Fax: 233-21-662375

Ministry of Roads & Transport
P.O. Box M. 57
Ministries, Accra
Hon. Edward Salia, Minister
Tel: 233-21-666465
Fax: 233-21-667114

Ministry of Mines and Energy
P.O. Box 40
Stadium, Accra
Hon. Ferdinand Ohene-Kena, Minister
Tel: 233-21-667151-3, 667090
Fax: 233-21-668262

Ministry of Works & Housing
P.O. Box M.43
Ministries, Accra
Hon. Isaac Adjei-Mensah, Minister
Tel: 233-21-662242/667689
Fax: 233-21-663268

Ministry of Employment & Social Welfare
P.O. Box M.84
Ministries, Accra
Hon. Mohammed Mumuni, Minister
Tel: 233-21-665349
Fax: 233-21-667251

Ministry of Food and Agriculture
P.O. Box M.37
Ministries, Accra
Hon. J. H. Owusu-Acheampong, Minister
Tel: 233-21-663036
Fax: 233-21-663250

Ministry of Communications
P.O. Box M.41
Ministries, Accra
Hon. John Mahama, Minister
Tel: 233-21-662772
Fax: 233-21-664067

Ghana Investment Promotion Center
P.O. Box M193
Accra
Mr. Kwesi Ahwoi - Executive Director
Tel: 233-21-665125/9
Fax: 233-21-663801
E-mail: gipc@ghastinet.gn.apc.org

Customs, Excise and Preventive Service
P.O. Box 68, Accra
Dr. Charles Asembri, Commissioner
Tel: 233-21-666841/2/662123
Fax: 233-21-660019

Divestiture Implementation Committee
P.O. Box C102, Cantonments, Accra
Mr. Emmanuel A. Agbodo, Executive Secretary
Tel: 233-21-772049/773119/760281
Fax: 233-21-773126
E-mail: dicgh@ncs.com.gh

Ghana Free Zones Board
Ministry of Trade & Industry Annex
P.O. Box M.47, Accra
Mr. George Aboagye, Executive Secretary

Tel: 233-21-780532/3/4/5/7
Fax: 233-21-780536
E-mail: freezone@africaonline.com.gh

Ghana Supply Commission
P.O. Box M 35, Accra
The Chief Executive
Tel: 233-21-228131
Fax: 233-21-668452

Ghana National Petroleum Corporation (GNPC)
Private Mail Bag, Tema
Mr. Tsatsu Tsikata, Chairman
Tel: 233-22-206020/204654/202823
233-21-774234 (Accra)
Fax: 233-21-232039
E-Mail: gnpc@ghana.com

Minerals Commission
P.O. Box M.248, Accra
Mr. Kofi Ansah, Chief Executive
Tel: 233-21-772786/779823/4
Fax: 233-21-773324

TRADE ASSOCIATIONS & CHAMBERS OF COMMERCE

American Chamber of Commerce (Ghana)
P.O. CT 2869
Cantonments, Accra
Ms. Kathleen Boohene, Executive Secretary
Tel: 233-21-763834, 028-215372
Fax: 233-21- 771426
E-mail: amchamgh@ghana.com
Website: http://www.amcham-africa.org

Ghana National Chamber of Commerce
65 Kojo Thompson
P.O. Box 2325, Accra
Mr. Ato Ampiah, President
Tel: 233-21-662-427
Fax: 233-21-662-210

The West African Enterprise Network
West Africa Headquarters
SSNIT Tower Block, 5th Block
P.M.B., Ministries Post Office
Accra
Tel: 233-21-780186
Fax: 233-21-669100
E-Mail: ababio@ghana.com

Private Enterprise Foundation
P.O. Box C1671, Cantonments - Accra

Mr. Kwesi Abeasi, Director General
Tel: 233-21-222313/231488
Fax: 233-21-231487

Ghana Chamber of Mines
Minerals House
No. 10, 6th Street
Airport Residential Area - Accra
Mr. John Bentum-Williams, Executive Director
Tel: 233-21-760652,761893
Fax: 233-21-760653
Email: chamine@ghana.com

Association of Ghana Industries (AGI)
Trade Fair Center
P.O. Box 8624, Accra-North
Dr. J. A. Addison, President
Tel: 233-21-777-283/775-311, ext. 697/723
Fax: 233-21-773143

Ghana Export Promotion Council
P.O. Box 146, Accra
Mr. Tawia Akyea, Executive Director
Tel: 233-21-228-813/30
Fax: 233-21-668-263

Ghana Stock Exchange
P. O. Box 1849, Accra
Mr. Yeboa Amoa, General Manager
Tel: 233-21-669908/669914/669935
Fax: 233-21-669913
E-Mail: stockex@ncs.com.gh

U.S. EMBASSY TRADE PERSONNEL

Ambassador Kathryn Dee Robinson
Ms. Denise Mathieu, Deputy Chief of Mission
Mr. Robert Merrigan, Economic/Commercial Officer
Ms. Chrish Kresge, Commercial Specialist (U.S. Dept. of Commerce)
Mr. Eric K. Adotey, Economic/Commercial Specialist
Ms. Abena Aidoo, Commercial Assistant/Librarian
Mr. Yaw Asante-Kwabiah, Agricultural Specialist

The local mailing address is:

Embassy of the United States of America
Ring Road East
P. O. Box 194
Accra, Ghana
Tel: (233-21) 775348/775297/775298
Fax: (233-21) 776008

The Commercial Service
c\o The United States Information Service (USIS)
Liberation and Castle Roads
P. O. Box 2288
Accra, Ghana
Tel: (233-21) 235096 (Direct)
229179 (Switchboard)
Fax: (233-21) 235096 or 776008
E-mail: comserv@ghana.com

OR:
The Foreign Agricultural Service
Ring Road East
Embassy of the United States
P. O. Box 194
Accra, Ghana
Tel: (233-21) 775348/775297/775298
Fax: (233-21) 778033
E-mail: fasaccra@ncs.com.gh

The Diplomatic Pouch address is:

Embassy of the United States of America
Accra - Department of State
Washington, DC 20521-2020

BANKS AND FINANCIAL INSTITUTIONS

COMMERCIAL BANKS

Commercial banks offer services such as current and savings accounts, telegraphic transfers, safe custody deposits, sale of traveler's checks and foreign transactions, including the establishment of letters of credit.

Ghana Commercial Bank Ltd.
P.O. Box 134
Accra
Tel: 233-21-666140
Fax: 233-21-662168

Standard Chartered Bank Ltd.
P.O. Box 768
Accra
Tel: 233-21-664591/9
Fax: 233-21-667751

Barclay's Bank Ltd.
P.O. Box 2949
Accra
Tel: 233-21-667392
Fax: 233-21-667420
The Trust Bank Ltd. (Formerly Meridien BIAO Bank)
P.O. Box 1862

Accra
Tel: 233-21-230486/665562/665605
Fax: 233-21-665710

Social Security Bank Ltd.
P.O. Box 13119
Accra
Tel: 233-21-667146/667147/667148
Fax: 233-21-668651

Agricultural Development Bank Ltd.
P.O. Box 4191
Accra
Tel: 233-21-662836
Fax: 233-21-662803

Bank for Housing and Construction Ltd.
P.O. Box M.1
Ministries Post Office, Accra
Tel: 233-21-220163
Fax: 233-21-229631

National Investment Bank Ltd.
P.O. Box 3726
Accra
Tel: 233-21-669301/662629
Fax: 233-21-669307

Cooperative Bank Ltd.
P.O. Box 5992
Accra
Tel: 233-21-228735/229438
Fax: 233-21-222292

Prudential Bank Ltd.
P.O. Box C628
Cantonments, Accra
Tel: 233-21-226322
Fax: 233-21-226803

International Commercial Bank Ltd.
P.O. Box 20057
Accra
Tel: 233-21-666190/663429/665779/669572
Fax: 233-21-668221

MERCHANT BANKS

Merchant banks offer services such as acceptances, new issues, private placings and public offers of shares for sale, underwriting of new issues and offers of shares for sale, corporate finance and consulting services, registrar's services for public and private companies, stockbroking services, management of investment portfolios and leasing and hire purchase services.

Merchant Bank Ghana Ltd.
P.O. Box 401
Accra
Tel: 233-21-666331
Fax: 233-21-667305

Ecobank Ghana Ltd.
Private Mail Bag
Accra
Tel: 233-21-229926/233-28-212020
Fax: 233-21-231934

CAL Merchant Bank Ltd.
P.O. Box 14596
Accra
Tel: 233-21-231098/231095/231912
Fax: 233-21-231104/231913

First Atlantic Merchant Bank Ltd.
P.O. Box C16120
Cantonments, Accra
Tel: 233-21-231433/231435
Fax: 233-21-231399

Metropolitan and Allied Bank Ltd.
P.O. Box C1778
Cantonments, Accra
Tel: 233-21-232774
Fax: 233-21-232728

For corresponding U.S. banks, see Chapter VIII, section 6.

PRINT MEDIA

Ghanaian Times
New Times Corporation
P.O. Box 2638
Accra
Tel: 233-21-228282 (6 lines)
Fax: 233-21-229398/220733
E-mail: newtimes@ghana.com

Daily Graphic
The Graphic Corporation
P.O. Box 742
Accra
Tel: 233-21-228903/228911/228938/228927
Fax: 233-21-234754
E-mail: graphic@ghana.com

Ghanaian Chronicle
General Portfolio Limited
Private Mail Bag
Accra-North
Tel: 233-21-232713/227789/232608
Fax: 233-21-232608
E-mail: chronicl@africaonline.com.gh
Website: www.ghanaian-chronicle.com

Business Chronicle
General Portfolio Limited
Private Mail Bag
Accra-North
Tel: 233-21-232713/227789/232608
Fax: 233-21-232608
E-mail: chroncl@africaonline.com.gh
Website: www.ghanaian-chronicle.com

Business & Financial Times
Strategic Development Associates
P.O. Box 2157
Accra
Tel: 233-21-223334/233-27-540404
Fax: 233-21-223334
E-mail: bft@ighmail.com

The Statesman
Kinesic Communications
P. O. Box 846
Accra
Tel: 233-21-233242
Fax: 233-21-233242

High Street Journal
Sheik Investments Ghana Ltd.
P.O. Box 588
Achimota
Tel/Fax: 233-21-500125
E-mail: hsjaccra@ghana.com

The Financial Post
Post Publications Limited
P.O. Box AN 8377
Accra-North
Accra
Tel: 233-21-223012/238038-9
Fax: 233-21-238038
E-mail: tfnpost@africaonline.com.gh

Contact Information for Advertising on Radio and TV:

TV

Ghana Broadcasting Corporation
P.O. Box 1633
Accra
Tel: 233-21-221107/221161
Fax: 233-21-221149/221153

Metro TV
P.O. Box C1609
Cantonments, Accra.
Tel: 233-21-765700/238590-1
Fax: 233-21-765703/234797
E-mail: metrotv@ighmail.com

TV3 Network
P.O. Box M. 83
Accra
Tel: 233-21-228697/763457-8
Fax: 233-21-228629

RADIO

Radio GAR (95.7 FM)
Ghana Broadcasting Corporation
P. O. Box 1633
Accra
Tel: 233-21-221147/97
Fax: 233-21-221163
E-mail: gar@ighmail.com

Radio Gold (90.5 FM)
Network Broadcasting Company Limited
P. O. Box 17298
Accra
Tel: 233-21-311977/300281/2/3
Fax: 233-21-300284
E-mail: radiogold@africaonline.com.gh
Website: www.radiogold90.5fm.com

Radio Joy (99.7 FM)
Multimedia Broadcasting Company Limited
P.O. Box 17202
Accra
Tel: 233-21-233558/233559/233560
Fax: 233-21-224405
E-mail: joyfm@ghana.com
Website: www.joy997fm.com.gh

Radio Choice (102.3 FM)
P.O. Box CT 3032
Cantonments, Accra
Tel: 233-21-760124
Fax: 233-21-773612

E-mail: choicefm@ghana.com
Website: www.choicefm.com

INTERNET SERVICE PROVIDERS

Africaonline Ghana Ltd.
2nd Floor, Rose Plaza
Kaneshie Industrial Area
P.O. Box 11241
Accra North
Tel: 233-21-226802
Fax: 233-21-226849
www.africaonline.com.gh

Internet Ghana
Kekulasi Court, Faanofa Road
P.O. Box 6745
Accra-Adabraka
Tel: 233-21-220622, 300385
Fax: 233-21-235836
www.internetghana.com
administrator@ighmail.com

Network Computer Systems Ltd. (NCS)
7 Sixth Avenue Ridge
P.O. Box PMB
Accra-Osu
Tel: 233-21-220622,238218,225472,773372,231191

For a good webpage on doing business in Ghana, plus rebroadcasts of all three Ghanaian TV networks on the internet, try going to www.ghanaclassifieds.com
The best webpages on tourism in Ghana are www.ncrc.org.gh and www.landtours.com

ADVERTISING AND BILLBOARDS

Dapeg Limited
P.O. Box 7398
Accra
Tel: 233-21-224677/227401
Fax: 233-21-302663
E-mail: dapeg@africaonline.com.gh

Design & Display Publicity Ltd.
19 Ring Road East, Osu
P.O. Box 5504
Accra-North, Accra
Tel: 233-21-777827
Fax: 233-21-774205
E-mail: argon@ghana.com

Icon Communications
P.O. Box C878
Cantonments, Accra
Tel: 233-21-232371-2/244405, Fax: 233-21-232336

Lintas Ghana Ltd.
Osu - Ako Adjei Park
P. O. Box 1262
Accra
Tel: 233-21-772321/772324/772481
Fax: 233-21-772498
E-mail: APLINTAS@ighmail.com

Media Majique & Research Systems
2nd Crescent Street, Asylum Down
P.O. Box 5893
Accra-North, Accra
Tel: 233-21-231604/226631
Fax: 233-21224062
E-mail: mmrs@ghana.com

MULTILATERAL FINANCIAL INSTITUTIONS

World Bank Field Office
Mr. Peter Harrold, Country Director
69 Dr. Isert Road
North Ridge Residential Area
Accra
Tel: 233-21-229681, Fax: 233-21-227887
E-mail: charrold@worldbank.org

IFC Liaison Office
150A Roman Road
Roman Ridge, Accra
Tel: 233-21-778109/779804-5/761152
Fax: 233-21-776245
E-mail: ifcghana@ghana.com

Africa Project Development Facility Satellite Office
150A Roman Road
Roman Ridge, Accra
Tel: 233-21-778109/779804-5/761152
Fax: 233-21-776245
E-mail: apdf@ghana.com

MARKET RESEARCH FIRMS

Boulders Advisors Limited
No.5, 2nd Dade Walk - Labone
P. O. Box C3664
Cantonments - Accra
Mr. Reginald N. France
Tel: 233-21-775516/771248

Fax: 233-21-771249
E-mail: boulders@ghana.com

CME Consulting Services
P. O. Box 9789
Airport - Accra
Mr. Y. Osafo Marfo
Tel: 233-21-773217/776013
Fax: 233-21-773740

Databank Financial Services Ltd.
5th Floor SSNIT Tower Block
P.M.B., Ministries, Accra
Mr. Ken Ofori-Atta, Chairman
Tel: 233-21-669417/669421/669110/665124
Fax: 233-21-669100
E-Mail: databank@africaonline.com.gh

Deloitte, Haskins & Sells
4, Liberation Rd.
P.O. Box 453, Accra
Mr. Joe Forson, Managing Partner
Tel: 233-21-775355/774169/773761
Fax: 233-21-775480
E-mail: deloitte@africaonline.com.gh

J.S. Addo Consultants
P. O. Box 9820
Airport - Accra
Mr. J.S. Addo
Tel: 233-21-669342
Fax: 233-21-226803

KAB Marketing Associates
1st Floor, Glemin House, Osu
P.O. Box 01854, Osu - Accra
Mr. Kofi Adom-Boakye
Tel: 233-21-302850
Tel: 233-27-557132/557512
Fax: 233-21-773279

Media Majique & Research Systems
P.O. Box 5893, Accra-North
Mr. Reginald Laryea
Tel: 233-21-226631/231604
Fax: 233-21-224062
E-mail: mmrs@ghana.com

Peat Marwick, Okoh & Co.
Mobil House, Liberia Rd.
P.O. Box 242, Accra
Mr. E.O. Asiedu, Partner
Tel: 233-21-664881-4

Fax: 233-21-667909
E-mail: asiedu@kpmg.africaonline.com.gh or kpmg-gh@kpmg.africaonline.com.gh

Plan Consult
P. O. Box C1367
Cantonments - Accra
Mr. Ebow Bannerman
Tel: 233-21-669165
Fax: 233-21-667141
E-mail: plancons@africaonline.com.gh

PriceWaterhouseCoopers
4th Floor, Gulf House, Legon Rd.
P.O. Box C1535, Cantonments, Accra
Ms. Victoria Cooper, Resident Partner
Mr. Felix Addo, Resident Partner
Tel: 233-21-506217/506218/776027
Fax: 233-21-506216/772137
E-mail: pwc@ghana.com

Research International Ghana Ltd.
Osu Ako Adjei Park
P.O. Box 1262, Accra
Mr. Attafuah, Technical Director
Tel: 233-21-776637/761141-3
Fax: 233-21-776711
E-mail: righana@ghana.com

Research Marketing Services
Mr. W. A. Krosah, Managing Director
Tel: 233-21-779731/2
Fax: 233-21-773928

WASHINGTON, D.C. CONTACTS FOR GHANA:

U.S. GOVERNMENT AGENCIES

U. S. Department of Commerce
International Trade Administration/Office of Africa
14th Street and Constitution Ave., NW
Washington, DC 20230
Mr. Douglas Wallace, Desk Officer - Ghana
Tel: (202) 482-4388
Fax: (202) 482-5198
E-mail: Douglas_Wallace@ita.doc.gov

The Trade Information Center (TIC)
Department of Commerce
Office of Export Promotion Coordination
International Trade Administration
14th Street and Constitution Ave., N.W. HCHB 7424
Washington, DC 20230
Tel: (202) 482-0543

Fax: (202) 482-4473
Website: http://www.ita.doc.gov/tic

Multilateral Development Bank Operations
Ms. Janet Thomas, Acting Director
Tel: (202) 482-3399
Fax: (202) 482-5179

U.S. Department of Agriculture
U.S. Foreign Agricultural Service
Trade Assistance and Promotion Office
14th and Independence Avenue, NW
Washington, DC 20250-1052
Tel: (202) 720-7420
Fax: (202) 690-4374 or 205-9728
E-mail: tapo@fas.usda.gov
Website: http://www.fas.usda.gov

U.S. Department of State
Africa Bureau-AF/W
Room 4250
John Olson, Desk Officer - Ghana
Washington, DC 20520
Tel: (202) 647-3391
Fax: (202) 647-4855

U.S. Department of Treasury
1500 Pennsylvania Avenue, NW
Washington, DC 20220
Mr. Ed Barber
Office of the Assistant Secretary of Int'l Affairs
IDB Room 5400
Tel: (202) 622-1231
Fax: (202) 622-1228

U.S.A.I.D. (United States Agency for International Development) AFR/ONI
Mr. Douglas Jerry Brown,
Agribusiness Advisor
1111 N. 19th Street, Rm. 210
Rosslyn, VA 22209
Tel: (703) 235-9082
Fax: (703) 235-5423

Overseas Private Investment Corporation (OPIC)
Mr. Sam Smoots, Regional Manager, Investment Development
Ms. Edith Quintrell, Regional Manager, Insurance
1100 New York Avenue, NW
Washington, DC 20527
Tel: (202) 336-8799
Fax: (202) 336-8700

U.S. Trade and Development Agency
Mr. John Richter, Regional Director for Africa

1621 N. Kent Street
Suite 300
Arlington, VA 22209-2131
Tel: (703) 875-4357
Fax: (703) 875-4009
E-mail: info@tda.gov

Web: www.tda.gov

Export Import Bank of the United States (EXIMBANK)
Ms. Annmarie Emmet
Coordinator for Africa
811 Vermont Avenue, NW, 7th Floor
Washington, DC 20571
Tel: (202) 566-8008
Fax: (202) 566-7524
E-mail: Annmarie.Emmet@exim.gov

TPCC Trade Information Center
Tel: (800) USA-TRADE

U.S. BASED MULTILATERAL FINANCIAL INSTITUTIONS

The World Bank
1818 H Street, NW
Washington, DC 20433
Tel: (202) 477-1234
Fax: (202) 477-6391

The International Finance Corporation
1818 N Street, NW
Washington, DC 20433
Tel: (202) 477-1234
Fax: (202) 477-3112

Multilateral Investment Guarantee Agency (MIGA)
1818 H Street, NW
Washington, DC 20433
Tel: (202) 473-3075
Fax: (202) 872-1521

Africa Growth Fund
1850 K Street, NW, Suite 390
Washington, DC 20006
Tel: (202) 293-1860
Fax: (202) 872-1521

The Corporate Council on Africa
1660 L Street, NW, Suite 301
Washington, DC 20036
Tel: 202-835-1115
Fax: 202-835-1117

LIST OF RECOMMENDED HOTELS

ACCOMMODATION IN GHANA

Ghana offers a wide range of hotel accommodation for her growing economy and tourist industry: Ghana's hotels are classified according to the international star-system with 5-stars as the highest and one-star being the minimum internationally acceptable quality. In addition, there are local budget hotels with minimum acceptable standards of sanitation and comfort. Only hotels with Ghana Tourist Board's license displayed are to be patronized.

REGION	NAME	LOCATION	ADDRESS	NO. OF ROOMS	NO. OF BEDS	GRADE	TARIFFS	¢
GREATER	La Beach Hotel	La	Box 1, Trade Fair	104	106	4-Star	Single	$240
ACCRA			Tel : 772501				Double	$270
			Fax : 772520				Twin	$270
	Golden Tulip Hotel	Cantonments	Box 16033 Airport-Accra	183	183	4-Star	Single	$192
			Tel : 775360				Double	$215
			Fax : 775361				Suite	$280
							Chalets	$3,000
								$4,000
								Per/Mnth
	Novotel, Accra	Accra-Central	Box 12720, Accra-North	181	180	4-Star	Single	$140
			Tel : 667546	(178)			Double	$160
			Telex: 233 2532 GX	Ops			Suite	$290
			Fax :233-21 667533					
	Hotel Shangri-La	Airport	Box 9201 K. I. A.	52	52	3-Star	Single	$100
		Residential	Tel : 777500/776993				Double	$132
		Area	Telex : 2561 GX				Twin	$154

			Fax : 774873					
	Hotel Wangara	Labone	Box 6565, Accra-North	50	93	3-Star	Single	$100
			Tel : 772525: 772438				Double	$135
			Fax : 23321 772438				Twin	$135
							Suite	$175
	Kingsby Hotel	New Achimota	Box 5496, Accra-North	57	99	3-Star	Double	$50
			Tel : 400742				Twin	$50
			400891				Suite	$80
	Mariset Plaza	Osu Ako-Adjei	Box 0608, Osu	19	23	3-Star	Single	$70+15%
			Tel : 774434				Double	$77+15%
							Twin	$75+15%
			Fax : 772085				Suite	$100+15%
	Nogahil Hotel	Achimota	Box C511, Cantonments	12	24	3-Star	Double	$105
			Tel : 500121/22				Suite	$135
			Fax : 501002					
	Paradise Beach Hotel	Ada Foah	Box 66, Ada Foah	44	48	3-Star	Single	$55
			Tel : (0968) 275/276/277				Double	$65
			Telex : 275				Suite	$120
	Secaps Hotel	Tetteh	Box 1176, Accra	28	34	3-Star	Single	$81
		Quarshie	Tel :				Double	$105

			500206/209					
		Circle						
	Apex Hotel	Kpehe	Box 53, G.P.O,Accra	10	18	2-Star	Double	45,000.00
			Tel : 229456/231908				Twin	50,000.00
	Courtesy Int. Hotel	Tema C.10	Box 4181, Tema	15	20	2-Star	Double	47,300.00
			Tel : 4152/712929	13			Suite	57,300.00
				(Ops)				
	Capital Court	Tesano	Box 7279, Accra-North	10	13	2-Star	Double	$45
	Hotel		Tel : 230845/6	7			Twin	$50
			Fax : 230835	(Ops)				
	El Elyon Hotel	Osu	Box C. 2416, Cantonments	16	21	2-Star	Double	$65
			Tel : 774421				Twin	$80
			Fax : 776343				Suite	$95
				ROOMS	BEDS			
GREATER	Ebis Hotel	Dzorwulu	Box 1903, Accra-North	15	15	2-Star	Single	$60
ACCRA			Tel : 775343/761846				Double	$75
			Fax: 774880					$85
	Granada Hotel	Airport	Box 6250, Accra-North	35	59	2-Star	Double	$50
		Residential	Tel : 775343				Suite	^$80
			Fax: 774880					

	Gye Nyame Hotel	Asylum Down	Box 8820, Accra-North	22	37	2-Star	Single	$35
			Tel : 223321				Double	$42
			223211				Twin	$50
			Fax : 233-21 226486				Suite	$60
	Holiday Hotel	Airport West	Box 8457, Accra-North	15	22	2-Star	Double	$60
		Res. Area	Tel : 773660				Twin	$70
			Fax : 233-21 773432				Suite	$80
	Hotel Salleria	Odorkor	Box 1459, Kaneshie	18	20	2-Star	Single	15,000.00
			Tel : 229672					20,000.00
			Fax: 229672				Double	28,000.00
							Suite	35,000.00
	Hotel de Joko	New Achimota	Box PMB, Accra	30	40	2-Star	Single	48,300.00
			Tel : 400413					57,000.00
			Fax : 302541				Double	69,000.00
							Twin	80,000.00
	Kaysens Executive	Tema Comm. 10	Box C. 927, Cantonments	10	20	2-Star	Single	40,250.00
			Tel : 302715/4362				Double	46,250.00
			Fax : 022 4262				Suite	69,500.00
	Korkdam Hotel	New Achimota	Box 4605, Accra	21	33	2-Star	Single	46,000.00
			Tel : 400423/400916				Double	51,750.00

			Fax: 400259				Twin	57,000.00
	King David Hotel	Kokomlemle	Box 10323, Accra-North	18	21	2-Star	Double	56,000.00
			Tel : 225280/229832					64,000.00
			Telex : D. K.266					
	Maglab Hotel	North Odorkor	Box 490, Kaneshie	11	22	2-Star	Twin	$60
			Tel : 229832/225280					
	Maple Leaf Hotel	New Achimota	Box 3787, Accra	31	51	2-Star	Double	74,000.00
			Tel : 400185					
			Fax : 400949					
	Mariset International	Airport	Box 0608, Osu	16	19	2-Star	Double	40,000.00
	Hotel	Residential	Tel : 775922	(14)			Twin	40,000.00
			Fax : 773198	OPS			Suite	48,000.00
	Miklin Hotel	East Legon	Box 17181, Accra	37	34	2-Star	Single	$60
			Tel : 500708	22			Double	$80
				(Ops)				
	Nick Hotel,	Tema C. 6	Box 11105, Tema	10	10	2-Star	Single	$42
			Tel : (0221) 4594				Double	$46
				ROOMS	BEDS			
GREATER	North Ridge	North Ridge	Box 1365.	27	50	2-Star	Single	$72

	Hotel		Accra					
ACCRA			Tel : 225809/230935				Double	$78
			Fax : 221417					
	Oak Royal Hotel	Tema Comm. 6	Box 1532, Tema	10	14	2-Star	Single	54,000.00
			Tel : 6926/6515				Double	58,000.00
			Fax : 6515					
	Parker House Hotel	North Odorkor	Box 18139 Airport, Accra	20	20	2-Star	Single	40,250.00
			Tel : 301705/4000078				Double	46,000.00
			Fax : 400133					
	Penta Hotel	Osu, R.E.	Box 7354, Accra-North	30	39	2-Star	Single	$50
			Tel : 775429				Double	$55
			Telex :2646				Suite	$70
			Fax : 773418					
	Sanaa Lodge	Tesano	Box 6461, Accra-North	30	52	2-Star	Double	$65
			Tel : 220443				Twin	$80
			Fax : 227494				Suite	$80
	Sherwood Park Hotel	Labone	Box 1111, Accra-North	10	14	2-Star	Single	$65
			Tel : 773881/773882				Double	$75
							Suite	$85
	Sunlodge Hotel	Tesano	Box 6909, Accra-North	12	20	2-Star	Single	42,000.00

			Tel : 229758/229795				Double	50,000.00
			Telex : 775524				Suite	70,000.00
	Sunrise Hotel	North Ridge	Box 2287, Accra	19	24	2-Star	Single	$71
			Tel : 224575				Double	83
			222201				Suite	$95
			Telex : 2469					
	Sunspot Hotel	Airport Rest. Area	Box 0165, Osu	14	19	2-Star	Single	36,000.00
			Tel : 773322	(12)			Double	42,000.00
				Ops			Twin	50,000.00
							Suite	50,000.00
	SSNIT Guest House	Ringway Estates	Box M. 149	18	22	2-Star	Single	86,400.00
			Tel : 226228/225366				Twin	104,000.00
			Fax : 225879					
			Telex : 2564					
ASHANTI	Hotel Georgia	Adiebeba	Box 2240, Kumasi	32	46	3-Star	Single	100,000.00
			Tel : 24154/23915				Double	130,000.00
							Twin	140,000.00
							Suite	160,000.00
	Hotel Royal Basin	Anwomaso,	Box 537, UST, Kumasi	15	25	3-Star	Double	80,000.00
		Kumasi	Tel : 60144				Suite	100,000.00

	Sir Max Hotel	Ahodwo,	Box 3733, Kumasi	21	21	3-Star	Double	75,000.00
		Kumasi	Tel : 25222/25278				Twin	65,000.00
							Suite	85,000.00
	Anyinam Lodge	Obuasi	Box 699, Obuasi	52	78	2-Star	Double	72,000.00
			Tel : 478/439				Twin	81,000.00
	Cicero Guest House	West Nhyiaeso	Box 1187, Kumasi	13	13	2-Star	Double	100,000.00
		Ext. Kumasi	Tel : 24473				Twin Suite	
	City Hotel	Ridge Kumasi	Box 1980, Kumasi	169	338	2-Star	Single	25,000.00
			Tel : 23293-9				Double	45,000.00
							Twin	55,000.00
	Hotel La Sab	Kwadaso Agric.	Box 1937, Kumasi	42	54	2-Star	Single	
		Kumasi	Tel : 26549/24111				Double	78,000.00
							Twin	120,000.00
							Suite	
	Hotel Rexmar	West Patasi,	Box 3179, Kumasi	20	20	2-Star	Single	116,500.00
		Kumasi	Tel : 22294/29111				Double	124,000.00
							Suite	155,000.00
	La Vikus Hotel	Danyame,	Box 4713, Kumasi	28	47	2-Star	Single	80,000.00

		Kumasi	Tel : 22975				Double	100,000.00
							Twin	110,000.00
							Suite	125,000.00
	Melody Hotel	Kroppo, Kumasi	Box 2049, Kumasi	30	30	2-Star	Single	19,000.00
			Tel : 26155				Double	35,000.00
							Twin	45,000.00
							Suite	85,000.00
	Noks Hotel	Asokwa,Kumasi	Box 8556, Kumasi	18	18	2-Star	Single	35,000.00
			Tel : 24162				Double	60,000.00
							Twin	75,000.00
							Suite	90,000.00
	New Orleans Guest House	Danyame, Kumasi	Box 4575, Kumasi	18	18	2-Star	Single	40,000.00
			Tel : 25966				Double	55,000.00
							Twin	77,000.00
	Roses Guest House	Nhyiaeso, Kumasi	Box 4176, Kumasi	12	12	2-Star	Double	80,000.00
			Tel : 24072					
EASTERN REGION	Volta Hotel	Akosombo	Box 35, Akosombo	35	52	3-Star	Single	$80
	P.L.M Azur		Tel : (0251-731)				Double	$90
			021-662639/49				Suite	$130

			Fax : (0251) 663791					
	St. James Hotel	Koforidua	Box C 87, Koforidua	28	51	2-Star	Single	
			Tel : (081)23165				Double	
			Fax : (081) 23165				Twin	57,500.00
	Mac Dic Hotel	Koforidua	Box 1189, Koforidua	10	20	2-Star	Twin	51,750.00
			Tel : 081-23294					
REGION	NAME	LOCATION	ADDRESS	NO. OF ROOMS	NO. OF BEDS	GRADE	TARIFFS	¢
VOLTA REGION	Villa Cisneros	Sogakope	Box 96, Sogakope	68	123	2 -Star	Single	32,200.00
			Tel : (0968) 311	(55)			Double	48,300.00
			Fax : 0968311	Op			Charlet	58,650.00
NORTH	Las Hotel	Hospital Road	Box 121,Tamale	22	37	2-Star	Single	25,000.00
		Tamale	Tel : 22158				Double	36,000.00
								40,000.00
								44,000.00
	Picorna Hotel	Kaladan Park	Box 1212, Tamale	18	22	2-Star	Single	23,000.00
		Tamale	Tel : 22070				Double	32,200.00
							Twin	36,800.00

REGION	NAME	LOCATION	ADDRESS	NO. OF ROOMS	NO. OF BEDS	GRADE	TARIFFS	¢
UPPER WEST	Upland Hotel	Kpaguri, Wa	Box 308, Wa	40	48	2-Star	Single	32,000.00
			Tel : 22180	Ops.			Double	27,000.00
								18,000.00
BRONG	Tropical Hotel	Sunyani	Box 507, Sunyani	40	56	2-Star	Single	11,500.00
AHAFO			Tel : 061 / 7179				Double	18,400.00
							Twin	34,500.00
							Suite	57,500.00
WESTERN REGION	Hillcrest Hotel	Takoradi	Box 634, Takoradi	18	24	3-Star	Double	126,500.00
			Tel : 22277/22773				Week end	92,000.00
			Fax : 031-24381/23646				Rate(cash)	
			E-Mail : Hillcrest Africa on					
			Line. Com. Gh.					
	Ahenfie Hotel	Takoradi	Box 0684, Takoradi	8	8	2-Star	Single	23,000.00
			Tel: 22966/24272				Double	29,000.00
			Fax : 031-22007				Twin	48,300.00
							Suite	57,500.00
	Busua Beach Resort	Busua	Box 80, Agona-Nkwanta	41	67	2-Star	Single	60,000.00
			Tel				Double	85,000.00

			21210/21858-9					
			21893/21897				(Sea front)	80,500.00
							Suite	
	Guest House Maggi	Takoradi	Box 0684, Takoradi	10	10	2-Star	Double	45,425.00
			Tel : 22575				Twin	51,750.00
	Hotel Animens	Takoradi	Box 0475, Takoradi	18	21	2-Star	Twin	82,110.00
			Tel : 24676/77				Exec.	72,220.00
			Fax: 031-22481					70,150.00
							Double	57,500.00
	Hotel Alrose	Takoradi	Box 748, Takoradi	12	13	2-Star	Twin	77,050.00
			Tel : 24230					88,550.00
			Fax : 21109-031					
	Lynka Hotel	Tarkwa	Box 267, Tarkwa	12	12	2-Star	Single	$50
			Tel/Fax : (0362) 412				Double	$60
							Double	$70
							Suite	$80
	Mercy Lodge (Hotel)	Takoradi	Box 1030, Takoradi	10	10	2-Star	Double	45,000.00
			Tel : 21823					57,000.00
			Fax : 031-				Twin	69,000.00

			22887					
	Planters Lodge	Takoradi	Box 1096, Takoradi	12	12	2-Star	Double	$80.50
			Tel : 22230				Regular	$73
			Fax : 031-22233				Guest	
	Westline Hotel	Takoradi	Box 0408, Takoradi	20	29	2-Star	Double	50,000.00
			Tel : 24676					65,000.00
			Fax : 24145-031					75,000.00
CENTRAL	Coconut Grove Beach	Elmina	Box 175, Elmina	33	33	3-Star	Single	$50
REGION	Resort		Tel : 3363733650				Double	$60
			Fax : 33646				Family	$85
							Suite	$85
	Biriwa Beach Hotel	Biriwa	Box 479, Cape Coast	10	18	2-Star	Single	$55
			Tel : 33111/33222				Double	$60
			Fax : 33666/33555					
	Hotel Tills No.1	Gomoa-Fetteh	Box 600, Madina	12	24	2-Star	Double	$35
			Tel (027) 550480				Executive	$50
			Fax : 027(558247)					
	Harmony Beach Hotel	Elmina	Box A. 125, Cape Coast	17	17	2-Star	Double	$40
			Tel : 33678/9				Suite(Q)	$50

			Fax : 33681				Suite(K)	$60
	Ntiamoah Memorial	Agona Swedru	Box 287, Agona Swedru	28	45	2-Star	Double	15,000.00
	Hotel		Tel : 041-273				Twin	30,000.00
			Fax : 041-273				A/C	45,000.00

LIST OF RECOMMENDED RESTAURANTS

ESTABLISHMENT GREATER ACCRA REGION	LOCATION	ADDRESS	GRADE	CUISINE	SEATING CAPACITY	AVERAGE COST PER MEAL	HOURS OF OPERATION
Acquarius Restaurant	Nyaniba Estates	Box 0537, Osu Tel : 774059	1	European (German)	48	8,000.00	Monday-Sunday 6.00pm-3.00am
Atlantic Restaurant	Tema C. 5	Box 1112, Tema Tel : 022-206121	1	Chinese	50	4,000.00 5,000.00	Monday-Sunday 12.00noon-3.00pm 6.00pm-10.30pm
Best Cuisine	Ridge	Box 2323, Accra Tel : 220258	1	Ghanaian, American Italian,Oriental Outdoor catering	100	3,800.00	Monday Sunday 12.00noon-3.00pm 6.00pm 11.30pm
Bella Napoli Restaurant	Cantonments	Private Mail Bag, Tel : 666920	1	Italian & Continental	112	8,000.00	Monday-Sunday 12.00noon-3.00pm 6.00pm-11.30pm
Chez Marie Lou Restaurant	Osu	Box 0662, Osu Tel : 774891	1	French	75	6,000.00	Monday-Sunday 6.00pm-12midnight
China House Restaurant	Osu	Box 01714, Osu-Accra Tel : 027	1	Chinese	40	6,000.00	Monday-Sunday 12.00noon-

		557251					3.00pm
Chopsticks Restaurant	Tema Comm. 1	Box B. 82, Tema Tel : 6424	1	Chinese	80	10,000.00	Monday-Sunday 12.00noon-3.00pm 7.00pm-10.00pm
Dynasty Chinese Restaurant	Osu-Re	Box 11717, Accra-North Tel : 775496	1	Chinese	150	4,200.00	Monday-Sunday 11.00am-3.00pm 6.00pm-11.30pm
Hinlone Chinese Restaurant	Labone	Box 1527, Tema Tel : 772782	1	Chinese		8,000.00	Monday-Sunday 12.00noon-3.00pm
Landing Rest.	Airport	Box 8124, Accra-North Tel :	1	Continental & African	150	8,000.00	Monday-Sunday 24 hours
La Bouquet Restaurant	Osu	Box 4334, Accra Tel : 772417	1	Continental, Lebanese	160	9.000.00	Monday-Sunday 12noon-3.00pm 7.00pm-11.pm
Manna Korean Restaurant	Tema C.12	Box 77, Trade Fair Tel : 6644	1	Korean, Chinese, Japanese	150	4,500.00	Monday-Sunday 12noon-3.00pm 6.30pm-10.30pm
May Flower Restaurant	Tema C. 11	Box 8009, Tema Tel : 6615/4970	1	Ghanaian, Continental, Chinese	65	3,500.00	Monday-Sunday 7.00am-12.00noon
Makaira Rest.	Labone	Box 7872, Accra		French	60	9,500.00	
Panda Chinese Restaurant	Osu	Box 632, Dansoman Tel : 777477	1	Chinese	60	8,000.00	Monday-Sunday 11.30am-3.30pm 6.30pm-11.30pm

Pearl of the East	Osu	Box 2098, Osu Tel : 774907	1	Chinese	100		
Regal Chinese Restaurant	Osu	Box 11577, Accra Tel : 773386	1	Chinese	200	8,000.00	Monday-Sunday 12.00noon-3.00pm 6.30pm-11.00pm
Ritz Specialities Restaurant	Abossey Okai	Box 15645, Accra-North Tel : 225883	1	Continental & Mid-Eastern	50	8,500.00	Monday-Sunday 12.00noon-3.00pm 7.00pm-11.00pm
Ristorante Sole Mio	Osu	Box 14492, Accra	1	Italian	80	8,000.00	Monday-Sunday 12.00noon-3.00pm 7.00pm-11.00pm
Bus Stop Restaurant	Ring Road Central	Box 380, Accra-North Tel : 220930	2	Continental & Snacks	200	9,400.00	Monday-Sunday 10.00am-1.00am
Edvy Restaurant	Adabraka	Box 6094, Accra-North Tel : 229348	2	Ghanaian, Chinese	100	6,000.00	Monday-Sunday 8.30am-6.00pm
Home Touch Restaurant	Burma Camp	Box 3370, Airport Tel : 777662	2	Ghanaian, Continental	100	6,000.00	Monday-Sunday 12.00noon-8.00pm
La Pergola Restaurant	Cantonments	Box 1121, Accra-North Tel : 234764	2	French & Ghanaian	60	6,000,00	Monday-Sunday 8.30am-11.00pm
New Club 400 Restaurant	Ring Way Estates	Box 987, Accra Tel ; 223723	2	Mid-Eastern	32	10,000.00	Monday-Sunday 12.00noon-3.00pm 7.00pm-12midnight
Papaye Rest	Osu	Box 10505.	2	Fast Foods	60	3,200.00	Mondav-

		Accra-North					Sunday 12.00noon-11.30pm
Paloma Snacks Restaurant	Ring Road East	Box 3727, Accra Tel : 223245	2	Fast Foods Continental, Snacks	72	3,000.00	Monday-Sunday 11.00am-12.midnight
Providence Catering Services	Osu	Box C 588, Cantonments Tel : 773625	2	Ghanaian, Continental, Oriental	60	4,000.00	Monday-Friday 10.00am-7.00pm
Theatre Gardens Restaurant	National Theatre	Box C. 680, Accra	2	Continental, Ghanaian	100	3,500.00	Monday-Sunday 7.30am-9.00pm
White Bell Rest	Ridge	Box 9003, K.I.A. Tel : 227066	2	Ghanaian, Continental & Fast Food	100	3,500.00	Monday-Friday 12.00noon-5.00pm
ESTABLISHMENT ASHANTI REGION	LOCATION	ADDRESS	GRADE	CUISINE	SEATING CAPACITY	AVERAGE COST PER MEAL	HOURS OF OPERATION
Chopsticks Restaurant	Nhyiaeso, Kumasi	Box : 8049, Kumasi Tel : 051-23221	1	Chinese	50		
Goldfinger Restaurant	Obuasi	Box : 250, Obuasi Tel : 365	1	Chinese & Continental	120		
Moti Mahal Restaurant	Danyame, Kumasi	Box 994, Kumasi Tel : 051-26499	1	Lebanese & Indian	170		
Royal Gardens	Hotel, Georgia,	Box : 55166, Kumasi	1	Chinese	50		
Chinese Rest.	Kumasi	Tel : 25733					
Sweet Garden Restaurant	La Vikus Hotel, Kumasi	Box 4317, Kumasi Tel : 051-25102	1	Chinese & Continental	60		
4 Aces Restaurant	Danyame, Kumasi	Box 657, Kumasi Tel : 051-	2	Lebanese & Continental	60		

		29855					
Adehyeman Gardens	Kejetia Playground, Kumasi	Box : 4917, Kumasi Tel : 051-26076	2	Ghanaian & Continental	250		
Jofel Catering Services	Asokwa, Kumasi	Box : M. 1466, Kumasi Tel :	2	Ghanaian & Continental	120		
ESTABLISHMENT BRONG-AHAFO	LOCATION	ADDRESS	GRADE	CUISINE	SEATING CAPACITY	AVERAGE COST PER MEAL	HOURS OF OPERATION
Tata Restaurant	Sunyani	Box 847, Sunyani Tel : 061-435	3	Ghanaian & Continental	60		
ESTABLISHMENT VOLTA REGION	LOCATION	ADDRESS	GRADE	CUISINE	SEATING CAPACITY	AVERAGE COST PER MEAL	HOURS OF OPERATION
Boarder Beach Rest.	Aflao		3	Ghanaian, Continental Snacks			
ESTABLISHMENT NORTHERN REGION	LOCATION	ADDRESS	GRADE	CUISINE	SEATING CAPACITY	AVERAGE COST PER MEAL	HOURS OF OPERATION
Sweet Gardens Restaurant	Nim Avenue Hospital Road, Tamale	Box 121, Tamale	2	Chinese	80	3,500.00 16,800.00	7.00am-4.00pm 6.00pm-9.30pm
ESTABLISHMENT WESTERN REGION	LOCATION	ADDRESS	GRADE	CUISINE	SEATING CAPACITY	AVERAGE COST PER MEAL	HOURS OF OPERATION
Africa Beach Restaurant	Takoradi	Box	2	Ghanaian, Continental, Chinese	24		
Harlem Home Cooking Services	Takoradi (near Harbour round-about)	Box 77, Takoradi Tel : (031)23577	3	Ghanaian,	56	3,000.00 4,000.00	10.30am-8.30pm
ESTABLISHMENT	LOCATION	ADDRESS	GRADE	CUISINE	SEATING	AVERAGE	HOURS OF

EASTERN REGION					CAPACITY	COST PER MEAL	OPERATION
Sophisticat Restaurant	Koforidua	Box 740 Tel : 081 23056	2	Continental, Ghanaian, Chinese	70	5,000.00	8.30am-10.00pm
Tamara Restaurant	Larteh	Box 62, Larteh Tel : 027 778186	2	Ghanaian, Continental	210	5,000.00 - 8,000.00 12,000.00	11.00am-10.00pm
Mothers Pride Restaurant	Amanase	Box 15646 Accra-North	3	Ghanaian/Continental	68	1,500.00 4,500.00	8.00am-9.00pm
Nkawkaw Rest Stop	Nkawkaw	Box 155 Tel : 081-2357	3	Ghanaian, Continental	50	2,000.00 3,500.00	7.00am-9.00pm
Odweanoma Rest (Goil)	Nkwakaw	Box 368 Koforidua Tel : 081-22459,	3	Ghanaian/Continental	58	2,400.00 3,000.00	8.00am-9.00pm
ESTABLISHMENT UPPER EAST REGION	LOCATION	ADDRESS	GRADE	CUISINE	SEATING CAPACITY	AVERAGE COST PER MEAL	HOURS OF OPERATION
Comme Ci, Comme Ca	Daporetindongo	Box Tel : 2355	3	Ghanaian & Continental	150	2,500.00 6,900.00	7.30am-3.00pm 6.00pm-10.00pm
ESTABLISHMENT CENTRAL REGION	LOCATION	ADDRESS	GRADE	CUISINE	SEATING CAPACITY	AVERAGE COST PER MEAL	HOURS OF OPERATION
Aggies Catering Services	Brenu Akkyinim	Box c/o NIB 937, Cape Coast	3	Ghanaian & Continental	60	3.000.00 10,000.00	8.00am-6.00pm

GLOSSARY

Abusua
: The family in Akan society

Adae
: Akan sacred day. According to the traditional lunar calendar, an *Adae* day occurs every fortnight.

Asafo
: Traditional Akan men's association and originally fighting companies.

Asante/Ashanti/Ashantee
: Akan group, geographically located to the central part of the country. Founders of the Asante Empire, and speakers of Asante-Twi language.

Asantehene
King of Asante.
Bosomtwi (Lake)
The only natural lake in Ghana. It is located about 32 km to the south-east of Kumase, the Asante capital.
CHW
Community Health Worker.
Consultative Assembly
A body elected by various organizations in 1991/92 to debate the constitutional proposals drawn out by a government-appointed Committee of Experts. The document agree upon by the Consultative Assembly was accepted in May of 1992 as the constitution for the Fourth Republic to be elected to power later in 1992/93.
CPP.
Convention People's Party (was in power from 1957-1966).
Global 2000
An organization founded and chaired by Mr. Jimmy Carter (former President of the United States) to aid Third World farmers with improved seedlings, financial assistance, and extension services. The goal was to create agricultural self-sufficiency in the selected countries. Ghana became a Global 2000 member in the mid- 1980s.
Homowo
Ga annual homecoming festival.
IMF.
International Monetary Fund.
JSS.
Junior Secondary School.
NCWD.
National Council on Women and Development.
NUGS.
National Union of Ghana Students.
Odwira
Annual Akan festival for the propitiation of the ancestors.
Ramadan
Muslim month of fasting.
SRC.
Students Representative Council (equal to SGAs in the United States).
SSS.
Senior Secondary School.
Tariqa
Muslim brotherhood.
TBA.
Traditional Birth Attendant.
Tendaana
Mole-Dagbane Earth cult and shrine.
TUC.
Trade Union Congress.
UNESCO
United Nations Education, Science, and Cultural Organization.
UNICEF
United Nations Children's Fund.
VHW.
Village Health Worker.
WHO.
World Health Organization (United Nations)

BASIC TITLES ON GHANA

IMPORTANT!

All publications are updated annually!

Please contact IBP, Inc. at ibpusa3@gmail.com for the latest ISBNs and additional information

TITLE
Ghana A "Spy" Guide - Strategic Information and Developments
Ghana A Spy" Guide"
Ghana Banking & Financial Market Handbook
Ghana Banking & Financial Market Handbook
Ghana Banking and Financial Sector Business and Investment Opportunities Handbook
Ghana Banking and Financial Sector Business and Investment Opportunities Handbook
Ghana Business and Investment Opportunities Yearbook
Ghana Business and Investment Opportunities Yearbook
Ghana Business and Investment Opportunities Yearbook Volume 1 Strategic Information and Opportunities
Ghana Business Intelligence Report - Practical Information, Opportunities, Contacts
Ghana Business Intelligence Report - Practical Information, Opportunities, Contacts
Ghana Business Law Handbook - Strategic Information and Basic Laws
Ghana Business Law Handbook - Strategic Information and Basic Laws
Ghana Business Law Handbook - Strategic Information and Basic Laws
Ghana Business Law Handbook - Strategic Information and Basic Laws
Ghana Business Success Guide - Basic Practical Information and Contacts
Ghana Company Laws and Regulations Handbook - Strategic Information and Basic Laws
Ghana Constitution and Citizenship Laws Handbook - Strategic Information and Basic Laws
Ghana Country Study Guide - Strategic Information and Developments
Ghana Country Study Guide - Strategic Information and Developments
Ghana Country Study Guide - Strategic Information and Developments Volume 1 Strategic Information and Developments
Ghana Criminal Laws, Regulations and Procedures Handbook - Strategic Information, Regulations, Procedures
Ghana Customs, Trade Regulations and Procedures Handbook
Ghana Customs, Trade Regulations and Procedures Handbook
Ghana Diplomatic Handbook - Strategic Information and Developments
Ghana Diplomatic Handbook - Strategic Information and Developments
Ghana Ecology & Nature Protection Handbook
Ghana Ecology & Nature Protection Handbook
Ghana Ecology & Nature Protection Laws and Regulation Handbook
Ghana Economic & Development Strategy Handbook
Ghana Economic & Development Strategy Handbook
Ghana Electoral, Political Parties Laws and Regulations Handbook - Strategic Information, Regulations, Procedures
Ghana Energy Policy, Laws and Regulation Handbook
Ghana Financial Market Business Opportunities and Regulations Handbook
Ghana Financial Market Business Opportunities and Regulations Handbook
Ghana Fishing and Aquaculture Industry Handbook - Strategic Information, Regulations,

TITLE
Opportunities
Ghana Foreign Policy and Government Guide
Ghana Foreign Policy and Government Guide
Ghana Healthcare Sector Organization, Management and Payment Systems Handbook - Strategic Information, Programs and Regulations
Ghana Immigration Laws and Regulations Handbook - Strategic Information and Basic Laws
Ghana Insolvency (Bankruptcy) Laws and Regulations Handbook - Strategic Information and Basic Laws
Ghana Investment and Business Guide - Strategic and Practical Information
Ghana Investment and Business Guide - Strategic and Practical Information
Ghana Investment and Business Guide - Strategic and Practical Information
Ghana Investment and Business Guide - Strategic and Practical Information
Ghana Investment and Business Guide Volume 2 Business, Investment Opportunities and Incentives
Ghana Investment and Business Profile - Basic Information and Contacts for Succesful investment and Business Activity
Ghana Investment, Trade Strategy and Agreements Handbook - Strategic Information and Basic Agreements
Ghana Labor Laws and Regulations Handbook - Strategic Information and Basic Laws
Ghana Land Ownership and Agriculture Laws Handbook
Ghana Mineral & Mining Sector Investment and Business Guide - Strategic and Practical Information
Ghana Mineral & Mining Sector Investment and Business Guide - Strategic and Practical Information
Ghana Mining Laws and Regulations Handbook
Ghana Privatization Programs and Regulations Handbook
Ghana Privatization Programs and Regulations Handbook
Ghana Recent Economic and Political Developments Yearbook
Ghana Recent Economic and Political Developments Yearbook
Ghana Recent Economic and Political Developments Yearbook
Ghana Tax Guide Volume 1 Strategic Information and Basic Regulations
Ghana Taxation Laws and Regulations Handbook
Ghana: How to Invest, Start and Run Profitable Business in Ghana Guide - Practical Information, Opportunities, Contacts

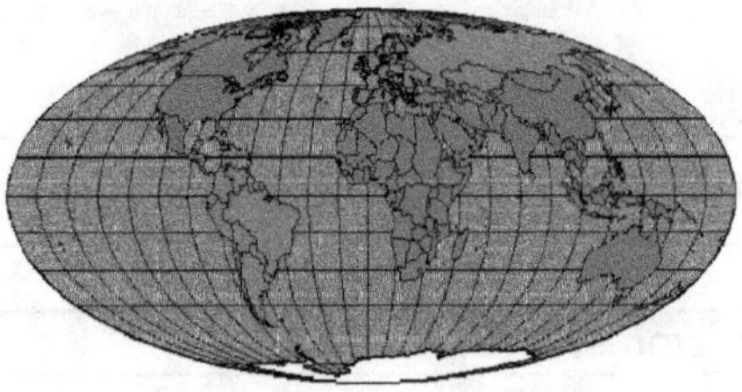

WORLD BUSINESS AND INVESTMENT OPPORTUNITIES YEARBOOK LIBRARY

World Business Information Catalog, USA: http://www.ibpus.com
Email: ibpusa3@gmail.com

Price: $99.95 Each

TITLE
Abkhazia (Republic of Abkhazia) Business and Investment Opportunities Yearbook Volume 1 Strategic, Practical Information and Opportunities
Afghanistan Business and Investment Opportunities Yearbook Volume 1 Strategic, Practical Information and Opportunities
Aland Business and Investment Opportunities Yearbook Volume 1 Strategic, Practical Information and Opportunities
Albania Business and Investment Opportunities Yearbook Volume 1 Strategic, Practical Information and Opportunities
Algeria Business and Investment Opportunities Yearbook Volume 1 Strategic, Practical Information and Opportunities
Andorra Business and Investment Opportunities Yearbook Volume 1 Strategic, Practical Information and Opportunities
Angola Business and Investment Opportunities Yearbook Volume 1 Strategic, Practical Information and Opportunities
Anguilla Business and Investment Opportunities Yearbook Volume 1 Strategic, Practical Information and Opportunities
Antigua and Barbuda Business and Investment Opportunities Yearbook Volume 1 Strategic, Practical Information and Opportunities
Antilles (Netherlands) Business and Investment Opportunities Yearbook Volume 1 Strategic, Practical Information and Opportunities
Argentina Business and Investment Opportunities Yearbook Volume 1 Strategic, Practical Information and Opportunities
Armenia Business and Investment Opportunities Yearbook Volume 1 Strategic, Practical Information and Opportunities
Aruba Business and Investment Opportunities Yearbook Volume 1 Strategic, Practical Information and Opportunities
Australia Business and Investment Opportunities Yearbook Volume 1 Strategic, Practical Information and Opportunities
Austria Business and Investment Opportunities Yearbook Volume 1 Strategic, Practical Information and Opportunities
Azerbaijan Business and Investment Opportunities Yearbook Volume 1 Strategic, Practical Information and Opportunities
Bahamas Business and Investment Opportunities Yearbook Volume 1 Strategic, Practical Information and Opportunities
Bahrain Business and Investment Opportunities Yearbook Volume 1 Strategic, Practical Information and Opportunities
Bangladesh Business and Investment Opportunities Yearbook Volume 1 Strategic, Practical Information and Opportunities
Barbados Business and Investment Opportunities Yearbook Volume 1 Strategic, Practical Information and Opportunities
Belarus Business and Investment Opportunities Yearbook Volume 1 Strategic, Practical Information and Opportunities

For additional analytical, business and investment opportunities information,
Please contact Global Investment & Business Center, USA
at (202) 546-2103. Fax: (202) 546-3275. E-mail: ibpusa3@gmail.com

TITLE
Belgium Business and Investment Opportunities Yearbook Volume 1 Strategic, Practical Information and Opportunities
Belize Business and Investment Opportunities Yearbook Volume 1 Strategic, Practical Information and Opportunities
Benin Business and Investment Opportunities Yearbook Volume 1 Strategic, Practical Information and Opportunities
Bermuda Business and Investment Opportunities Yearbook Volume 1 Strategic, Practical Information and Opportunities
Bhutan Business and Investment Opportunities Yearbook Volume 1 Strategic, Practical Information and Opportunities
Bolivia Business and Investment Opportunities Yearbook Volume 1 Strategic, Practical Information and Opportunities
Bosnia and Herzegovina Business and Investment Opportunities Yearbook Volume 1 Strategic, Practical Information and Opportunities
Botswana Business and Investment Opportunities Yearbook Volume 1 Strategic, Practical Information and Opportunities
Brazil Business and Investment Opportunities Yearbook Volume 1 Strategic, Practical Information and Opportunities
Brunei Business and Investment Opportunities Yearbook Volume 1 Strategic, Practical Information and Opportunities
Bulgaria Business and Investment Opportunities Yearbook Volume 1 Strategic, Practical Information and Opportunities
Burkina Faso Business and Investment Opportunities Yearbook Volume 1 Strategic, Practical Information and Opportunities
Burundi Business and Investment Opportunities Yearbook Volume 1 Strategic, Practical Information and Opportunities
Cambodia Business and Investment Opportunities Yearbook Volume 1 Strategic, Practical Information and Opportunities
Cameroon Business and Investment Opportunities Yearbook Volume 1 Strategic, Practical Information and Opportunities
Canada Business and Investment Opportunities Yearbook Volume 1 Strategic, Practical Information and Opportunities
Cape Verde Business and Investment Opportunities Yearbook Volume 1 Strategic, Practical Information and Opportunities
Cayman Islands Business and Investment Opportunities Yearbook Volume 1 Strategic, Practical Information and Opportunities
Central African Republic Business and Investment Opportunities Yearbook Volume 1 Strategic, Practical Information and Opportunities
Chad Business and Investment Opportunities Yearbook Volume 1 Strategic, Practical Information and Opportunities
Chile Business and Investment Opportunities Yearbook Volume 1 Strategic, Practical Information and Opportunities
China Business and Investment Opportunities Yearbook Volume 1 Strategic, Practical Information and Opportunities
Colombia Business and Investment Opportunities Yearbook Volume 1 Strategic, Practical Information and Opportunities
Comoros Business and Investment Opportunities Yearbook Volume 1 Strategic, Practical Information and Opportunities
Congo Business and Investment Opportunities Yearbook Volume 1 Strategic, Practical Information and Opportunities
Congo, Democratic Republic Business and Investment Opportunities Yearbook Volume 1 Strategic, Practical Information and Opportunities
Cook Islands Business and Investment Opportunities Yearbook Volume 1 Strategic, Practical Information and Opportunities
Costa Rica Business and Investment Opportunities Yearbook Volume 1 Strategic, Practical Information and Opportunities

TITLE
Cote d'Ivoire Business and Investment Opportunities Yearbook Volume 1 Strategic, Practical Information and Opportunities
Croatia Business and Investment Opportunities Yearbook Volume 1 Strategic, Practical Information and Opportunities
Cuba Business and Investment Opportunities Yearbook Volume 1 Strategic, Practical Information and Opportunities
Cyprus Business and Investment Opportunities Yearbook Volume 1 Strategic, Practical Information and Opportunities
Czech Republic Business and Investment Opportunities Yearbook Volume 1 Strategic, Practical Information and Opportunities
Denmark Business and Investment Opportunities Yearbook Volume 1 Strategic, Practical Information and Opportunities
Djibouti Business and Investment Opportunities Yearbook Volume 1 Strategic, Practical Information and Opportunities
Dominica Business and Investment Opportunities Yearbook Volume 1 Strategic, Practical Information and Opportunities
Dominican Republic Business and Investment Opportunities Yearbook Volume 1 Strategic, Practical Information and Opportunities
Ecuador Business and Investment Opportunities Yearbook Volume 1 Strategic, Practical Information and Opportunities
Egypt Business and Investment Opportunities Yearbook Volume 1 Strategic, Practical Information and Opportunities
El Salvador Business and Investment Opportunities Yearbook Volume 1 Strategic, Practical Information and Opportunities
Equatorial Guinea Business and Investment Opportunities Yearbook Volume 1 Strategic, Practical Information and Opportunities
Eritrea Business and Investment Opportunities Yearbook Volume 1 Strategic, Practical Information and Opportunities
Estonia Business and Investment Opportunities Yearbook Volume 1 Strategic, Practical Information and Opportunities
Ethiopia Business and Investment Opportunities Yearbook Volume 1 Strategic, Practical Information and Opportunities
Falkland Islands Business and Investment Opportunities Yearbook Volume 1 Strategic, Practical Information and Opportunities
Faroes Islands Business and Investment Opportunities Yearbook Volume 1 Strategic, Practical Information and Opportunities
Fiji Business and Investment Opportunities Yearbook Volume 1 Strategic, Practical Information and Opportunities
Finland Business and Investment Opportunities Yearbook Volume 1 Strategic, Practical Information and Opportunities
France Business and Investment Opportunities Yearbook Volume 1 Strategic, Practical Information and Opportunities
Gabon Business and Investment Opportunities Yearbook Volume 1 Strategic, Practical Information and Opportunities
Gambia Business and Investment Opportunities Yearbook Volume 1 Strategic, Practical Information and Opportunities
Georgia Business and Investment Opportunities Yearbook Volume 1 Strategic, Practical Information and Opportunities
Germany Business and Investment Opportunities Yearbook Volume 1 Strategic, Practical Information and Opportunities
Ghana Business and Investment Opportunities Yearbook Volume 1 Strategic, Practical Information and Opportunities
Gibraltar Business and Investment Opportunities Yearbook Volume 1 Strategic, Practical Information and Opportunities
Greece Business and Investment Opportunities Yearbook Volume 1 Strategic, Practical Information and Opportunities

TITLE
Greenland Business and Investment Opportunities Yearbook Volume 1 Strategic, Practical Information and Opportunities
Grenada Business and Investment Opportunities Yearbook Volume 1 Strategic, Practical Information and Opportunities
Guam Business and Investment Opportunities Yearbook Volume 1 Strategic, Practical Information and Opportunities
Guatemala Business and Investment Opportunities Yearbook Volume 1 Strategic, Practical Information and Opportunities
Guernsey Business and Investment Opportunities Yearbook Volume 1 Strategic, Practical Information and Opportunities
Guinea Business and Investment Opportunities Yearbook Volume 1 Strategic, Practical Information and Opportunities
Guinea-Bissau Business and Investment Opportunities Yearbook Volume 1 Strategic, Practical Information and Opportunities
Guyana Business and Investment Opportunities Yearbook Volume 1 Strategic, Practical Information and Opportunities
Haiti Business and Investment Opportunities Yearbook Volume 1 Strategic, Practical Information and Opportunities
Honduras Business and Investment Opportunities Yearbook Volume 1 Strategic, Practical Information and Opportunities
Hungary Business and Investment Opportunities Yearbook Volume 1 Strategic, Practical Information and Opportunities
Iceland Business and Investment Opportunities Yearbook Volume 1 Strategic, Practical Information and Opportunities
India Business and Investment Opportunities Yearbook Volume 1 Strategic, Practical Information and Opportunities
Indonesia Business and Investment Opportunities Yearbook Volume 1 Strategic, Practical Information and Opportunities
Iran Business and Investment Opportunities Yearbook Volume 1 Strategic, Practical Information and Opportunities
Iraq Business and Investment Opportunities Yearbook Volume 1 Strategic, Practical Information and Opportunities
Ireland Business and Investment Opportunities Yearbook Volume 1 Strategic, Practical Information and Opportunities
Israel Business and Investment Opportunities Yearbook Volume 1 Strategic, Practical Information and Opportunities
Italy Business and Investment Opportunities Yearbook Volume 1 Strategic, Practical Information and Opportunities
Jamaica Business and Investment Opportunities Yearbook Volume 1 Strategic, Practical Information and Opportunities
Japan Business and Investment Opportunities Yearbook Volume 1 Strategic, Practical Information and Opportunities
Jersey Business and Investment Opportunities Yearbook Volume 1 Strategic, Practical Information and Opportunities
Jordan Business and Investment Opportunities Yearbook Volume 1 Strategic, Practical Information and Opportunities
Kazakhstan Business and Investment Opportunities Yearbook Volume 1 Strategic, Practical Information and Opportunities
Kenya Business and Investment Opportunities Yearbook Volume 1 Strategic, Practical Information and Opportunities
Kiribati Business and Investment Opportunities Yearbook Volume 1 Strategic, Practical Information and Opportunities
Korea, North Business and Investment Opportunities Yearbook Volume 1 Strategic, Practical Information and Opportunities
Korea, South Business and Investment Opportunities Yearbook Volume 1 Strategic, Practical Information and Opportunities

TITLE
Kosovo Business and Investment Opportunities Yearbook Volume 1 Strategic, Practical Information and Opportunities
Kurdistan Business and Investment Opportunities Yearbook Volume 1 Strategic, Practical Information and Opportunities
Kuwait Business and Investment Opportunities Yearbook Volume 1 Strategic, Practical Information and Opportunities
Kyrgyzstan Business and Investment Opportunities Yearbook Volume 1 Strategic, Practical Information and Opportunities
Laos Business and Investment Opportunities Yearbook Volume 1 Strategic, Practical Information and Opportunities
Latvia Business and Investment Opportunities Yearbook Volume 1 Strategic, Practical Information and Opportunities
Lebanon Business and Investment Opportunities Yearbook Volume 1 Strategic, Practical Information and Opportunities
Lesotho Business and Investment Opportunities Yearbook Volume 1 Strategic, Practical Information and Opportunities
Liberia Business and Investment Opportunities Yearbook Volume 1 Strategic, Practical Information and Opportunities
Libya Business and Investment Opportunities Yearbook Volume 1 Strategic, Practical Information and Opportunities
Liechtenstein Business and Investment Opportunities Yearbook Volume 1 Strategic, Practical Information and Opportunities
Lithuania Business and Investment Opportunities Yearbook Volume 1 Strategic, Practical Information and Opportunities
Luxembourg Business and Investment Opportunities Yearbook Volume 1 Strategic, Practical Information and Opportunities
Macao Business and Investment Opportunities Yearbook Volume 1 Strategic, Practical Information and Opportunities
Macedonia Business and Investment Opportunities Yearbook Volume 1 Strategic, Practical Information and Opportunities
Madagascar Business and Investment Opportunities Yearbook Volume 1 Strategic, Practical Information and Opportunities
Madeira Business and Investment Opportunities Yearbook Volume 1 Strategic, Practical Information and Opportunities
Malawi Business and Investment Opportunities Yearbook Volume 1 Strategic, Practical Information and Opportunities
Malaysia Business and Investment Opportunities Yearbook Volume 1 Strategic, Practical Information and Opportunities
Maldives Business and Investment Opportunities Yearbook Volume 1 Strategic, Practical Information and Opportunities
Mali Business and Investment Opportunities Yearbook Volume 1 Strategic, Practical Information and Opportunities
Malta Business and Investment Opportunities Yearbook Volume 1 Strategic, Practical Information and Opportunities
Man Business and Investment Opportunities Yearbook Volume 1 Strategic, Practical Information and Opportunities
Marshall Islands Business and Investment Opportunities Yearbook Volume 1 Strategic, Practical Information and Opportunities
Mauritania Business and Investment Opportunities Yearbook Volume 1 Strategic, Practical Information and Opportunities
Mauritius Business and Investment Opportunities Yearbook Volume 1 Strategic, Practical Information and Opportunities
Mayotte Business and Investment Opportunities Yearbook Volume 1 Strategic, Practical Information and Opportunities
Mexico Business and Investment Opportunities Yearbook Volume 1 Strategic, Practical Information and Opportunities

Title
Kuwait Energy Policy, Laws and Regulations Handbook
Libya Energy Policy, Laws and Regulations Handbook
Malaysia Energy Policy, Laws and Regulations Handbook
Mexico Energy Policy, Laws and Regulations Handbook
Morocco Energy Policy, Laws and Regulations Handbook
Namibia Energy Policy, Laws and Regulations Handbook
New Zealand Energy Policy, Laws and Regulations Handbook
Nigeria Energy Policy, Laws and Regulations Handbook
Norway Energy Policy, Laws and Regulations Handbook
Oman Energy Policy, Laws and Regulations Handbook
Pakistan Energy Policy, Laws and Regulations Handbook
Papua New Guinea Energy Policy, Laws and Regulations Handbook
Papua New Guinea Oil & Gas Sector Energy Policy, Laws and Regulations Handbook
Peru Energy Policy, Laws and Regulations Handbook
Philippines Energy Policy, Laws and Regulations Handbook
Qatar Energy Policy, Laws and Regulations Handbook
Sri Lanka Energy Policy, Laws and Regulations Handbook
Romania Energy Policy, Laws and Regulations Handbook
Russia Energy Policy, Laws and Regulations Handbook
Saudi Arabia Energy Policy, Laws and Regulations Handbook
Sudan Energy Policy, Laws and Regulations Handbook
Suriname Energy Policy, Laws and Regulations Handbook
Syria Energy Policy, Laws and Regulations Handbook
Trinidad and Tobago Oil & Gas Sector Energy Policy, Laws and Regulations Handbook
Tunisia Energy Policy, Laws and Regulations Handbook
Turkey Energy Policy, Laws and Regulations Handbook
Turkmenistan Energy Policy, Laws and Regulations Handbook
Ukraine Oil & Gas Sector Energy Policy, Laws and Regulations Handbook
United Arab Emirates Energy Policy, Laws and Regulations Handbook
United Kingdom Energy Policy, Laws and Regulations Handbook
United Kingdom Oil & Gas Sector Energy Policy, Laws and Regulations Handbook
United States Energy Policy, Laws and Regulations Handbook
Venezuela Energy Policy, Laws and Regulations Handbook
Vietnam Energy Policy, Laws and Regulations Handbook
Vietnam Energy Policy, Laws and Regulations Handbook
Yemen Energy Policy, Laws and Regulations Handbook

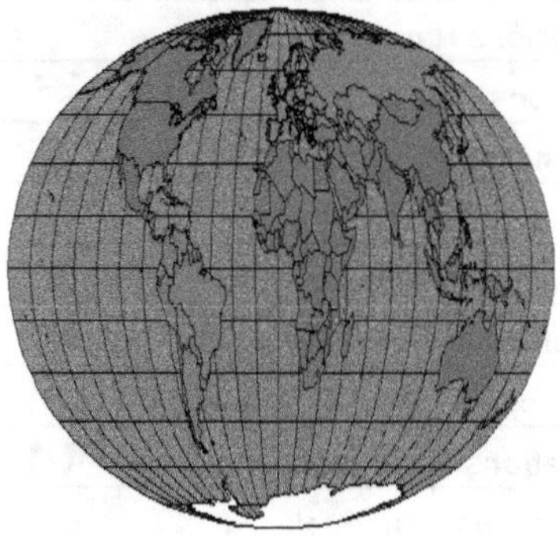

WORLD ENERGY POLICY, BUSINESS & INVESTMENT OPPORTUNITIES LIBRARY

Price: $149.95 Each

Title
Albania Energy Policy, Laws and Regulations Handbook
Algeria Energy Policy, Laws and Regulations Handbook
Angola Energy Policy, Laws and Regulations Handbook
Australia Energy Policy, Laws and Regulations Handbook
Azerbaijan Energy Policy, Laws and Regulations Handbook
Bahrain Energy Policy, Laws and Regulations Handbook
Bangladesh Energy Policy, Laws and Regulations Handbook
Benin Energy Policy, Laws and Regulations Handbook
Brazil Energy Policy, Laws and Regulations Handbook
Brunei Energy Policy, Laws and Regulations Handbook
Cameroon Energy Policy, Laws and Regulations Handbook
Canada Energy Policy, Laws and Regulations Handbook
China Energy Policy, Laws and Regulations Handbook
Colombia Oil & Gas Sector Energy Policy, Laws and Regulations Handbook
Congo Energy Policy, Laws and Regulations Handbook
Congo, Dem. Republic Energy Policy, Laws and Regulations Handbook
Cote d'Ivoire Energy Policy, Laws and Regulations Handbook
Dubai Energy Policy, Laws and Regulations Handbook
Ecuador Energy Policy, Laws and Regulations Handbook
Egypt Energy Policy, Laws and Regulations Handbook
Equatorial Guinea Energy Policy, Laws and Regulations Handbook
Gabon Energy Policy, Laws and Regulations Handbook
India Energy Policy, Laws and Regulations Handbook
Indonesia Energy Policy, Laws and Regulations Handbook
Iran Energy Policy, Laws and Regulations Handbook
Iraq Energy Policy, Laws and Regulations Handbook
Kazakhstan Energy Policy, Laws and Regulations Handbook

TITLE
Uganda Business and Investment Opportunities Yearbook Volume 1 Strategic, Practical Information and Opportunities
Ukraine Business and Investment Opportunities Yearbook Volume 1 Strategic, Practical Information and Opportunities
United Arab Emirates Business and Investment Opportunities Yearbook Volume 1 Strategic, Practical Information and Opportunities
United Kingdom Business and Investment Opportunities Yearbook Volume 1 Strategic, Practical Information and Opportunities
United States Business and Investment Opportunities Yearbook Volume 1 Strategic, Practical Information and Opportunities
Uruguay Business and Investment Opportunities Yearbook Volume 1 Strategic, Practical Information and Opportunities
Uzbekistan Business and Investment Opportunities Yearbook Volume 1 Strategic, Practical Information and Opportunities
Vanuatu Business and Investment Opportunities Yearbook Volume 1 Strategic, Practical Information and Opportunities
Vatican City (Holy See) Business and Investment Opportunities Yearbook Volume 1 Strategic, Practical Information and Opportunities
Venezuela Business and Investment Opportunities Yearbook Volume 1 Strategic, Practical Information and Opportunities
Vietnam Business and Investment Opportunities Yearbook Volume 1 Strategic, Practical Information and Opportunities
Virgin Islands, British Business and Investment Opportunities Yearbook Volume 1 Strategic, Practical Information and Opportunities
Wake Atoll Business and Investment Opportunities Yearbook Volume 1 Strategic, Practical Information and Opportunities
Wallis & Futuna Business and Investment Opportunities Yearbook Volume 1 Strategic, Practical Information and Opportunities
Western Sahara Business and Investment Opportunities Yearbook Volume 1 Strategic, Practical Information and Opportunities
Yemen Business and Investment Opportunities Yearbook Volume 1 Strategic, Practical Information and Opportunities
Zambia Business and Investment Opportunities Yearbook Volume 1 Strategic, Practical Information and Opportunities
Zimbabwe Business and Investment Opportunities Yearbook Volume 1 Strategic, Practical Information and Opportunities

TITLE
Slovenia Business and Investment Opportunities Yearbook Volume 1 Strategic, Practical Information and Opportunities
Solomon Islands Business and Investment Opportunities Yearbook Volume 1 Strategic, Practical Information and Opportunities
Somalia Business and Investment Opportunities Yearbook Volume 1 Strategic, Practical Information and Opportunities
South Africa Business and Investment Opportunities Yearbook Volume 1 Strategic, Practical Information and Opportunities
Spain Business and Investment Opportunities Yearbook Volume 1 Strategic, Practical Information and Opportunities
Sri Lanka Business and Investment Opportunities Yearbook Volume 1 Strategic, Practical Information and Opportunities
St. Helena Business and Investment Opportunities Yearbook Volume 1 Strategic, Practical Information and Opportunities
St. Pierre & Miquelon Business and Investment Opportunities Yearbook Volume 1 Strategic, Practical Information and Opportunities
Sudan (Republic of the Sudan) Business and Investment Opportunities Yearbook Volume 1 Strategic, Practical Information and Opportunities
Sudan South Business and Investment Opportunities Yearbook Volume 1 Strategic, Practical Information and Opportunities
Suriname Business and Investment Opportunities Yearbook Volume 1 Strategic, Practical Information and Opportunities
Swaziland Business and Investment Opportunities Yearbook Volume 1 Strategic, Practical Information and Opportunities
Sweden Business and Investment Opportunities Yearbook Volume 1 Strategic, Practical Information and Opportunities
Switzerland Business and Investment Opportunities Yearbook Volume 1 Strategic, Practical Information and Opportunities
Syria Business and Investment Opportunities Yearbook Volume 1 Strategic, Practical Information and Opportunities
Taiwan Business and Investment Opportunities Yearbook Volume 1 Strategic, Practical Information and Opportunities
Tajikistan Business and Investment Opportunities Yearbook Volume 1 Strategic, Practical Information and Opportunities
Tanzania Business and Investment Opportunities Yearbook Volume 1 Strategic, Practical Information and Opportunities
Thailand Business and Investment Opportunities Yearbook Volume 1 Strategic, Practical Information and Opportunities
Timor Leste (Democratic Republic of Timor-Leste) Business and Investment Opportunities Yearbook Volume 1 Strategic, Practical Information and Opportunities
Togo Business and Investment Opportunities Yearbook Volume 1 Strategic, Practical Information and Opportunities
Tonga Business and Investment Opportunities Yearbook Volume 1 Strategic, Practical Information and Opportunities
Trinidad and Tobago Business and Investment Opportunities Yearbook Volume 1 Strategic, Practical Information and Opportunities
Tunisia Business and Investment Opportunities Yearbook Volume 1 Strategic, Practical Information and Opportunities
Turkey Business and Investment Opportunities Yearbook Volume 1 Strategic, Practical Information and Opportunities
Turkmenistan Business and Investment Opportunities Yearbook Volume 1 Strategic, Practical Information and Opportunities
Turks & Caicos Business and Investment Opportunities Yearbook Volume 1 Strategic, Practical Information and Opportunities
Tuvalu Business and Investment Opportunities Yearbook Volume 1 Strategic, Practical Information and Opportunities

TITLE
Papua New Guinea Business and Investment Opportunities Yearbook Volume 1 Strategic, Practical Information and Opportunities
Paraguay Business and Investment Opportunities Yearbook Volume 1 Strategic, Practical Information and Opportunities
Peru Business and Investment Opportunities Yearbook Volume 1 Strategic, Practical Information and Opportunities
Philippines Business and Investment Opportunities Yearbook Volume 1 Strategic, Practical Information and Opportunities
Pitcairn Islands Business and Investment Opportunities Yearbook Volume 1 Strategic, Practical Information and Opportunities
Poland Business and Investment Opportunities Yearbook Volume 1 Strategic, Practical Information and Opportunities
Polynesia French Business and Investment Opportunities Yearbook Volume 1 Strategic, Practical Information and Opportunities
Portugal Business and Investment Opportunities Yearbook Volume 1 Strategic, Practical Information and Opportunities
Qatar Business and Investment Opportunities Yearbook Volume 1 Strategic, Practical Information and Opportunities
Romania Business and Investment Opportunities Yearbook Volume 1 Strategic, Practical Information and Opportunities
Russia Business and Investment Opportunities Yearbook Volume 1 Strategic, Practical Information and Opportunities
Rwanda Business and Investment Opportunities Yearbook Volume 1 Strategic, Practical Information and Opportunities
Sahrawi Arab Democratic Republic Volume 1 Strategic Information and Developments
Saint Kitts and Nevis Business and Investment Opportunities Yearbook Volume 1 Strategic, Practical Information and Opportunities
Saint Lucia Business and Investment Opportunities Yearbook Volume 1 Strategic, Practical Information and Opportunities
Saint Vincent and The Grenadines Business and Investment Opportunities Yearbook Volume 1 Strategic, Practical Information and Opportunities
Samoa (American) A Business and Investment Opportunities Yearbook Volume 1 Strategic, Practical Information and Opportunities
Samoa (Western) Business and Investment Opportunities Yearbook Volume 1 Strategic, Practical Information and Opportunities
San Marino Business and Investment Opportunities Yearbook Volume 1 Strategic, Practical Information and Opportunities
Sao Tome and Principe Business and Investment Opportunities Yearbook Volume 1 Strategic, Practical Information and Opportunities
Saudi Arabia Business and Investment Opportunities Yearbook Volume 1 Strategic, Practical Information and Opportunities
Scotland Business and Investment Opportunities Yearbook Volume 1 Strategic, Practical Information and Opportunities
Senegal Business and Investment Opportunities Yearbook Volume 1 Strategic, Practical Information and Opportunities
Serbia Business and Investment Opportunities Yearbook Volume 1 Strategic, Practical Information and Opportunities
Seychelles Business and Investment Opportunities Yearbook Volume 1 Strategic, Practical Information and Opportunities
Sierra Leone Business and Investment Opportunities Yearbook Volume 1 Strategic, Practical Information and Opportunities
Singapore Business and Investment Opportunities Yearbook Volume 1 Strategic, Practical Information and Opportunities
Slovakia Business and Investment Opportunities Yearbook Volume 1 Strategic, Practical Information and Opportunities

TITLE
Micronesia Business and Investment Opportunities Yearbook Volume 1 Strategic, Practical Information and Opportunities
Moldova Business and Investment Opportunities Yearbook Volume 1 Strategic, Practical Information and Opportunities
Monaco Business and Investment Opportunities Yearbook Volume 1 Strategic, Practical Information and Opportunities
Mongolia Business and Investment Opportunities Yearbook Volume 1 Strategic, Practical Information and Opportunities
Montserrat Business and Investment Opportunities Yearbook Volume 1 Strategic, Practical Information and Opportunities
Montenegro Business and Investment Opportunities Yearbook Volume 1 Strategic, Practical Information and Opportunities
Morocco Business and Investment Opportunities Yearbook Volume 1 Strategic, Practical Information and Opportunities
Mozambique Business and Investment Opportunities Yearbook Volume 1 Strategic, Practical Information and Opportunities
Myanmar Business and Investment Opportunities Yearbook Volume 1 Strategic, Practical Information and Opportunities
Nagorno-Karabakh Republic Business and Investment Opportunities Yearbook Volume 1 Strategic, Practical Information and Opportunities
Namibia Business and Investment Opportunities Yearbook Volume 1 Strategic, Practical Information and Opportunities
Nauru Business and Investment Opportunities Yearbook Volume 1 Strategic, Practical Information and Opportunities
Nepal Business and Investment Opportunities Yearbook Volume 1 Strategic, Practical Information and Opportunities
Netherlands Business and Investment Opportunities Yearbook Volume 1 Strategic, Practical Information and Opportunities
New Caledonia Business and Investment Opportunities Yearbook Volume 1 Strategic, Practical Information and Opportunities
New Zealand Business and Investment Opportunities Yearbook Volume 1 Strategic, Practical Information and Opportunities
Nicaragua Business and Investment Opportunities Yearbook Volume 1 Strategic, Practical Information and Opportunities
Niger Business and Investment Opportunities Yearbook Volume 1 Strategic, Practical Information and Opportunities
Nigeria Business and Investment Opportunities Yearbook Volume 1 Strategic, Practical Information and Opportunities
Niue Business and Investment Opportunities Yearbook Volume 1 Strategic, Practical Information and Opportunities
Northern Cyprus (Turkish Republic of Northern Cyprus) Business and Investment Opportunities Yearbook Volume 1 Strategic, Practical Information and Opportunities
Northern Mariana Islands Business and Investment Opportunities Yearbook Volume 1 Strategic, Practical Information and Opportunities
Norway Business and Investment Opportunities Yearbook Volume 1 Strategic, Practical Information and Opportunities
Oman Business and Investment Opportunities Yearbook Volume 1 Strategic, Practical Information and Opportunities
Pakistan Business and Investment Opportunities Yearbook Volume 1 Strategic, Practical Information and Opportunities
Palau Business and Investment Opportunities Yearbook Volume 1 Strategic, Practical Information and Opportunities
Palestine (West Bank & Gaza) Business and Investment Opportunities Yearbook Volume 1 Strategic, Practical Information and Opportunities
Panama Business and Investment Opportunities Yearbook Volume 1 Strategic, Practical Information and Opportunities

www.ingramcontent.com/pod-product-compliance
Lightning Source LLC
LaVergne TN
LVHW080031210926
848481LV00011B/3158